Evoking the rugged individualism of Frost's "The Road Not Taken" and Thoreau's censure, "The mass of men lead lives of quiet desperation", Michael seeks the unfamiliar and the challenging. His restless journey leads us around the world, not as a spectator, but as a participant. He embraces uncertainty and loneliness for the awareness and richness of life they can bring. Read this to your grandchildren; there is hope some of them can become true individuals.

Peter Luthy
UK/USA/Switzerland

So much has happened since I read this book and started focusing on ego-minimisation and substance. I am truly convinced that putting my ego aside has enabled me to achieve much more than when it was tying me to the ground, forcing me to re-think all my actions and reactions because of social pressure. Life is a lot more natural now, and thus much more rewarding. I have also had job offers from two major energy companies, thanks in part to my new sense of what is or isn't important. This book has completely changed the way I approach life; hopefully it will help others, too.

Anne-Ségolène Capelle (28)
Chemical engineering doctoral student

I have read my share of post-colonial stories. But Michael's story of the bush boy of good lineage takes us on a journey of self-discovery that is both moving and fascinating. The story includes throwbacks to an ancestral buccaneering spirit, but also shows how that spirit can adapt to the risk-filled world of money. It is told with a raw honesty that comes from knowing that he has little time left to live, and draws on the ego-freeing principles in Zen Buddhism that he has internalised. It is a story I commend for those who are not afraid to brave our turbulent world.

Professor Wang Gungwu
World authority on China and its overseas diaspora

An entertaining tale of Michael, with his insatiable curiosity, keen wit and irresistible charm, travelling around the world, exploring places and enjoying people, handling the peaks and valleys on his journey with great spirit and balance. What better way to live?

Chris Tan
Founder, Ivory Capital, Singapore

Michael, in our minds, will forever be dressed in a *dhoti*, kimono, *longyi*, *barong* or some other exotic garb. From the first page of his memoir, his life appears as truly extraordinary and exciting, revealing the variety and uniqueness of his and his family's lifelong global adventures. Great reading for intimate friends – and for strangers, who will soon be caught up in the fascination that is Michael.

Reuben and Arlene Mark
Former chairman and CEO, Colgate Palmolive, USA

Stories maketh the man, and Michael's voyage – from Africa to Japan, to Mongolia to Hong Kong and so on – truly outlines what kind of man he is, and what kind of life he has led. A worthwhile read for any strong-willed, independent individual looking to make something of life – the way Michael has.

India du Cann (24)
Fashion industry professional

It's hard to write my "comments", simply because I was so greatly moved. It's the glorification of adventure, but also the value of monasticism — the blending of a pioneer with that of a Buddhist monk. It's the story of how hardship breeds hope, which breeds personal success.

Nothing can go wrong if you have the right attitude, a sense of purpose, resourcefulness and good energy. Though I'm not sure this is just a book — more like a memoir/autobiography/life prescription manual/adventure tale/legacy reading for the younger generations. Or all of the above.

The continuous struggle of minimising the demands of your ego while maximising your inherent curiosity and need to explore comes out very clearly in the book, and is utterly interesting and relevant in today's world. I also loved the connectivity and commentary of the various "travel stories/incidents" with major world events (political, economic, social, and financial). It made the book extra lively and "current".

Vasilis Kertsikoff
Ship-owner, Greece

It was an effortless and quite delightful read, and I did not want it to end. The story goes beyond simply describing a life full of thrills, adventures, achievements and failures. It describes a state of mind needed to best withstand what life has to offer (or take), which is a valuable lesson in itself for a young man like myself, and should become a part of my own voyage through life.

Lucas Langlois (24)
Nuclear engineering student

A friend of over 30 years, Michael has always been a thinker and a doer. I am sure his memoir will confirm this remarkable character, and at the same time gives the readers the enjoyment of following Michael's interesting life journey.

Dr. Vichit Surapongchai
Chairman Siam Commercial Bank, Bangkok, Thailand

Michael is one of those larger than life fellows; driven by an insatiable curiosity and desire for adventure that took him from a mountaintop Buddhist monastery in Japan to the board rooms of the most prestigious investment banks in the world. It has been a privilege and an honour to meet him, and I hope that this book will help others like myself to benefit from his wisdom and passionate thirst for life.

Thierry Capelle
Director, Shell Chemicals UK, global lead, NBD Chemicals

Michael's memoir presents a fascinating and incredible life journey from colonist farming, adventures on four continents, eccentric human encounters and the mental strength of a Buddhist monk to high risk-taking entrepreneurship, the haute finance of investment banking and his frequent fights to overcome health problems. I am grateful for his warm friendship.

Onno Ruding
Former Finance Minister of The Netherlands and retired vice chairman of Citibank

Michael Dobbs-Higginson's action-packed and free life has been turned into a lively, picturesque memoir. From his provincial Rhodesian roots to becoming a monk, sailing the Atlantic before GPS, trying out drugs, and entering banking, and much more, he reveals himself to be an honest, curious and daring performer in a book where you hear his voice talking directly to you.

Professor Jason Wilson
Professor emeritus and author

The book richly confirms Michael Dobbs-Higginson as a deeply original thinker and creative actor. The range of his experiences is extraordinary. Of particular importance, the book underlines the significance of Asia to our national future. Overall a gripping read.

Sir John Boyd
Former Ambassador to Japan and Honorary Chairman of Asia House, London, UK

A truly breath-taking saga of Michael's journeys, both physical and spiritual. From Zimbabwe to Canada, Japan to Hong Kong, Michael's tale delights and inspires all who hear of it. His embrace of both Eastern and Western religions and cultures is truly a model for our divisive times. He is a businessman, a father, an adventurer, a hitchhiker, and above all an inspiration for anyone who seeks to lead a fulfilling and meaningful life.

Maximillian Peel (12)
School student

Michael was always one to tell a good story, and I am delighted that he has now decided to share his many lively and at times outrageous anecdotes in this fascinating memoir. I used to see him fairly often while he was living in Hong Kong, but even I did not know the half of his remarkable life.

Michael was a larger than life character at a time when you could dream big dreams, and see them come true. This book will tell you more about entrepreneurship than a year at business school.

David KP Li
Chairman and chief executive, The Bank of East Asia, Hong Kong

A Raindrop in the Ocean is a fascinating account, taking the narrator (and the reader with him) from the African bush on a global journey of discovery and intense personal experiences. The author's immense curiosity, paired with deep spirituality and astonishing fearlessness, transpires on every page, and showcases beautifully what life may have on offer if we just embrace the challenge. A wonderfully inspiring life story, especially for young readers — to awaken the desire for real experiences and discovery…and to switch that smartphone off.

Britta Pfister
Managing Director of Rothschild Trust, Singapore

I loved the book, and read it compulsively. It lifted my spirits.

Natasha Bhatia
Co-Founder, private equity firm, UK

An amazing and inspiring book where the author reveals his extraordinary and challenging life, while introducing his life philosophy, which he acquired during his training to become a Buddhist monk in Japan – the Buddhist wisdom of keeping one's balance by minimising ego to help deal with any hardship, or, indeed, success. I can't wait to introduce my husband and children to it.

Kana Sugiyama
Former member of the Japanese Foreign Service and lawyer

A Raindrop in the Ocean is Michael's tremendous journey through life, an incredible testimony to how he chose to live it. From Africa to Asia and Europe. From Christianity to Buddhism. Oscillating between entrepreneurship and jobs in large corporations. From a single man to a family patriarch. Always with a hunger to discover, an independence of mind, an incredible openness to others, and firm life values never to be broken. This is a beautiful book: a reminder that freedom must be used.

Thierry de Panafieu
Private equity investor

A RAINDROP IN THE OCEAN

THE LIFE OF A GLOBAL

ADVENTURER

MICHAEL DOBBS-HIGGINSON

Published in 2017
by Eye Books
29A Barrow Street
Much Wenlock
Shropshire
TF13 6EN
www.eye-books.com

ISBN: 978-1785630323

Copyright © Michael Dobbs-Higginson 2017
Cover design by Chris Shamwana
Typesetting and design by Clio Mitchell

British Library Cataloguing in Publication Data
A catalogue record for this book is available from the British Library

Printed by CPI Group (UK) Ltd, Croydon CR0 4YY

Dedication

My adventure through life was primarily influenced by two people: my mother, who both started me off on this adventure and gave me the initial freedom to do so, and Marie-Therese, my wife of now some forty-seven years, who provided me an unshakeable foundation from which to keep exploring the world by trying all manner of new things, with their attendant risks, rewards and, often, pain. All of which experiences were very interesting, and thus, instructive.

These memoirs are also dedicated to all those people who have the courage to be really curious, and who are willing to challenge the established order by focusing on the substance, as opposed to the form, of what life can offer. And who are willing to take the risks, including the alienation, that usually go with such an approach.

Prologue

THE DAWN WAS shortly to break through the light mist. Wearing only a T-shirt, shorts and flip-flops, with neither money nor passport, I trudged along the tracks of the railway, taking two sleepers at a time and doing my best to stay calm. It was four o'clock in the morning and I was alone in the middle of the Gobi Desert. The Mongolian capital, Ulan Bator, was four hundred miles to the north-west, and Beijing was the same distance to the south-east. I had known many disconcerting, isolated situations in my life, but I had never felt such disquiet as I did now. It was only my second time in China, but I was painfully aware that it had become a ruthless, unsentimental place during the Cultural Revolution, where life was cheap. Anything could happen to me, and nobody would care that I was just a hapless traveller with a potentially fatal sense of curiosity. I cursed the folly that had got me into this predicament.

Up ahead, I heard a light ting-ting-ting sound. It was a sign of life, and it sounded unthreatening, so I hastened towards it. As the sound grew louder, I saw a figure bending over the rails. It was a rail-tapper, dressed in standard-issue Chairman Mao suit and cap, tap-tap-tapping the track to test for cracks in the metal.

I emerged out of the mist and said good morning to him in the best Mandarin I could muster. To my consternation, instead of greeting me back, he screamed in terror, dropped his hammer and ran off as fast his legs would carry him.

Now I had really blown it. I could just imagine him calling the police and bringing out all the local villagers to search for me. Since I had no papers on me, I could see myself being thrown into a bamboo cage and paraded through the town, while the villagers threw rotten vegetables at me. But I had missed my train and there wouldn't be another one for a week. What the hell was I going to do?

The only other time I had visited China was in 1964, on a fleeting call at Shanghai on a freighter. Now, following the conclusion of the Cultural Revolution, my wife and I had managed to get a two-week transit visa through this magnificent country on the Trans-Siberian Railway. That meant starting the journey in Mongolia, where we stayed with the British ambassador in Ulan Bator. We then embarked on the train ride across four hundred miles of undulating grassland steppes to the Chinese border.

It was around 3am by the time we reached the border, where Outer Mongolia became Inner Mongolia and we were formally in China. We stopped at a small station before the next main station of Erenhot/Erlian. Being of a curious disposition, as well as wanting to stretch my legs, I got off for a wander around the station to see if I could find anyone to talk to. Marie-Thérèse called after me to keep an eye on the train to make sure I did not miss it, because this was only a weekly service. I told her not to worry. There was bound to be a whistle to call any passengers back on board.

There was no sign life on the platform but I walked around the back of the station building and found a fellow writing at a desk in an office. He nearly fell off his chair when he saw me, because a white face must have been such a rarity in those parts, but he knew I was a passenger from the train, so he was not too alarmed. We started exchanging Chinese ideograms by way of rudimentary communication. He asked who I was, and I wrote the word for England. We became fairly engrossed in our little conversation, so I completely lost track of the time, and it was with a sudden shock that I remembered my train. I had not heard any whistle, but I had been distracted, and in any case I was now completely out of sight and earshot of the platform. Giving him a cursory bow and wave, I hastened back to the platform. My heart sank as my worst fears were confirmed: the train was no longer there.

I looked frantically around for someone who might be able to help me but as I did so the lights started going out one by one. Trying not to panic, I headed back to the office where I had been talking to this fellow a few minutes earlier, but now that door was locked. The situation was turning rapidly into a nightmare.

There seemed to me no alternative but to start walking along the railway tracks in the direction of Beijing. There was a road at the front of the station, but I was mindful of the paranoid atmosphere in China: anyone seeing me wandering the highways might assume I had been dropped in by the CIA, and there was no knowing what might happen to me. Sticking to the track seemed the safest policy.

My encounter with the rail-tapper confirmed all my worst fears about the situation where foreigners were concerned. As this poor chap ran off into the dawn, I decided in my jittery state that the best thing was to return to the station, which might have opened again by now. But when I got there, it was still locked. I decided then to set off the other way along the tracks, the way we had come. Four hundred miles was an impossibly long distance on foot, but moving back in the direction of Ulan Bator felt better than staying where I was.

For as long as I could remember, I had woken up every morning and wondered what adventure the day would hold. The taste for it is in my blood. An ancestor on my father's side, despite being a wealthy landowner in Barbados, decided to become a pirate and was subsequently known as the Gentleman Pirate. He became an associate of the infamous Blackbeard and ended his life on the hangman's scaffold in Charles Town, South Carolina. My father, the son of a British army officer, was born in Tianjin, China, and my Anglo-Irish mother's family distinguished themselves in London, Ireland, the Americas and India. I myself was born in a farmhouse with no electricity, in the isolated British colony of Southern Rhodesia – now known as Zimbabwe. From my mother, a free-thinking quasi-mystic, who cut a striking figure in our remote colonial outpost, I had learned not to fear being an outsider, and to take risks at an early age. Had I now taken one risk too many?

Nearly twenty years earlier, I had abandoned the country of my birth and set off to be a medical student at Trinity College, Dublin, with which my mother's family had been involved since it was founded in 1592. After a year of studies, I decided that I was both not patient enough to deal with sick people for the rest of my life, and far too curious about the rest of the world to be restricted to this profession. So I left and began a six-year odyssey around the world. It took me from a cultural college in Germany to a Vancouver logging camp, from a stevedore's job in San Francisco to a mountaintop Buddhist monastery in Japan, from a jail cell in rural Oregon to an opium den in Laos, to crossing the Atlantic in a seven-metre sloop with no GPS to some serious climbing in the Canadian Rockies – and my accommodation ranged from one of the finest stately homes in England to the freezing floor of a Canadian public lavatory.

At every turn, I was driven by intense curiosity and had learned not to be daunted by physically difficult or emotionally isolating challenges. I had built up five businesses in Tokyo and then lost everything when the CIA threatened my life. Having been ordained as a lay Buddhist monk, I had learned to control my emotions by trying to minimise the demands of my ego, and I had never fallen prey to panic or despair.

But my current situation was as testing as any I had ever known. Where was my wife? Would we ever see each other again? If we did not, it would be entirely my fault.

After I had stumbled on for about three miles, I saw a large railway shed ahead of me with tracks going into it. The interior was brightly lit and full of noise, and my heart lifted, because now at least I might find some people to whom I could explain my predicament.

As I walked in, I saw an astonishing sight. On the train track in front of me sat a row of bogies – effectively the chassis and wheels of a train and nothing else – from which the carriage itself seemed to have been stripped away. I walked further into the shed and saw that the train itself was suspended ten feet off the ground, carriage by carriage, on a row of cranes. And there, at one of the windows, to my amazement and huge relief, was Marie-Thérèse, looking down at me, equally flabbergasted and delighted to see me.

The shed, it turned out, was a rail gauge-changing station: the Chinese use the standard international gauge but the Mongolians use the Russian one, which is about three and a half inches wider. That means that all carriages much be lifted off their bogies in a procedure that can take several hours. Because it was so laborious, it was no wonder that they ran so few trains on that line, but as my wife and I were joyously united, and as I prepared my speech of abject apology for not heeding her warning, I thanked my lucky stars that it all took so long. If the train really had gone off to Beijing without me, I am not at all confident I would have survived to tell the tale.

Forty years on, I am still telling my tales, but the time I have left to do so is limited. I was recently diagnosed with an incurable lung disease, which my specialists tell me, gives me only around two years to live.

I am generally calm about the prospect of dying. For this, I thank the Buddhist belief system which has enriched my life and helped me get through the toughest events in it. I have always focused on substance not form, being driven by curiosity, and attempting to minimise the demands of my ego. This three-part formula has served me well, leading to success in my business career as well as immense personal fulfilment. It surprises some people that I could be a committed Buddhist – I am ordained as a Zen monk – while holding senior positions in the business world and setting up multi-million-pound ventures. To me, there is no contradiction. The assumption that there should be derives from the common association of Buddhism with the kind of people who are most obviously drawn to it in the West. As a religious philosophy, it is not solely about chanting cross-legged to a soundtrack of wind chimes while preaching peace, love and harmony. If it were, how could Japan – where two-thirds of the population is Buddhist – ever have become the world's third largest economy? Rather, it is a belief system honed over more than two thousand years, which has an application to all areas of life. My aim in writing about my life's adventures is to provide a fuller and more complete account of this practical wisdom I learned in Japan, and to challenge some of those preconceptions about the spiritual teachings of the East.

The title, *A Raindrop in the Ocean*, refers to a Buddhist meditation *koan* or problem. It is partly a metaphysical enquiry: if a raindrop falls into the ocean, does it cease to exist? The answer is both yes and no: the raindrop is still there, but it is no longer an isolated thing, as it has lost the "skin" (aka ego) that was formerly around the water of the raindrop. This gives us a way of understanding how a person can have two apparently contradictory properties at the same time: the body/ego (form – a separate entity) and the soul (substance – part of the whole), which is a useful lesson for approaching the complexities of the world. It is thus a metaphor for the relationship between the individual and the rest of the world. It is about leaving the ego behind (the border demanding individual ego recognition) and accepting being an indivisible part of a greater whole. Before the monastery, I tried "to eat life before it ate me", but since the monastery, I have tried "to be dispassionately passionate" – the dispassion is the removal of the ego, while the passion is absolutely necessary for communication with others and taking joy from being alive, which is not the monastic way. I still have a long way to go in achieving this latter goal.

I have spent my life since my monastic sojourn attempting to be a raindrop in the ocean. A great deal of enjoyment has been mine along the way, and the process has never been less than fascinating. Having learned to be fully engaged by life, I have not felt bored in a very long time.

I:

Boyhood in the African Bush

IT WAS A HOT morning on the high-veld and I was in my usual garb of a pair of shorts and virtually nothing else, about to go off into the bush with one of the cattle herders, Twalika — my favourite, as he was always patient in explaining the ways of the bush and the wildlife that inhabited it. There were snakes everywhere, and I knew it was important to watch out for the puff adders that enjoyed basking in the sun while they lay in wait for small animals on the paths around my grandfather's farm. Unlike most other snakes, they were too sluggish to slither away, but they were not slow to bite, and their venom could easily kill a small boy. Nevertheless, six years old and fearless, I liked to run everywhere barefoot, and today was no exception. With a spear in my hand and my fox terrier, Toki, running on ahead, we set out on the path through my grandfather's tobacco fields. The rows of squat green plants were just coming into flower and the sweet scent of the pink blooms perfumed the air.

A couple of fields away lay the nearest of the five villages on my grandfather's land. I often liked to sneak away on Saturday nights to sit with the village children at the *kraal*, the centre of the mud and lathe houses, and watch the adults drink *skokiaan*, a vile-smelling home-brewed liquor that made them laugh loudly and dance. The men of the village were out in the fields at this time in the morning, but there were a few children roaming around, and an old woman sat in the doorway of her grass-thatched hut cutting vegetables into a stew-pot. We waved at her and called hello in *Chilapalapa*, the pidgin language that I had been taught to use with the Shona villagers, but we did not stop because Toki was pressing ahead and I did not want to lose sight of him. I had a vivid memory of a leopard snatching another of our dogs off the veranda of our house, and I had no intention of letting any such accident befall Toki…

Beyond the village was an irrigation channel. It was dry at this time of year but it was a good route to follow and we now walked along its sun-baked path, humming a song I had learned from Nursey, who had sung the same songs to my father, and his brother and sister, when they were children in China. Some way along this channel was a spreading mahogany tree with just enough footholds for me to climb into the lower branches and survey the surrounding plateau. I hauled myself up, my bare toes curling nimbly around the bole, and settled into a comfortable perch, where I pulled from my pocket a slab of cake I had stolen from the kitchen. Toki looked up at me imploringly so I tore off a chunk and dropped it down to him, as well as giving a piece to Twalika. My vantage point was just high enough to see the low roof of our house, which my father had built from bricks that he and a team of village helpers had made from mud and straw and baked in the sun. Away to the north, too far to see, was my grandparents' farmhouse, which was larger than ours and full of treasures my grandfather had brought from the East. The one I liked best was a huge lacquered screen on which animals were painted: extraordinary creatures of a kind we did not have in Africa. There were tigers and griffins and dragons, and they puzzled me because I thought we had every conceivable animal on the farm. Glossing over the fact that several of them were mythological, my grandfather explained that they didn't live in our part of the world: rather, they lived in China. After hearing his explanation, I had decided that one day I would travel to Asia to see these exotic creatures for myself.

Until that day came, however, I still had plenty to explore on my doorstep. In the opposite direction from my grandfather's house, further along the irrigation channel, was one of the dams that the farm used for irrigation and fishing when it was full. Having realised he was not getting any more cake, Toki had wandered off in that direction and I decided I had better jump down and follow.

When we reached the dam, I could see my dog sniffing around a bulky object on the floor of the dry basin. It was hidden behind some stones, and from the stink and the cloud of flies, I assumed it was a dead animal.

"Come away, Toki," I called.

He looked up to acknowledge my arrival, but it was clear he had no intention of leaving his noxious-smelling discovery alone. As Twalika and I approached, I tried to make out what kind of animal it could be. The most likely possibility was one of my grandfather's cattle, in which case Twalika would have to report this discovery to our headman. But the shape looked too small for that. Perhaps it was a calf. Bones were sticking out of what dark skin remained, and whatever it was looked as if it had already become a meal for the fish before the damn dried up. Twalika tried to persuade me to leave, as he was clearly very agitated. Holding my hand over my nose to try and fend off the stench, I tiptoed closer. Now, with horror, I saw that the shape was not the remains of a dead animal. I was looking at a dead body.

For all my fearless nature, I was trembling now.

"Come here, Toki," I called, my voice shrill and hesitant in the eerie silence that seemed to have descended on this part of the bush.

Backing away, I grabbed Toki by the scruff of the neck to pull him with me, then began to run as fast as my bare feet would carry me back to our house, with Twalika following me closely.

I found my mother in the kitchen talking to our cook in *Chilapalapa* about lunch.

"There's a dead man in the dam!" I blurted out.

My mother was normally calm in a crisis, but she looked alarmed and promptly dispatched one of the kitchen boys to look for my father. Then she hugged me close and asked me to tell her precisely what I had seen, which I did.

"What do you think killed him?" I asked.

I knew there were lions and hyenas out there, because we could hear them at night, and I was under no illusions about the dangers of such wild creatures.

"Let's wait until your father goes to find out," she said.

I did not know this at the time, but my mother knew at once that no animal had killed this man. It was impossible to recognise him but it was probable that he was a stranger to our farm. He had no doubt been murdered in order to harvest his organs so a witch-doctor could used them for his *muti*, or potions, in black magic rituals. The police were called, but nobody was ever charged because this kind of thing was a fact of life, albeit infrequent, in the bush of Southern Rhodesia. For me, as the discoverer of the body, it was a rough early awakening to the fact that life could be pretty brutal.

I also learned not entirely to dismiss black magic as primitive superstition. There was a time when one of the men on our farm became very ill. The local mini-clinic could do nothing for him so my father sent him off by bus to the general hospital in Salisbury, the capital, and monitored his health by public telephone. In those days of very limited long-distance communication, we had a system where one ring was for a neighbour twenty miles away, two were for a slightly closer neighbour, and three meant the call was for us. When the call came through, the hospital told us the man was definitely dying.

My father shook his head and looked at my mother. "I'm sure it's black magic," he said.

He called in his headman and told him: "I know perfectly well your wife is a witch-doctor. Bring her here at once."

The man looked at his feet.

"If you don't, there will be very severe consequences," my father said.

His wife was duly brought to my father. I was standing watching when she arrived, fascinated to see what an actual witch would look like. But to my disappointment she looked no different from any of the other village women.

"Have you put a spell on this man?" my father wanted to know.

"No, sir!" she insisted. "Honestly, I have not!"

My father picked up his *sjambok*, a whip made of rolled hippopotamus hide, and raised it to make it clear he meant business. The threat had the desired effect and the woman changed her tune immediately.

"All right, all right," she pleaded. "I did put a spell on him, because he liked a girl and she liked him, but somebody else wanted her. That man paid me to put a spell on him. I will take the spell off now, I swear to you, sir. Please do not whip me."

She disappeared back to the village, and about three hours later we received a call from the general hospital some one hundred kilometres away. The man had got out of bed, they told us, and was coming home.

I have no idea how one explains that in a rational way. But incidents like it informed my world view as I grew up in this remote, unsophisticated outpost of the British Empire.

My grandfather had arrived in Southern Rhodesia in the 1920s. He was a brigadier-general who had lost a leg in the First World War. Like many men of his class and generation he had a nursery nickname that stuck with him for the rest of his life; his was Piglet. That may make him sound frivolous to modern ears, but in truth he was gruff and rather distant, as befitted a man who had spent the first half of his life in the Victorian era. Clean-shaven with a shiny bald head baked as a brown as the bricks of our house, he clumped around on his wooden leg, issuing orders in a military manner, and according his grandchildren a half-hour audience every day before his dinner. We referred to him as Grandpa, but to his face we called him 'Sir' – as indeed did our father.

His real name was Cecil Pickford Higginson, and he had been born in Liverpool, where my great-grandfather was a coal merchant. The family had previously owned sugar plantations in the Caribbean, and our most exciting direct ancestor was a renegade called Stede Bonnet, nicknamed the Gentleman Pirate. He decided that being a pirate was more profitable than owning a sugar plantation, and he fell in with the notorious Blackbeard. Eventually, he was hanged in South Carolina in 1718. By respectable contrast, my grandfather went to public school in the UK and then the Army Staff College at Camberley in Surrey. He served as a captain in the Shropshire Light Infantry in the Boxer Rebellion in Beijing before going off to the Boer War in South Africa, where he was mentioned in dispatches twice and decorated with the DSO. Later, he went back to China, where my father was born in the northern port city of Tianjin in 1910. He then commanded a battalion in the First World War, but lost his leg in the first year and was invalided out. He was made a Companion of the Order of St Michael and George.

He could have settled into a comfortable retirement in the Home Counties, but he had fallen in love with Africa during his time there and he decided he would go back. The British

government was offering land grants to help settle Southern
Rhodesia, the crown colony between the Limpopo river in
the south and the Zambezi river in the north, occupying a
part of Africa named after the British empire-builder Cecil
Rhodes. My grandfather acquired a parcel of land in central
Mashonaland, some fifty miles north of the capital, Salisbury.
His two sons and a daughter were at public school in England,
and he let them stay on. But he made it clear to them that there
was no question of their going on to university. Instead they
were required, at the age of seventeen or eighteen, to help him
build his own little empire in Rhodesia. To sweeten this pill,
he secured land grants for them, too, and they all ended up
building their own houses on what was effectively a sprawling
family estate.

The settlers of their era were creating farms out of raw bush.
Traditional African agriculture was based on a slash-and-burn
model, and there was no notion of crop rotation before the
colonials arrived. Whatever the rights and wrongs of their
unilaterally taking ownership of the land, they undoubtedly
made it more productive. This fertile region, and Rhodesia
generally, acquired a reputation as the breadbasket of Africa.

Life was not all witch-doctors and mud bricks. My
grandparents made money from their tobacco crop when the
Second World War broke out, and my grandmother – whom we
called Granny Maud – wintered every year in the smartest hotel
in Cape Town. She came from a military family in Hampshire
and she loved wearing extravagant hats. She also enjoyed the
constant support of Nursey. A Devonshire girl, whose real
name was Miss Bristow, she had gone with the family to China

as an 18-year-old and stayed on with our family for the rest of her life. She had ruled my father's nursery with a rod of iron, and she did the same for us children, her ferocity only slightly undermined by the rich West Country burr she had never lost.

The real adventurer in the family was my mother. She was born in Ireland to an old and distinguished family. One of her ancestors was Lord Mayor of London in the reign of Queen Elizabeth I. Another became High Sheriff of County Antrim and built Castle Dobbs, an elegant mansion which still stands near Carrickfergus in Northern Ireland. Yet another Dobbs forebear was appointed Surveyor of Ireland in the 1720s and then immigrated to the US where he became the seventh governor of North Carolina, acquiring a vast estate of four hundred thousand acres. Under the British system, where the eldest son of a wealthy family inherited everything and the rest had to go off and find something else to do, a succession of younger sons and their descendants built railways in South America, and helped run the East India Company and the British Raj. My mother's great-grandfather, Major-General Richard Dobbs, spent more than thirty years in the colonial administration in southern India, where he befriended the fabulously rich and cultured Maharaja of Mysore (now the State of Karnataka). He even had a village, Dobbspet (just north of Bangalore), named after him.

I therefore grew up with tales of derring-do by my mother's side of the family. She and my father were coincidentally at the same English public school, Sherborne in Dorset, but they did not know each other there because he was four years older, and in any case the boys' and the girls' schools were completely separate. So far, so conventional. But at the age of nineteen, my mother set out for the United States on her own, which was an extraordinary undertaking for a young woman in the early 1930s. Her plan was to attend the first-ever school of osteopathy in Kirksville, Missouri, which had opened the year before her arrival.

On her way, she had her first great adventure, which, remarkably, only emerged by accident. I was her first-born, and the most like her in character, so she spent a lot of time talking to me. One day I discovered the word 'divorce' in a book and asked my mother what it meant. She duly told me, and then I asked, as small children are inclined to do, if she had ever been divorced herself.

"Actually, I have," she said. And it all came out.

In order to get to Missouri from the East Coast, she had hitch-hiked. She accepted one lift from a handsome young man with a big smile and the pair of them ended up getting caught in a snowstorm. By her account, they were trapped in the car for three whole days. Obviously, it was very cold, and to keep each other warm they huddled close. The driver cannot be blamed for noticing the attractions of his clear-skinned young Irish passenger with the twinkling brown eyes, and one thing led to another. But he was apparently a man of honour, as ten days later he married her. After such a limited courtship, the relationship did not last, and my mother divorced him after three months, whereupon she proceeded calmly to Kirksville and qualified as an osteopath. She confided all this to me without inhibition in our car outside a shopping centre in Salisbury when I was seven years old. If she had not, we might none of us have ever known the story.

After she had finished her training she went back to her parents in Ireland, but she was in no mood to settle down. She decided she wanted to see Africa. War had already broken out but she managed to book passage for Cape Town on a liner which set out from the Port of London in November 1939.

On the voyage south she met my father's mother, who was trying to get back to the farm in Mashonaland after a trip home to the UK, now that the war had started. Since my mother was a good-looking gal with an engaging manner, and my grandmother was probably bored by the long sea voyage, it was natural that they should strike up a friendship, and at some stage Granny Maud told my mother: "You must come to stay with us in Rhodesia."

"I'd love to," said my mother, who knew an invitation to adventure when she heard one.

They duly exchanged addresses and for a while nothing came of it. My mother disembarked in Cape Town as planned and travelled overland to Johannesburg, where she started practising osteopathy. But the policies of the largely Boer government in South Africa were restrictive and dehumanising. The system was not yet officially known as apartheid, but she hated the rigid separation between blacks and whites. While neighbouring Southern Rhodesia also had racial laws, and she would come to disapprove of them profoundly, the colony seemed at the time to represent a softer version of the situation in South Africa. So she sent a letter to the elegantly dressed Mrs Higginson from the ship and asked if she could come to visit. She received a reply by return of post in the affirmative, at which she packed her bags and set off for Salisbury, some six hundred miles to the north.

The train journey was long and slow, and she was tired but excited when she arrived. Waiting for her at the station was her hostess's son Bill, who was tall, slim, good-looking and charming. He was also shy and did not have much to say on the bumpy, three-hour drive on the dust road back to the farm. But it cannot have escaped his attention as they bounced along over the high-veld that this remarkably spirited, vivacious young woman was also quite easy on the eye.

Conditions on my grandparents' farm were primitive. There was no electricity, and my mother had to get used to finding cobras in the bathroom, black or green mambas in the fruit orchard, and the sight of elephants trampling the vegetable garden. Few of her contemporaries at Sherborne School for Girls would have lasted longer than a week, but my mother loved it. She got on as well as ever with Granny Maud, and she charmed my gruff grandfather. She also continued to get to know young Bill. I do not believe, from what she told me many years later, that she had fallen head over heels in love with him, but she liked him well enough. She was also certain that she liked this new life in Rhodesia, and she was keen to start having children. Because my father was reticent by nature, she could not foresee him taking the initiative, and even though there had been no indication from my grandparents that she was outstaying her welcome, she was eager to put her future on a proper footing. It had not escaped her attention that 1940 which was a leap year, which meant that, according to custom, it was acceptable for a woman to propose to a man on the 29th of February. So that was what she did.

It took my father completely by surprise but he must have been aware that this was a propitious turn of events, not least because there were very few eligible white women out in the bush, and he was unlikely to do half as well if he turned the proposal down. So he swallowed whatever pride he felt at this reversal of the traditional roles and blurted out: "Yes, yes, Elizabeth, of course I'll marry you. Absolutely!"

They were married on the 25th of July, and I was born eleven months later, on 20 June 1941. My brother Brian arrived in 1943, and our sister Ann two years after that.

The war in Europe was a long way away from Rhodesia but, like men all over the Commonwealth, my father felt duty-bound to sign up. He took flying lessons from a local pilot and went off to join the Royal Air Force in 1943, where he eventually ended up as an instructor. It meant he saw very little active service during the war, which kept him safe, even if he had few stories to tell when he returned. Meanwhile his brother and sister stayed behind and followed my grandfather's lead in selling tobacco to the troops. It made them a lot of money, and we ended up as the poor relations of the family. But, on balance, I was proud that my father volunteered.

The main difference the war made to my life was that my mother decided she no longer wanted to stay alone on the farm. She took us instead to live in a rented house in Salisbury, where she could earn a living as an osteopath. From then on, we only saw the farm during school holidays. When my father came back from the war he also realised he had lost the will to run a large operation on the land. He gave his farm back to my grandfather, who incorporated it into his own estate, and my parents bought twenty-five acres of land some twenty minutes' drive from the city centre of Salisbury. It was a fairly sleepy place as capital cities go, caught in something of a time-warp, and in those days it had quite large plots of land, so people had space. That was particularly true for us: our property was huge considering that it was only twenty minutes from the city centre. My father built a rambling one-storey thatched-roof home for us – a typical farmer's house transplanted into the city. The only other building visible was my rich uncle's mansion at the top of the hill adjoining our property. Otherwise, we felt we were living in the country.

At the bottom of our property, we had a swamp area known as a *vlei*, and a yellow gum tree plantation from which my father used to sell the timber. He set himself up as an agent for British firms importing and selling their products into Rhodesia, and he also turned about twelve of our twenty-five acres into a market garden, growing vegetables to sell to hotels and restaurants in Salisbury, with the help of a workforce of about fifteen. We ate vegetables straight out of the earth, and fruit straight off the trees. We children were all given our own personal peach tree and we had bananas, guavas, grapefruit, oranges and passion fruit, which we called *granadillas*. There was also a large open field of about five acres where my father grew grass to rear young calves until they were yearlings. For a small boy, the haystacks were a great delight. It was possible to hollow them out inside and make a den, completely out of sight of any grown-ups. The hay could be prickly on bare legs, but it was not hard to scavenge old towels and cushions from the house to make the interior quite comfortable. I would crawl inside and be master of my own little home, and if I was feeling hospitable, I could entertain guests.

I was apparently a difficult child. Not in terms of tantrums, but I had inherited the Dobbs adventure gene and I got into all sorts of scrapes. My first experience of hospital was when I was two years old. I was teasing Toki with a piece of bread; as he jumped at it, I pulled away so he snapped his teeth in mid-air. It was a good game. Unfortunately, on my last attempt, I snatched the bread away very close to my mouth, and he closed his teeth on my lip, tearing it apart. I needed stitches and I had my first, awful taste of chloroform, which in those days was used as an anaesthetic. Another time, I was chasing a girl in my school playground with my shoelaces undone. I tripped, gashed my head open and needed five more stitches. Then there was the day I was pushing my sister on a swing. I was swinging her higher and higher because I enjoyed her squeals as she went up and up. Then I was distracted by something and looked to one side, only to turn back and receive a sharp upper-cut from the descending seat. It lifted me off the ground and cut my jaw open, which meant more chloroform and stitches. It ought to have made me more careful, but it seemed not to. I had an accident on a picnic in the bush when I was crossing a river with a Coke bottle in my hand; I slipped on a rock and smashed the bottle, cutting both tendons in my right forefinger. Another time I was taken to the circus, where I saw trick cyclists standing on the saddle of their bikes and using strings to operate the handlebars. Naturally I thought I could do that too, so I tried it on a hill. I came off almost immediately and cut open my eye, needing another five stitches. Perhaps the most spectacular incident came when I was running with my brother and sister towards our uncle's pool. I had shouted, "Last one in's an ass!" and I was too busy telling my brother over my shoulder that he was going to be the ass to notice that the pool was empty. I only realised when I was in mid-air, at which point I started frantically back-pedalling like a cartoon character. I crashed down onto the concrete bottom and broke my ankle.

I was so difficult to keep out of trouble that Granny Maud offered to pay for me to attend an exclusive prep school called Ruzawi, about forty-five miles east of Salisbury. I was duly packed off there at the age of six. Before I went, my mother sat me down for a serious talk.

"It's very important," she said, "to behave in a moral way."

As well as being an adventurer, my mother was very religious, and devoted a lot of time to prayer in the little chapel she had created in our house. She even claimed to have had visions. She was a Christian and I was baptised an Anglican, but she had a great interest in comparative religions and philosophy, and she now tried to impress some of this thinking on me.

"You will find that many people in life focus on form: what one looks like, how one is dressed, all the things that are on the surface that you first see when you look. But you will have a much richer life if you do the more difficult thing, which is to focus on substance – all the things that are below the surface." Years later I came to the conclusion that Moses had missed a very important commandment; namely "thou shalt have no prejudice", as so often prejudice is based on a person's form – the colour of the skin, his beliefs, her ethnicity and his way of being. And thus, his/her substance is never given a chance to be understood, let alone appreciated.

She explained, and I more or less grasped, that, in human terms, substance is the essence of the person, the business of the soul, and therefore who that person is, in value terms. To find the substance, ignore the clothing, the accent, and so on. It is more important to find out what the person believes in, what drives him or her. This focus on substance, my mother told me, represented the main foundation on which to build one's own moral value system. Real advancement in life was not a question of money or form; it was an advancement of the spirit.

She also had a warning: "Focusing on substance can be a long, hard and rather lonely road, because most people go with the flow and focus on form," she said. "But if you succeed, you'll see that it is worth the effort."

These were weighty messages for a six-year-old boy to absorb, but I did my best to apply the idea of moral values when I arrived at school. One day, for example, I saw some senior boys competing to see how far they could hit frogs with a cricket bat.

"Please don't do that," I said. "It's cruel."

"Who do you think you are, you little twerp?" the largest of them demanded.

"You're killing them," I persisted. "It's not nice to kill frogs like that."

I was probably lucky to escape without a kicking.

On another occasion, I stepped in to stop some bullies tormenting a smaller boy. My intervention was successful, because they stopped persecuting him. Unfortunately, however, they transferred their attention to me, and instead of being grateful to me for helping him out, the smaller boy tried to ingratiate himself with them by cheering them on. It was a useful lesson in the weakness of human nature, but I also realised I would need to learn to fight back if I was going to carry on trying to take the moral high ground.

Since I had been a voracious reader from an early age, I was more advanced than my peers and was moved up a class. That made me the youngest, and when I also turned out to be smart, the abuse intensified. In the end the bullying proved too much. I was not robust enough to deal with it, and after a couple of years my parents took me out of Ruzawi and put me in a day school near our home instead. It was around this time that my grandfather died, heralding the end of an era on the farm.

At twelve I was sent away again, this time to a public school called Plumtree, in the village of Plumtree. It was right out in the bush, on the border with Botswana. This one-horse town was originally a simple siding on the railway line between Mafeking and Bulawayo, Rhodesia's second city. The school was founded at the turn of the twentieth century by the Railway Mission to cater for the nine children of the station master, a man called Smith. They were represented for posterity by nine plums in a plum tree on the school crest. The school had since established itself as one of the best in the country. It was set up along the lines of a British public school, complete with a "fagging" system where junior boys acted as servants to senior ones. The fag-master, as the senior boy was known, was allowed to hand out reasonable punishments, but mine was an out-and-out sadist who took it upon himself to brand me with an immersion heater, leaving my right thigh disfigured by a circular brand. It was horrific conduct, but not the kind of thing one snitched about if one knew what was good for one.

At the same time, I was falling foul of the school authorities. In my own mind I was not especially unruly. To me the world was a kaleidoscope of potential new adventures, and I was driven by curiosity and willingness to experiment. Unfortunately, that did not always sit well with the disciplinary attitudes of a colonial public school of the 1950s. I soon became the most-caned boy at Plumtree. Being blessed with what I have come to realise is an abnormally high pain threshold, I dealt with this with some nonchalance, which merely reinforced the masters' conviction that I had a bad attitude.

As well as thwacking one's buttocks with a cane, which was a common sanction in schools all over the world in those days, Plumtree had developed another distinctive collective punishment of its own. My House had a large, wide-spreading *marula* tree, a species common all over southern Africa – elephants in particular love to eat their bark and fruit. These trees had fruit the size of golf balls that would ripen and burst in springtime, attracting a plague of flies, birds and monkeys, and when they fell to the ground and rotted, they stank and attracted even more insects. Badly behaved boys were therefore sent up these trees before the berries ripened fully to knock them off. When I was fourteen, I was one of those sent up – as was my brother Brian, who had by that time joined me at the school, although, conversely, he was generally a model student. Being fairly athletic, as well as wanting to outdo my younger brother, I set out to climb further and higher than anyone else. Unburdened by fear, I managed to reach the very top, about fifteen metres from the ground. I was thoroughly enjoying throwing berries at the people below me, including my brother, who was safely in the middle of the tree, when there was a sharp crack. The branch I was sitting on snapped, tipping me towards the ground. In those frantic split seconds I grabbed in vain at the boughs of the tree as I plunged past. Salvation of sorts came in the form of one of the lowest branches. I smashed into it but immediately felt a searing pain in my left thigh. What was more, the branch had not stopped my fall completely. Instead, it had flipped me round so I was now falling head-first. I landed on the sandy earth floor with my arms outstretched, and according to the onlookers I actually bounced about a foot. When I came to rest, my left femur was sticking three inches out of my shorts, dripping bone marrow onto the khaki cotton. I had also broken my left elbow and several bones in each wrist.

"I'm wrecked," I groaned, as my horrified brother jumped down from the tree and bent over me. "I'm completely wrecked."

I repeated the same phrase over and over, but, strangely, I apparently did not cry.

Because it was a Saturday morning, it took about forty-five minutes for the school doctor to arrive. He brought his station wagon and I was manhandled onto a mattress in the back. The nearest hospital was more than fifty miles away in Bulawayo. In those days, many of the bush roads in Rhodesia were made with what were called strips: two widths of tarmac, each a little broader than the tyre of a car, which was a cheap way of providing a macadam road. There was dirt or gravel in between and dried ridges of earth called corrugations on each side. It was fine for normal driving but if one wanted to overtake, one would have one's right wheels on the strip and the others on the corrugated earth at the side of the road. I was losing a lot of blood so we needed to go fast and there was a lot of overtaking. Every time it happened my bones jangled and grated together, and it was all I could do not to scream.

We eventually reached Bulawayo, and as they were wheeling me onto the X-ray machine I finally passed out. The blood loss cannot have helped, and also the pain was too much to take. For some reason, I did not feel it in the most obvious place, the horribly broken femur sticking out of my thigh, or in my broken left elbow. But the agony of my two wrists more than made up for that.

I woke up some hours later in the male ward. I was still alive, which was something. If the broken bone had hit my femoral artery, everyone agreed I might very well not have been. But I was alarmed to find that both my arms and my left leg were strapped to the ceiling. The really bad news was that I was likely to have to stay in that position for the next six weeks.

I was already beginning to acquire the habit of treating every experience as an interesting adventure, and a hospital is precisely the kind of place where one can find all manner of positive things, provided one is in the frame of mind to look. First and foremost, I discovered that people can be extraordinarily kind. I was unable to read because my arms were tied up to the ceiling, so some of the men on the ward volunteered to turn the pages of a book for half an hour at a time. It was a tedious job, because they had to keep quiet while I was reading, so it was very generous of them. I also discovered that there is always somebody worse off than oneself. After I had been there a couple of weeks, a young lad came in with an extreme form of rheumatoid arthritis. It had completely deformed all his joints and largely blinded him, and it was likely to be terminal. It was a useful reminder to me that I should stop feeling sorry for myself and be thankful that what I had was not much worse.

The final benefit for a confident, tolerably good-looking fourteen-year-old boy confined to a hospital bed for two months was that it put me in close proximity to nurses.

Young people in hospitals tend to be treated differently from other patients. Being injured or ill is an unpleasant experience whatever one's age, but children and teenagers are generally considered unlucky to have ended up in hospital so early in life, and everyone is inclined to make a fuss of them. As a reasonably well-mannered young lad, I did my best to return the compliment by being bright and attentive back, and I managed to be particularly bright and attentive towards the succession of pretty young women just a few years older than myself who were on hand to tuck me in, plump up my pillows, give me bed baths, brush my teeth and generally minister to me around the clock. There really were worse fates, I decided. All the men on my ward flirted with the nurses, most of them in a far more robust and confident manner than I ever dared; but I began to notice that, in my case, some of the flirtation was returned. One nurse in particular, a trim blonde called Mary who must have been about eighteen, and had the same sun-burnished, outdoors complexion as I did, seemed more than happy to tarry at my bedside. When I was finally released from my ceiling straps and encouraged to take faltering steps to try to regain the use of my legs, it was Mary who first brought me out into the sunshine, and as I put my hand in hers for support, it was the most comfortable thing in the world to hold onto it. Emboldened, I attempted a kiss one day when we had reached a relatively secluded part of the hospital grounds, and I was delighted to find that I had not misread the signals.

I spent a total of two months in that hospital, and the last few weeks flew by in the excitement of a furtive affair. But there were obvious limits to what we could get up to, not least because Mary could have been sacked if her matron learned how far our friendship had developed. Nevertheless, youth and ingenuity helped us push the boundaries of what was possible in that restricted environment, and there was a tearful moment when I was told I could leave and we finally had to part.

We told each other that we should certainly try and see one another again. I had a pleasant vision of entertaining Mary at my home in Salisbury, as my parents were very relaxed about our having friends to visit, even to stay. But it was such a long way from Bulawayo, I could not see it happening. We agreed that we would keep in touch by letter.

When I came back to school after missing a term I was largely untouchable. The governors had found out about boys being punished by being sent up trees, and they had also learned about the fagging incident, because the doctors had discovered the branding on my thigh in hospital. The headmaster offered to resign. My family said that was not necessary. They could have gone much further and sued the school, because I had so nearly died, but that might have destroyed the place, so they decided to forgive. Their magnanimity meant the school could continue unscathed, but I emerged with a useful advantage over what I regarded as the establishment.

I had already attracted a dissident group of about ten or fifteen boys – they were not the brightest people in the school, I have to say – and we now grew in confidence. The school authorities had made it very clear that my free-thinking attitude and my spirit of adventure did not fit in with their idea of education. My long period outside the school, along with my exposure to great suffering and the excitement of my affair, made me feel like even more of an outsider, and my general sense of alienation from what I saw as the narrow values of the school made me determined to follow my own path. I led raids on neighbouring orchards at night to get fruit from farmers, only stopping when one farmer shot at us. And I climbed the school bell tower at two o'clock in the morning and unhooked the bell used to wake everybody up at six-thirty. The next morning, the African employee known as the bellboy (even though he was an adult) tried to ring it, but it would not sound. Eventually the housemasters woke up at around seven or seven-thirty and had to go around rousing the boys themselves. They knew it was I who did it, but nobody could prove it.

I had been back at school for almost two terms when a younger boy came to find me in the library, where I was doing some prep, to tell me I had a visitor. She was waiting for me in my housemaster's study, he said. My first thought was alarm. Had something happened to Granny Maud, or to my father or sister, and my mother had driven all the way from Salisbury to tell us in person? There was no sign of anyone being sent to fetch my brother with the same message, but I was worried nonetheless as I hurried along the corridor. Yet when I turned the corner next to the housemaster's office and saw who was standing there, my mouth fell open in astonishment. It was not my mother, but Mary. I had never seen her out of her nurse's uniform before, and she looked ravishing in a summer frock and raised heels. But she was blushing to the roots of her hair.

"Hello," I said. "This is a surprise. We're not normally allowed..."

"So Mr. Barrett has been explaining," she said.

"Well I hope he can make an exception since you've come all this way."

My housemaster was opening and closing his mouth without any words coming out. He was clearly conflicted between his desire to bawl me out, or worse, and the need to be courteous in front of this really rather pretty young woman. I calculated that I still just about had the advantage of the situation, and the best thing Mary and I could do was make ourselves scarce. So I thanked the headmaster for fetching me and off we strolled in the direction of Mary's car for a picnic in the bush.

No woman had ever turned up to visit a boy – junior or senior – in the history of the school. When I walked back into the building later in the afternoon, it was fair to say my standing had increased to a level that threatened to make me even more independent than I already was.

In the meantime, I had also discovered an entrepreneurial streak. Boys in the school were heavily dependent on the tuck shop for sweets. The shop was open at various set times in the day, and of course it only took cash, which we were allowed to draw once a week from our respective housemasters. I sensed an opportunity. If I could get hold of some stock of my own, I could sell it on credit at all times of the day or night and charge a premium for the service, provided I could be sure of collecting my debts. If I made all my product myself, I would solve my supply problems and also be able to add a large margin. So I initially started with peppermint and chocolate creams that needed no cooking. Then when I got my first study, I bought a stove and started producing fudge and coconut ice. If I had exams, I would stir fudge while trying to translate tracts of Latin. I engaged a couple of hefty rugby forwards to collect my debts for me, whom I also paid in sweets. As I charged a mark-up of several hundred percent, I was soon doing very nicely. From the age of fifteen I also ran the school photography society. I took all the school photos and made a profit by selling the pictures to the students in them; nobody else seemed to be interested in photography so I had a complete monopoly. And in a third arm of my nascent business empire, I caught small wild animals such as lemurs, which I sold to a pet shop in Salisbury. As I rose through the school I got younger boys to catch grasshoppers to feed them until I could get them to the city at term-end.

The income came in very handy. In those days, there was a white population of about one hundred and fifty thousand in Southern Rhodesia, compared with a black population of two and a half million. The whites consisted of the oldest pioneer families, newer families like mine from the second wave of settlement, and more recent immigrants who had arrived in the late Forties and Fifties, to escape rationing and the general post-war gloom in Britain. There were social classes – working, middle and upper – just as there were back in the old country. We were economically at the bottom of the upper when compared to my friends in Salisbury. For example, most of them were given cars by their parents, whereas if I wanted one, I would have to buy my own. My "business" activities now enabled me to buy an ancient Ford Prefect. A friend, whose father had the largest garage in Salisbury, said he would help me fix it, which he did, up to a point. Despite his best efforts I still had to reverse up the steeper hills because it could not manage them in first gear, and the steering was also rather eccentric. One had to wrench the wheel from left to right to make turns, as opposed to gliding smoothly. It was hard work, but it got me to parties in the holidays. Fortunately, a number of girls appreciated my being very different from most other young men of my age, and I could drive them around in it too.

My holidays were spent flitting from party to party in the small confines of what passed for Rhodesian society. One night, when I was seventeen, I was coming back from one of these parties at two in the morning when I swerved to avoid a rabbit. I was only doing about twenty miles an hour because I was coming around a corner, but as the steering was so bad, I could not re-correct my course and I ended up rolling the car into a ditch. Since no one had seat belts in those days, I rolled around with it. As the car and I came to rest I could hear petrol dripping out of the tank. I had been smoking when the crash happened, so I knew there was a lit cigarette somewhere in the car. I grabbed at the door handle and scrambled frantically to get out before the car blew up with me inside it. I fumbled the door open, leapt to a safe distance and waited. Somehow the cigarette must have put itself out, because there was no explosion. So I stood there, staring disconsolately at my battered, now undriveable car. With no other option available at that time of night, I set out to walk the couple of miles back home.

The whole house was asleep but I went straight in to my father to wake him up.

"I've crashed my car," I whispered breathlessly as he turned his light on. "What should we do?"

I was distressed and dishevelled, so I must have been an alarming sight.

My father looked at me and sighed.

"I'll arrange for somebody to pick it up in the morning," he said.

I waited for him to ask if I was all right, but the enquiry never came. He simply assumed, because I got in these scrapes all the time, that I must be. It didn't particularly surprise or upset me. He was a good man and definitely a gentleman in his dealings with the world around him, but we had little in common.

As far as the practical arrangements were concerned, he was as good as his word, and the next morning he arranged for the car to be picked up and brought back to the house. I then managed to sell it for a modest sum to an African mechanic who thought he was getting a good deal. He was unaware of the dodgy steering or the fact that he would have to reverse up hills, but if he was a mechanic I was confident he would be able to fix that. With the small amount of money I got from him,

I bought a second-hand Indian Warrior motorbike, which was very rare in Rhodesia at the time.

Subsequently, my friend Gordon Littleford, the son of an American tobacco auctioneer, had a Triumph, as did another friend, and the three of us became a very moderate trio of Hell's Angels. We cruised our motorbikes loudly and at great speed around Salisbury, with the occasional brave girl on the back.

Most schoolboys did not talk about politics or the unequal status of whites and blacks in our self-governing colony. To my discredit, I was more interested in discussing girls and having a good time. I did, however, discuss these things with my mother, who was an active proponent of integration. At that time in Southern Rhodesia it was against the law for a white person and a black person to have sex with each other. It was like the segregation in the Deep South of America, only more so. My mother wrote a series of letters on the subject – one would call them blogs nowadays – which she sent to Sir Roy Wrelensky, the country's prime minister. She was eventually invited by him to go to England and deliver a series of promotional lectures on the case for change. But her advocacy did not go down well with a certain redneck element among the colonial farmers. Indeed, after I had already left Rhodesia in 1959, a fire-bomb was thrown at our house. It only managed to burn an old hedge, but it irritated my father immensely.

I had grown up with many of our staff, and the imbalance in our relationship with them was unavoidable. Every Saturday, my father distributed their weekly food supplies. When I was about seven years old, he started delegating that task to me if he was going out with my mother for the evening. My job was to watch the head 'boy' ladle out food and sacks and to say when each person had enough. We also had a system of passes, whereby employees could not leave the property without written permission. I used to sign these passes for grown men and women, and without my, or my parents' signature, a man of, say, fifty was not allowed to leave our property. I cannot pretend that I questioned this practice as a child, because to me it was just the way things were. I am also sure that such remarkable responsibility at such an early age gave me a level of confidence which set me up for my own adult life. But it came at the expense of the human dignity of our staff. As I began to think critically about the world around me, it seemed a particularly stark example of the way black people were belittled and infantilised by colonial rule. Not only was it wrong, it was also likely to leave a bitter legacy.

The attitudes of some of the white population were deeply shocking. There was a right-wing group of farmers who used to treat their black employees truly as slaves. For example, they would put an Alsatian dog in a mealie bag – the big hessian sack that was used to carry cornflour – and force their staff to beat this dog in the bag with sticks. To a dog, Africans and Europeans have a different scent, so the Alsatian would forever afterwards associate violence and pain with the African smell and be rabid towards black people. It was calculating and ugly. One of my contemporaries, whose father had a huge estate and was known as 'Boss' Lilford, actually killed one of his black employees and got off scot-free, without even being charged.

And I had a so-called friend, who, after a drunken party, saw a black man riding his bicycle on the road and tried to run him down. He drove the man into a ditch and very nearly killed him, laughing madly as he did it. I wrestled with the steering wheel and eventually managed to pull him away. If I had not, the incident could have been much worse.

An immediate, specific example of the violence inherent in pre-Independence Africa was the fact that my parents lost friends and acquaintances to the Mau Mau rebellion against the British in Kenya (1952-1960), which involved brutal attacks on civilians, including women and children. After the Congo gained its independence in June, 1960, a breakaway splinter group of Kantanga tribesmen went on a killing rampage and indiscriminately slaughtered thousands, including European nurses, nuns and priests who had devoted their lives to looking after the local people. Their good works had been no defence against the horrible, destructive violence that had flared up after decades of Belgian colonial rule. They had all been swept up in an orgy of awfulness by the Katanga. Not only had many of the women been raped, they had also been mutilated, in some cases having their breasts hacked off.

Although by the time this last event happened, I had already left Rhodesia, it merely confirmed my reasons for leaving. I had started to see that in post-colonial Africa, it would take many decades before some sort of balance could be achieved. I could understand where the anger and hatred came from. The Belgian colonial regime was widely regarded as the cruellest in Africa, and it had sown a bitter legacy. I also understood how violence could rampage in such an unchecked way. The African world had originally been a tribal one, with village elders who were respected and passed on the oral traditions to the younger ones. That continued from generation to generation in a virtuous circle. But when white colonialists arrived, they drew arbitrary lines on the map, dividing tribes down the middle and often pushing together people who had traditionally hated each other. They also introduced the idea of money, with the result that young Africans left the tribal environment to head for the cities and mines or white men's farms. Having made money, these young men no longer needed the elders, and the tribal bonds were further weakened. So colonialism had stripped away their culture, and there was no correcting system if ever violence erupted.

All these factors combined to make me feel it was pointless to remain in this closed, two-dimensional society. To my mind, what was happening in other countries might very well happen in Rhodesia too. I had no love for the present order, but I had little optimism for the future, either. Furthermore, I was very curious about the rest of the world – the UK and Ireland, where my family had sprung from, America, where my mother had studied, and which represented all that was new and exciting, and of course the mysterious and far distant Asia, which would be the focus of more than fifty years of my life.

Mindful of my mother's Irish roots, in early 1959, I applied for a place at Trinity College, Dublin, intending to study medicine there, starting in September of that year. To my satisfaction, I was accepted, but I needed Latin at a level that I had not yet reached, so I had to do an intensive course concluding with an exam. The day after I had taken it, I went into the school dining hall for the evening meal, and after I had eaten I walked around the entire hall saying goodbye to all my friends. When the headmaster did the roll-call that evening, I was not there. Somebody called out that they thought I had left the school, and it was true. Even though there were still another six weeks until the end of term, I had packed and sent my luggage on, then hitch-hiked to Bulawayo late at night, where I stayed with a friend. The following day I hitched on to Salisbury, which was nearly three hundred miles, so it took me the whole day. It was in the lap of the gods whether I had done enough to get through the Latin exam to confirm my place at Trinity, but after six years I was not prepared to put up with the stuffy boarding school environment of Plumtree even one day longer.

By the time I reached home, my parents had already received a call from school, so they were waiting for me. My housemaster told them I had left Plumtree in the same manner that I had participated in the school, and that I was a disgrace. My father was upset, but frankly he was so used to being upset he did not have a great deal to say. My mother just looked amused. Some forty-five years later, I learned that my housemaster had recorded that he had expelled me, – but after I had voluntarily left, thus giving a new dimension to the word expelled!

The news came that I had passed that vital Latin exam, so everything was in place for me to ship out. I got a summer job as a photographer on *The Rhodesia Herald*, and spent a pleasant few weeks taking pictures of social gatherings and traffic accidents. As the summer ended, I prepared for departure. I was leaving Rhodesia, and in my own mind I had already decided this was no longer the place for me. I was leaving permanently.

2:

My Odyssey Begins

I HAD GROWN UP among people who had lived their formative years in Britain or Ireland, and who spent a good deal of their time shuddering about the climate back there, so it was no surprise to find that conditions on the western fringes of Europe were damp and chilly. If anything, the grey skies of Dublin were not as bad as I had expected: every sunny day was a revelation, because I had never quite believed that such things were possible in Ireland. The main cultural adjustment for me was having to wear so many clothes in a new world where short trousers were spurned for anyone over the age of eleven.

But there were ample compensations. I had spent my entire life to date in the intellectual backwater of colonial Africa, so I had almost no culture written on me. My home city of Salisbury had been founded barely more than half a century ago. Now I found myself in the Georgian quadrangles of Trinity College, an institution dating back to the reign of Queen Elizabeth the First. History was everywhere in the city, from the stately old merchants' houses to the down-at-heel Victorian tenements, and Dublin was tight-knit and dense compared with the relaxed, largely single-storey sprawl of the Rhodesian capital. I was proud of my family roots in this historic place, and I was determined to soak up every new experience here.

Unfortunately, my fellow first-year students were disappointing companions. Growing up in the bush, I had matured early. I had been getting drunk and going with girls since I was twelve or thirteen, so these pursuits held no illicit thrill for me. The same could not be said for the unwashed puppies straight from English public schools among whom I found myself. They pitched themselves into these new experiences with great enthusiasm and not much discipline, and I had no desire to join them, which left me fairly isolated. Fortunately, the second-year students were much more grown up. They were the last generation of students to have done their National Service, which meant they had already engaged in the real, adult world. They had stories to tell of the Malayan Emergency or fighting the Mau Mau, and they were more interesting company all round.

Despite that, I only had one real friend at Trinity, a like-minded Englishman in the year above me named Simon Boreham. He and I concluded that the key to any sort of social success in campus life was to be eccentric, and in pursuit of this aim, we hit on the idea of attempting to travel the hundred-odd miles from Dublin to Belfast on foot. It would be an arduous trip, but we managed to secure sponsorship from Urney's, which was the household-name chocolate brand in Ireland. Their participation would help us attract the attention of the media, and, happily, the sponsorship was offered in kind, so we were given huge cartons of chocolate bars to sustain us on our

journey. We did some practice walking around Dublin for about
a month. On the day of our departure, we finished our lectures
and then met up at six o'clock in the evening at Trinity's main
gates, amid a large gathering of press and students, who were
either cheering us on or heckling. We had our last cigarettes –
I had taken to using an ivory cigarette holder – and then set
off on our way, smiling and waving confidently. Naturally, we
also set about eating our chocolate rations, which we foolishly
mixed with segments of orange.

We had left the city limits of Dublin when we began to
realise this might not have been the best idea: it was clear that
this mixture had a powerful emetic effect when consumed in
any quantity. After about fifteen miles, we were in crisis. With
no facilities in sight, we had no alternative but to pollute the
side of the road.

After another fifteen miles I discovered that I had another
problem. The fracture in my left femur after my accident in
the *marula* tree had left me with one leg shorter than the other.
Consciously or otherwise, I had developed the habit of never
fully extending my right knee, as a way of compensating for the
difference in leg length. This knee was now inflamed, and it hurt
like hell. I tried to soldier on, but it was becoming impossible,
and when we saw the welcoming lights of a roadside pub, we
dragged ourselves inside. It was well after hours but the place
was still going strong, and we drowned our sorrows over our
failure to complete the walk, and then slunk back into college
the next morning on the bus. Our return was marked by
general derision, although we earned a degree of sympathy for
our sorry tale of the emetic effects of chocolate bars. Urney's,

for obvious reasons, dropped us like a hot potato. The sole consolation was that the press which had helped wave us off had better things to focus on.

That humiliation took some living down, and it did nothing to improve my social standing. However, my isolation from my peers was trivial alongside the biggest disappointment of Trinity: the course itself. We had to begin by studying pre-med, which was little more than a rehash of my science A-levels at school, so I was not stretched. Furthermore, now that I had medic friends in the years above me, I could see that they had a level of commitment and dedication to medicine that I could not match. Comparing myself with them, I could see that many of them were cut out to be healers in a way that I was not, and I was by no means certain that I had the patience to spend all my professional life with sick people. I realised it had been a mistake to try to study this subject, and I resolved to leave Trinity at the end of my first year. More than anything else, I was curious about the world, and hungry for as diverse a range of experiences as possible.

I passed all my exams bar chemistry, which I did not even bother to sit, because I had already made my decision. A far better education for me would be to set out to see as much of the globe as I could, learning whatever the world could teach me as I went. It might be rash to enter adult life without a degree of some kind, but I could always get one somewhere else later on. And ultimately, I had already decided, I wanted to follow a piece of advice my mother had given me before I left Rhodesia: that I should go to live for a while in a Buddhist monastery in Asia in order to explore the spiritual philosophies of the East.

Precisely how I could make that happen was something I had yet to work out. In the event, it would take me several years, a cross-continental trek in North America and numerous jobs and adventures before I got there.

Eight months later, I was in Frankfurt, and the alarm clock with its two big bells on either side was trilling away so enthusiastically that it threatened to jump off the side-table. As I did every morning, I flung out a bare arm to try and slap the button on the top that would stop the din. I missed a couple of times before I finally hit it.

"You have to get it faster, otherwise Wilhelm will hear," whispered the woman by my side. She was ten years older than I, but her skin was soft and sweet-smelling, and getting out of the bed was the last thing I wanted to do.

"I'm trying, Traute," I whispered back. "I'm just not at my best at six o'clock in the morning."

Stumbling around in the dark, I pulled on some pyjama trousers and a dressing gown and gave my companion a kiss on the lips.

"*Biss spater,*" Traute whispered after me. See you later.

I opened the door to find a dishevelled male shape in the doorway. It was Traute's husband, Walter.

"*Guten Morgen,*" I whispered.

"*Morgen,* Michael," he whispered gruffly back, and clapped me amiably on the arm. As I squeezed past him, he slipped inside the room.

There were two doors opposite me, one ajar and the other firmly closed. Softly, I entered the open doorway and got into the warm bed that Walter had just vacated.

"Morning, Rachel," I whispered to the shape under the covers alongside me.

There was no reply, just the soft sound of breathing. Turning away from her, I pulled my side of the covers over me and closed my eyes in the hope of another decent hour's sleep before I had to get up again.

I had started my exploration of Europe by lodging with a family near Bonn, the small, functional capital of the demilitarised, chastened West Germany. There I briefly worked as a builder in a mental asylum, until a resident attacked one of my workmates with a hammer and tried to put a nail in his head, whereupon I decided that the job was not worth the danger. I then managed to get a scholarship to a *Heimvolkshochschule*, or cultural college, in an old monastery near the East German border, where I spent six months learning German folk dancing, attending lectures on German culture and cleaning endless supplies of potatoes, which were a staple of the post-war German diet – as well as picking up enough of the language to get by.

After the course was over, I went to stay with a cousin in Frankfurt and got a job stapling circulars together for the German railway workers' union. It was tedious work, but there was no danger of being attacked with a hammer.

One night in Frankfurt, I met Rachel. Originally from South Africa, she was trim and attractive, with black hair, and about seven years' my senior. She told me she was the mistress of a married German artist in his late thirties named Walter, with the full knowledge and consent of his wife. This Walter was looking for someone to help him sell his chocolate-box paintings of Bavarian country scenes to the American military, and when Rachel told him about me, he decided I was the ideal candidate because I was a native English speaker and, hopefully, I was confident enough to knock on doors. The job sounded more interesting than stapling circulars all day, so I accepted, and every evening Rachel drove me around the US military bases. I would go and knock on doors clutching a couple of paintings. Sometimes I was seen off like a mad dog, sometimes I would be allowed in, and occasionally I even sold a painting.

I was invited to live in Walter's shambolic flat. Initially, the arrangement was that I would share Rachel's room, which was unorthodox, considering that there was nothing romantic between us and she was attached to Walter. But the domestic set-up would soon become more unorthodox still. Once I moved in, Walter's wife Traute took a shine to me. She was a sad-looking woman, and certainly no beauty, but she was thoroughly pleasant, and her melancholy demeanour intrigued me. The four of us worked out a deal: I would live with Traute, and Walter would live with his girlfriend, in the same house, in two separate bedrooms. But Walter and Traute had a seven-year-old son who was too young to be told about the unconventional circumstances in which he was growing up. So we agreed that, every morning, when little Wilhelm got up to go to school, we would re-arrange ourselves so that he could say good morning to mummy and daddy in their bedroom and have his breakfast with them. Somehow we managed to get away with it, and the only downside to this otherwise blissful arrangement was that Wilhelm was an early riser; he got up at six-thirty, which meant the rest of us had to swap beds at six.

This *ménage à quatre* worked wonderfully for a few weeks, but all good things come to an end and I was anxious not to get too comfortable, because I had a world to explore. High on my immediate agenda was Berlin.

Since the post-war division of Germany into two states, the old capital of the Weimar Republic and the Third Reich was surrounded entirely by communist East Germany. The city was formally divided into four sectors, controlled by the Americans, the British, the French and the Russians. In reality, however, it was divided in two: the part controlled by the Western allies effectively belonged to West Germany, and, even in its truncated form, was that country's largest city. It was accessible by air or by a road corridor through East Germany. The Soviet-controlled sector of the city, which included the old Prussian centre and many of the great buildings of the city's nineteenth- and early twentieth-century heyday, was the capital of East Germany.

After hitch-hiking along the road corridor, I checked into a hostel in West Berlin and spent a few days exploring. The obvious first impression was that it looked very different to the German cities I had seen so far. Frankfurt and the area around Bonn had been relatively untouched by Allied bombing, but Berlin was visibly shattered.

For me, East Berlin was the real attraction, partly because it contained many great architectural jewels – the cathedral and the great museums on an island in the Spree, and the heart of the old government quarter – but also because it offered a glimpse into the hidden world of the Eastern Bloc, with its brutal concrete buildings and its chilly Stalinist order. I discovered that it was easy to cross into the East, on the other side of the now deserted Potsdamer Platz, without even showing a passport. Every day, tens of thousands of East Berliners commuted to work in West Berlin on the S-Bahn railway. There was also plenty of traffic in the other direction, from shoppers seeking the few goods of quality made by the East Germans, which were a fraction of the price of those in West Berlin, and which were bought using black market exchange rates.

I joined these bargain hunters and went across on the S-Bahn. Once there, the atmosphere changed abruptly: the place felt immediately hostile, and at times a little scary. Cold War tensions were intensifying, and Berlin was famous as a listening post for spies from both sides. As a result, I felt I was being watched everywhere. It was impossible to know if anybody really did care about a young traveller from colonial Africa, or whether I was just being paranoid. This became a real dilemma as I began to explore some of the camera shops in the crumbling heart of the city.

Because of the weak currency, the specialist photographic equipment that East Germany excelled in was a complete steal in the Eastern sector. The problem was that the official tourist exchange rate bore no relation to the actual value of the currency. There were strong restrictions against black market exchange, and there was a potential jail sentence if one was caught. In the West, the idea of the security services stalking an ordinary tourist committing a minor breach of currency laws would have been absurd, and maybe it was absurd in the East too, but never having lived in an authoritarian country, I had no sense of what was likely and what was not. After a lot of agitated humming and hawing, I decided it was worth the risk.

I found a black-market money-changer and did my deal, having done my best to discreetly establish that no homburg-hatted agent was watching me from behind a newspaper or from a shadowy doorway. A couple of hours later I was the proud, if nervous, owner of a wonderful Exakta camera with some superb Jena lenses and other equipment, at a third of the normal cost. All I had to do was get it back to the West. I installed it with the rest of my camera gear to make it look as if I had owned it all the time, and got back on an S-Bahn train across the border, doing my best impression of a carefree tourist with nothing to fear. Happily, nobody stopped me, and perhaps it really was absurd to be so worried.

I was fortunate in my timing, however. Nine months later, the communist government in East Germany shocked the world when it started building a fortified wall between East and West Berlin, complete with razor-wire and military checkpoints. Crossing became much more difficult for tourists like me, and all but impossible for residents on the eastern side. For the next twenty-eight years, any East German caught trying to climb the Berlin Wall to escape to the West was liable to be shot dead in the attempt.

A rendezvous with my mother in London, and her gift of fifty pounds, gave me the balance of funds I needed to visit my Trinity friend Simon in Canada, where he was now enjoying an odyssey of his own.

In those days, meeting up with other people on the move

was a complicated business. The only way of contacting fellow travellers was to write to them at the *poste restante* – a public mailbox at the city's general post office – of whichever place one expected them to have reached. One would suggest a meeting at some prominent landmark on a particular day, and then the same thing the following day if that did not work out, and one would just have to hope that the other person received the letter. It is hard nowadays to imagine how anyone ever managed to pull that off, but it was a normal part of travelling back then, and it was how I made contact with Simon. Once I had docked at the head of the half-frozen St Lawrence River, he and I duly had our reunion in Montreal. He showed me around the city for a few days and then we put French Canada behind us, setting out on the long train journey across the endlessly flat landscape of wheat plains to Calgary, the oil city at the foot of the Rocky Mountains.

We had nowhere to stay when we arrived, and very little money. But we saw a newspaper advert looking for encyclopaedia salesmen. I had already sold paintings to the US military, so door-to-door selling to civilians was well within my comfort zone, and I started shifting the volumes with some success. The job had lows and highs: I was punched a couple of times, but I was also seduced a couple of times. On one occasion, the two may even have been related.

The itinerant life was not for Simon, however, and after a while he decided to return to England. I waved him off and settled back into my routine as a solo traveller. I was good at being self-sufficient, and I was confident in my ability to make new friends whenever I had a need for company. I continued selling encyclopaedias, but one day, when I got back to the hostel where I had been staying and put my hand in my pocket to pay in advance for the night ahead, I found that my wallet was not there. I checked the other pocket, then the back ones and every pocket of my coat, and I frantically turned my bag inside out. But I did not recall putting it any of those places, and as each part of my search proved fruitless, I realised it was much more likely the wallet had fallen out of my pocket on the electric trolleybus back from the suburb where I had been hawking my wares. I did not even have the change for a phone call, so I raced off to the bus station to see if there was a lost property office. It was still open, but nothing matching the description of my wallet had yet been handed in, and frankly I could not imagine it ever happening. Even if someone did hand it in, the chances of it still having any cash in it were remote, and while I was sorry to have lost the wallet itself, because it had been a gift from my parents two or three years earlier, the loss of the money inside was of much greater practical significance. I always spent cash sparingly and I knew how to get by on very little, but suddenly I did not have a cent to my name.

Retracing my steps to the hostel, I told the owner what had happened and pleaded to be allowed to stay for a few days before I got my next pay packet from the encyclopaedia company. He shook his head and said it was out of the question. He did not even look me in the eye.

I had no choice but to pack up my few possessions and move on, trying to assess my options as I did so. If the worst came to the worst, I could eat by pilfering food from a market. But shelter was going to be more of a problem. I had been so busy pounding the streets selling my encyclopaedia subscriptions that I had made few local contacts, and certainly nobody I knew well enough to ask if I could stay for a few days. There was no such thing as a Rhodesian consulate in Calgary where I could go to ask for an emergency loan. But I had to find somewhere to sleep: even though the winter was drawing to a close, it was still bitterly cold at night, so it was not just a matter of comfort, but of survival. Downtown Calgary was beginning to look like a lonely place as darkness fell and the last commuters disappeared. I found myself wandering aimlessly in search of inspiration, and my path took me into the Memorial Park, a formal garden outside the city's main library. It had once been the pride of the city but now had a sad and neglected air. At the centre of the park stood a large equestrian statue commemorating the Canadian soldiers who died in the Boer War. The bronze cavalryman wore a wide-brimmed hat to keep the southern African sun out of his eyes, a memory of home that served to emphasise all the more my present cold and miserable state.

I continued my forlorn trudge along the formal paths of the garden. Over in the trees at the fringe of the park was a small, stone-fronted building with a dim yellow bulb glowing over the doorway. I had been there once before: these were the public conveniences, and they had left little positive impression on me at the time. Now, however, I saw the building in a new light. Here at least was a place where I could get out of the wind and snow. I checked that it was open all night and unattended, which it seemed indeed to be. After spending a further couple of hours searching for scraps of food, I came back at the end of the evening and managed to settle myself into a fairly discreet corner. I passed a fitful night on the dank, hard-tiled floor, using my rucksack as a pillow. Not many people came in to use the facilities, and most of those who did looked at me warily and made themselves scarce as quickly as they could.

The next day I was drained. I had running cold water on hand to give myself a basic wash, but there was no soap, and I had spent the night in my clothes so I felt fairly gruesome. One glance in the grimy mirror told me that I was in no fit state to go out knocking on suburban doors to sell encyclopaedia subscriptions. In any case, I did not even have the trolleybus fare to get there. Thus I began the classic spiral down into homelessness. My own jealously guarded territory became my safe space, and I felt a degree of security there that would have been impossible to imagine myself feeling just a week earlier. But with the search for food and the need to protect myself in my shelter becoming my all-consuming priorities, it was hard to think about anything beyond the confines of this narrow world. At night, drunks would taunt me, and some of them found it amusing to relieve themselves directly onto my sleeping bag. I did my best to fend them off, but I was also anxious not to get into fights. So I became meek and diminished. Seeing how quickly my circumstances threatened to transform me was a revelatory experience, and I discovered a new respect for the homeless people I might previously have walked past.

As I shivered at night, I could easily see how tempting it might be to insulate myself against cold and loneliness with cheap beer or worse. But I told myself I must fight such thoughts: keeping my head above the surface was a constant struggle, but

I needed even greater strength if I was to pull myself out of this situation.

For two weeks I scoured the job ads in every discarded newspaper I could lay my hands on, and eventually a notice caught my eye. A resort hotel up in the Rockies was looking for a photography assistant in preparation for the summer season, and crucially the post came with accommodation. Fortunately, I still had my precious East German equipment, guarded with my life, inside my rucksack. I managed to beg enough small change together to make a phone call, and somehow I made myself presentable enough for an interview downtown. I do not know whether it was desperation helping me talk a good talk, or simply an absence of other suitable candidates, but they told me the next day that I was hired. They were even prepared to give me a complimentary rail ticket. So I rolled up my poor, abused sleeping bag and said goodbye to Calgary. I was unlikely to forget my stay there.

The Chateau Lake Louise was a vast lakeside mansion originally built in the late nineteenth century by the Canadian Pacific Railway as a way of luring affluent travellers to the west of the country by rail. My work there involved photographing guests and managing the camera accessories shop in the hotel lobby. I was grateful for a comfortable room and very decent food, and once the summer season started, I got on well with the students who came to work through their long vacation. But my time there came to an abrupt end after a clash with my German boss, who had shown from the outset a tendency to order me around. As I became more established, I knew I was doing my

job well and I determined to stand up to him. I duly did so –
and I was told to pack up my stuff and leave. I could see it was
fruitless to argue: I had miscalculated and lost. But the loss was
not that great. I knew my way around the resort by then, and
before the day was out I had a new job as a soda jerk at a nearby
hotel. After a short interlude there, I fell in with three English
girls who had a big, clapped-out Chevrolet which they wanted
to drive down to the southern United States and then across
to New York. Mindful that it would be useful to have a man
along, they asked if I would like to join them.

   Our journey took us south, across the border into Washington
State. Technically a US visa was required, but the border officials
were fairly relaxed on the matter if a traveller had, as I did, a
valid Canadian visa. We drove on through Oregon and into
California, where we saw the Yosemite National Park, and then
continued across the desert to Las Vegas. In those days, guests
were given a free room in the hope that they would gamble. I
had very little money, so I was not inclined to throw it away
on the gaming tables, but we spent a couple of days seeing the
sinful sights and eating and drinking largely for free. Then we
drove on to the Grand Canyon, where I convinced the girls to
walk down with me and spend the night on the canyon floor.
It was not a restful night: a skunk ambled across our little
campsite and when two of the girls woke up and saw it, they
started shrieking. They were so scared they ended up spending
the rest of the night halfway up a tree.

   The next day, after the arduous climb back out of the
Canyon, the girls wanted to carry on to Phoenix, but I had
had my fill of tourism. Although my travels so far had been

haphazard and fairly aimless, I had resolved by now that my ultimate destination was Asia. I was following the lure of those mythical dragons and griffins my grandfather had told me about, and it would also be my opportunity to learn more about the great religions of the East, as my mother had urged. In that context, to head back towards the East Coast of the US felt like going in the opposite direction. So we said our goodbyes and I hitched a ride towards Los Angeles with an English couple. This journey was chiefly memorable for the sandstorm that blew up midway across the Mojave Desert. We were forced to pull over for an hour, and it was remarkable to be inside the cocoon of the car, with fine dust coming through the cracks and the air intake. When the storm finally passed, we got out to inspect the damage and found that the blue car was now silver, having lost its entire paint job in the assault.

Three days later, I was back in Oregon, where I woke up in jail.

The English couple had put me up for a night in Los Angeles, from where I continued up to San Francisco, where Gordon Littleford, my motorbike mate from Rhodesia, now lived with his family, across the bay in Oakland. I heard from them that one could 'dead-head' cars — delivering them long distance as a way of getting there oneself — and after they helped me find an appropriate agency, I got a contract to drive a car to Seattle.

The fee for driving the car from California to Washington State was enough for the petrol and minimal food, but it did not leave much over for hotels and proper meals. By nightfall I had got as far as Grants Pass, a small town in Oregon, and I was dog-tired. The car was too cramped to sleep in, so I had an idea. I asked for directions to the local highway patrol office to see if I could stay the night in one of their cells. The patrolman said that would not be possible, but perhaps I would have more luck at the local police station in town. I did as he suggested and repeated my request at the front desk. The officer on duty looked bemused at first but then he shrugged and said: "Okay, but I'm going to have to book you for vagrancy."

It would be my first (and last) arrest, but I did not see what harm it could do. So I had my photograph and fingerprints taken, then he took away my shoelaces and my belt and led me into the back of the station. He gestured towards a large, bare room equipped with what felt like a searchlight on the ceiling – the bulb must have been two hundred watts – with an open toilet in the corner and a number of empty bunks.

I stared at the cell.

"What's this?" I said.

"This is the drunk tank," the officer said.

"But I'm not drunk."

"It's fine, this is where you're going to sleep."

I had been hoping for a single cell with a nice comfortable bed, but when I said as much, he seemed to find that hilarious. It was a small town and he was probably bored, so the whole episode was clearly amusing him. On the other hand, if he had been busier, he might just have told me to get lost and I would have had to sleep in the car after all, so I had to count what blessings I could find. At least there were no other occupants that night.

He woke me up at six the following morning.

"Out," he said.

I went back to sleep. I had a long drive ahead of me and I needed all the rest I could get. Besides, I was twenty years old, and I was not good at early mornings.

The officer came back ten minutes later and said: "If you're not out in five minutes, you'll stay in here for the week."

I leapt out of bed with great alacrity, and he gave back my shoelaces, belt, wallet and watch. I went on my way, and I have no doubt he chuckled over the story for the rest of the week.

When I reached Seattle later that day, I had no more money in my pocket than I had had in the morning. But I had at least discovered a way of getting a free bed for the night, so I decided to try my luck once again. I rang what I hoped was a local police office from a phone booth, and got straight through to an operator at the city's central police station. I explained my predicament.

"You really don't want to be in one of the cells here," the operator said. "We have all sorts of unpleasant people – rapists, murderers, drug dealers. You might be assaulted in one of the general holding cells. Why don't you just come up and see us in the telephone operators' room?"

I did as she suggested and found the woman I had spoken to on the third floor of the police station. She and five colleagues faced a large switchboard on which a light would blink whenever a call came, whereupon one of them would grab a cable and stick it in the socket for that line.

I caught their end of the various conversations.

"I see, you've just found a dead man in your garden. We'll send a squad car round, ma'am."

"So, to be clear, your father has just assaulted you?"

"Calm down, sir. You say you've just killed your wife?"

The woman had not been joking when she said they had plenty of serious crime in this city.

As I stood in the doorway, one of these operators turned and said, "You must be Michael. Come and sit down with me."

She walked me to some chairs in the corner of the room and said: "We really can't organise for you to stay in jail. But some of us have children of your age who are travelling, and we hope that people will help them if they get into difficulties. So we'd like to help you."

They had collected fifty bucks to put me up in a cheap hotel across the road.

"Please, with our compliments, have a safe journey onwards," she said.

I was touched beyond words and I went around the room giving each of these kind middle-aged ladies a big kiss of gratitude. That took them by surprise, because America is not much of a kissing culture, but I was overwhelmed by their generosity to a complete stranger.

A friend from Lake Louise had invited me to visit him at his fraternity house in the University of British Columbia. After delivering the car, I used what was left from my donation from my telephone operator friends to buy a bus ticket to Vancouver, a hundred and fifty miles away. I ended up attending some courses that took my fancy at UBC for a few weeks because I was living free at the fraternity house and my friend there kindly gave me a small loan. I didn't ask for permission to do so, I simply joined the other students at lectures, and the professors never even noticed. I imagine they were more worried about students cutting classes than about strangers taking extra ones.

I knew, however, that I had to get a job if I was ever going to earn enough to get to Asia, and I managed to secure a position in a Vancouver department store selling gloves. I am by nature a good salesman. I had run my own sweet business at school, so I knew I had commercial flair, and my interest in other people was genuine. Unfortunately, those skills were of little use in my department, when there was scarcely a customer in sight from one hour to the next. With winter having started, most who wanted gloves already had them, and I said no more than fifteen or twenty words a day. It might have worked better had I been allowed to approach people and tell them I had a great deal for them, but that was not the style of the store. So I stood there all day, shuffling gloves from one tray to another. It was one of the only times in my life that I have suffered genuine, profound boredom. My frustration must have been obvious, because the manager fired me after three days.

I needed to find something more constructive, and I had heard there was a logging camp at Port Alice, at the far north-western end of Vancouver Island. It was a remote place. The island was visible across the bay from the city, but it then extended three hundred miles northwards, and that was where the camp was. Since there was no road there, it was only accessible by boat or seaplane.

I made my enquiries and discovered that the place was run on a Catch-22 arrangement: only union members were allowed in, but it was impossible to join the union without having a job.

Despite that, I managed to talk my way into the company's

Vancouver office.

"What can you do?" asked the recruitment manager dubiously.

"I'll do anything," I said truthfully. "I'm fit and willing, and I'm a fast learner."

"Well, you could be a logger," he said, not looking convinced by his own words. "But it's a tough job. You have to start at the bottom as a choker-man. You put a choker chain around the trunk of a felled tree so the crane can haul it up. Then it goes on a trailer to the pulp mill. It's the worst job, and accidents happen." He looked down at the dog-eared *résumé* I had optimistically offered him. "This medicine course you say you did. Did you do any chemistry?"

"Yes, certainly. A year of it."

There was no need to tell him I never wrote the exam. He did not have the air of a man who would care.

"In that case we have an opening in the pulp mill," he said. "We need a lab assistant to analyse the pulp as it gets processed. You'll need to work shifts, but I'm sure you could handle that."

I agreed, and I was officially accepted into the camp.

It was a tough place, populated by refugees from the normal world. Most of these loggers and pulp mill workers would come and work like crazy for three to six months and then go to Vancouver and blow their earnings on booze and prostitutes, after which they would come back and repeat the cycle. I stuck out a mile. My affectation of smoking with an ivory cigarette holder caused a good deal of mirth. Although I was fit, I was tall and thin, rather than burly like my lumberjack colleagues, which added to their amusement. And of course I spoke with an odd accent. Rhodesian sounds like a softer version of South African, without that harsh Afrikaner throatiness, and my own version of it was an educated one, so to their ears I simply sounded English. But I could cope with being teased, and to the amateur social anthropologist in me, everything about them was interesting.

My shift colleague in the pulp mill laboratory was another matter. He was a working-class Englishman called John who had somehow found his way to Canada in middle age. He was disgruntled and unhappy, and I guess he saw in me the other side of life: I had chosen to go there, and I would probably go on to something else, whereas he was forced to remain in that place. Whatever the reason, he made it clear he hated me from the day I walked in and said good evening to him.

Every day after that I would say good morning or good evening, and every day he would studiously ignore me as we tested the pulp that was being cooked in giant vats. It was not persecution on his part, so much as an absolute refusal to co-operate. I had learned at school not to waste energy worrying about hostility when it was clearly the other person's problem not mine. John had to live with himself, and I was doing fine living with myself. But it was nonetheless a frustrating experience to spend many months working alongside someone who, for no rational reason, hated me and had no intention of moderating that attitude.

The pulp mill manager invited me for dinner from time to time — I imagine because he was bored and isolated too, and I was a better conversational prospect than just about anyone else in the camp. That was my only social life, and when I was due a couple of weeks' vacation, I had no desire to go back to Vancouver to drink away my hard-earned cash like my workmates. Instead I discovered there was a log cabin on a lake, about fifteen miles inland from the pulp mill, where I would be allowed to stay.

The only way to get there was on foot. I arrived laden with my basic rations for two weeks – mainly cans, cereals and powdered milk. The cabin itself more than lived up to its billing. It consisted of just one room, with rather primitive cooking facilities, but it was barely ten metres from a lake on which there was an ethereally beautiful mist every morning, and the whole place was surrounded by virgin forest. After the crudeness of the logging camp, the peace and isolation was a joy – at first, at any rate. At that age, because of my general curiosity, I was essentially a gregarious person. With nobody else for miles, a limited supply of books and no telephone or radio, I began to feel the weight of loneliness. The only noises were the sounds of the forest, and after four or five days I started talking to myself. I realised that being truly alone is something few people ever experience – except prisoners in solitary confinement. Unlike them, I could walk outside and admire the scenery. I could also have trekked back to the camp any time I liked, so I was not trapped. But staying was one of the toughest things I had ever done.

At the end of the two weeks I knew I had had enough, but I was also encouraged that I had been able to take it. It reinforced the ambition that I had been steadily developing: once I finally got to Asia, I would seek out a monastery where I would further test my powers of endurance, in every sense of the word, which would help me to tackle the far more difficult task of making spiritual progress. I had every intention of taking seriously my mother's instruction to explore the world's great belief systems. With its focus on self-knowledge and awareness of one's place within the universe, Buddhism was the philosophy that interested me the most. I was beginning to sense that I might be more or less able to handle its disciplines.

Back in camp, I resumed my place in the kind of world where solitude was an impossible aspiration. The bunkhouse was rife with drinking and gambling, and the room next to mine was occupied by a particularly burly French Canadian who used to invite all his mates in to get loudly drunk with him. One night I was woken by a monumental crash as a fist came through the wall about a foot above my face. I heard drunken laughter through a hole in the well.

"Did you get the English bastard?"

"No, I missed," said the owner of the fist.

The pugilist was clearly on a roll now and thought he would have another go. So there was another loud crunch, but this time it was followed by a howl of agony.

"Christ, I think I've broken my wrist!"

He had punched straight into a joist, so the game came to an end and I could go back to sleep.

After I had accumulated a couple of thousand dollars in savings, I packed my bag and returned to the United States, once again getting by on my Canadian visa.

Having been toughened up in the logging camp, I now felt I could handle anything. Staying once more at the Littlefords' place in Oakland, I presented myself at the Alameda docks, the heart of the port of San Francisco. The selection process was haphazard: one had to turn up with a bunch of other deadbeats at six in the morning and hope to be picked by the foreman. Fortunately, because I was fresh and eager, I was selected most of the time.

On my first day, keen to show that I was capable of hard work, I was rushing around moving crates when the foreman came up to me and said: "Hey kid, see that pile of bags over there?"

"Yes," I said, following where he was pointing.

"I want you over there and fast asleep in five minutes, for the next two hours. We're in no rush here. You're making us all look bad." After that I slowed my pace.

The other eye-opener, in these days before the advent of containers, was the number of deliberate accidents. A crate from Japan would somehow 'fall off the forklift' and break open. Suddenly there were all these Sony radios lying on the floor and everyone was stuffing them in their bags.

"Help yourself!" someone would say.

I declined. I didn't want to seem priggish, but I disapproved. Although I had no intention of snitching, this large-scale, deliberate pilfering seemed pretty venal to me.

There was plenty of time for other pursuits outside working hours. I made contact with Jane, an English girl I had met in Vancouver, who was now living in San Francisco. At her apartment one day I picked up a book which would change my life. Entitled *The Chrysanthemum and the Sword*, it had been written immediately after the war by an American anthropologist called Ruth Benedict. She had never set foot in Japan – it was impossible for Westerners to do so in the war years – and she had written the book at the behest of the US Office of War Information, which wanted to predict the behaviour of the Japanese by gaining a better understanding of their national culture. Despite this unpromising genesis, it had come to be accepted as the seminal work on the country, and it made a convincing attempt to describe the code of behaviour in Japan and to explain why the Japanese were so perplexingly different to most other people in the world. One of Ruth Benedict's arguments was that most early societies, once they had the tools, tried to control their natural environment, and from there went on to try to control everything else, but the Japanese had never tried to control nature – they had simply accepted that they were part of it. Typhoons, volcanic eruptions, earthquakes and tsunamis had, over the centuries, given them an absolute sense of the immutability of the natural world, and as a result, they lived closer to a state of nature than any other nation, both literally and figuratively. In nature, there is only survival and balance, and a recognition of that fact had had a major impact on their spiritual philosophy, and their attitude to one another. Since it was inappropriate to impose ideals of fairness and order upon nature's random and often brutal acts, many Japanese did not experience guilt, because they did not believe in fairness, even as an ideal. This seemed to me a startlingly good way of understanding their behaviour during the Second World War: while undeniably appalling, it was perfectly consistent with the standards evolved by their civilisation. They did what they had always done, and they did unto others as they did to their own people. What the Germans did under Hitler was abhorrent and a complete break with their Christian belief system and culture.

It made me see that railing against this reality or assessing blame for their wartime conduct served little purpose, and by the end of the book I was gripped by this fascinating country and its culture, marked off by place, time and history from the rest of the world, and in many respects remaining as Japanese as it had been for hundreds or even a thousand years. Now, more than ever, I was determined to see Japan for myself and immerse myself in its culture.

I set to thinking seriously about the practicalities of getting there. I heard that the US Coast and Geodetic Survey was looking for sailors to crew one of its survey ships. It was heading up to Alaska and then down to Hawaii and back to San Francisco. That was a good enough start – it would get me halfway to Japan without my having to part with a cent, and I would get paid into the bargain. Along with one of Gordon Littleford's brothers, I went to sign up. Thanks to my lab experience at the pulp mill, I was immediately taken on. One of the ship's tasks was to analyse seawater samples at different depths, and my job was to run the lab where this was done. It was very similar to the task at the logging camp, except that I would not have to spend all my working hours in the company of someone who openly disliked me. It sounded excellent.

We embarked for the northern seas and encountered some seriously rough weather off Kodiak Island in the Gulf of Alaska. Waves would rear ten or fifteen metres over the stern of the boat, and we crashed up and down with them. It was hairy stuff but we got through it intact. In due course we carried on down towards Hawaii. But as we sailed into the central Pacific, I realised I might have a problem. When I signed on, I had told the Coast Guard recruiting officer that I was the son of an American diplomat stationed in Africa, in order to cover the fact that I did not have a US visa in my passport or a social security number. In those days, if one said that kind of thing with sufficient confidence, and looked the part, one could get away with it. But now one of the senior sailors tipped me off that we were all automatically being checked out because of the quasi-secret nature of the survey work, and I would be in a mess if they realised I had effectively entered the country illegally.

"Your best option is to jump ship in Hawaii before things catch up with you," he advised. "If they do catch you, you'll be deported and then you'll never be able to get back into the United States."

It sounded good advice. I notified the captain that I had a family emergency, whereupon I was given my last pay check and wished good luck. I now found myself on the quayside in Honolulu, halfway across the Pacific and with cash in my pocket.

I fell under the wing of some friendly local Hawaiians, who took me to live on a plantation in the Kona district, famous for its coffee, on the Big Island. We picked coffee beans by day and in our time off we hunted wild boars with knives and spears – or at least, I went with them while they did it. Leaping on a wild pig with a huge blade was a little too muscular for me, but I enjoyed eating the roast meat. Unfortunately, I lost a front tooth and I had to return to Honolulu, where I got it fixed – at no cost – on the US naval base, as my navy PX Card was still valid. I then managed to get a job in a parking garage in Honolulu, where I became friendly with a native Hawaiian who ran a surfing concession on Waikiki Beach. I had started surfing on family holidays in Durban and Mozambique, and had become quite good at it since arriving in Hawaii.

"Look," my friend said one day, "one of my buddies has just dropped out, and you can surf, so why don't you come and join me, teaching tourists?"

Within the space of a year I had been a paintings and glove salesman, a lumberjack, a stevedore, and a naval lab technician. Now I was to become a professional surfer. And although I could not know it when I took the job, this role would give me an introduction that would determine the course of the rest of my life.

Waikiki was a busy beach with lots of tourists, ninety percent of them from the US mainland. Some were young and fit and genuinely wanted to surf, but many were bloated landlubbers who merely played with the idea. There were a few Asian tourists too, and one afternoon a young Japanese guy in shirt and swimming trunks, with a completely shaved head, approached me.

"Want to rahn suffing," he announced.

"What?" I asked.

"Want rahn suffing," he repeated.

I said I was sorry, I really could not understand what he meant.

"Suffing!" he said, getting agitated now.

"Ah," I said as the penny finally dropped. "You want to learn surfing!"

The conversation became less stilted as my ear grew used to his accent. He told me his name was Koichi, and he had only just arrived in Hawaii. He had been sent by his temple in a monastery complex in Mount Koya to open a similar temple on Oahu, the island where Honolulu sits.

As I listened to him, an idea was forming. I had already established through my own research that anyone who wanted to go into a Japanese monastery was expected to lie on the front steps for a number of days, and sometimes for as much as a couple of weeks, in rain or snow, to show how serious they were about becoming a monk. But I had also learned from reading *The Chrysanthemum and the Sword* that if I did Koichi a favour, he would feel a sense of obligation to me, as his abbot probably would, because I had helped one of his monks. That was the Japanese way.

"I'll tell you what," I said. "It's my ambition to go to a monastery in Japan, and I would be very grateful for an introduction to your abbot. If you're able to give me one, I will give you free surfing lessons. I'll also help you find a place to live and look after you while you settle in."

Koichi considered for a moment and then told me he would accept the deal. I duly spent a couple of months teaching him to surf and I took him under my wing, as other people had taken me under theirs.

I had been calculating to some extent, because I had not known him when I made my offer. But I was confident it had been a good idea. I already had enough money from the logging camp, the survey vessel and the surfing to buy a ticket on a liner to Yokohama, and now I had an *entrée* into a Buddhist monastery. I was about to put into practice my mother's advice of investigating one of the great religious philosophies of the world at its source. All I had to do was book my passage.

3:

Stripped Bare
on the Mountain

THE ONLY WORD of Japanese I knew was *sayonara*. It had entered
the global vocabulary thanks to the recent hit film of that
name, starring Marlon Brando. The word meant 'goodbye', and
since I was keen to stay in this country for a while, I would
have to acquire some more vocabulary pretty quickly. But I
realised, as I stood on the bitterly cold quayside of Yokohama
in January 1963, that I was going to need some help. In every
other non-English-speaking country I had visited, I could read
the letters on the public notices even if I did not know what
they meant, and paying attention to the signs was a good way
of picking up words. There was no such possibility here. Aside
from some Roman lettering up the side of a steel lattice tower
that looked like a theme park attraction, but was in fact an
immense lighthouse, the only familiar marks on any of the
signage around me were numerals.

My first task was to find my way to the railway station. On
the quayside, I walked up to man in a business suit to ask if he

spoke English in an elaborately polite manner, even attempting a little bow, which I hoped approximated to Japanese customs. Whether it did that or not, I was patiently directed to the station, where I managed to buy myself a ticket for the relatively short journey along the industrialised bay to Tokyo.

Arriving in the capital, I checked into a cheap hotel for a couple of nights to try to orient myself to my new surroundings. On my first day, I walked until my knee screamed. There was nothing ancient or picturesque to see. Most of the city seemed to be a jumble of knocked-together buildings, with an oasis of clean modern towers at the centre. But it was no less interesting for that. The whole place was crowded but disciplined: the armies of neatly-dressed businessmen filling the pavements all seemed to be going in the same direction, and the city felt hectic but somehow efficient at the same time, like a finely-geared machine. It was striking that mine seemed to be the only Caucasian face. The war was now nearly twenty years in the past, but Japan was still a pariah nation where few outsiders wanted to come, and few of the inhabitants had ever left. In those years, Japanese citizens were not allowed passports unless they had a *bona fide* reason for travelling abroad on business, and even then, they were granted a one-trip document which had to be given back when they returned.

Everything was an adventure for me, even the most basic tasks, such as feeding myself. Fortunately, the cheap restaurants provided menus which included photos of the dishes, at which one could point. Once I was presented with the food, I then had to work out how to get it into my mouth equipped with only a pair of chopsticks. This required a level of manual dexterity

I did not yet possess, but hunger was a powerful incentive and I attempted to study the grip used by other diners. I took comfort from the fact that it seemed perfectly acceptable to lift the bowl to one's mouth and slurp soup or shovel food down in a way that would have horrified Nursey.

I could have carried on exploring for weeks, and although I knew that my friend Koichi's introduction to his abbot was unlikely to expire, I nonetheless wanted to travel to Mount Koya as quickly as possible. That was the real purpose of this long journey, and getting to know the rest of the country could wait.

It was a whole day's trip by train from Tokyo to Osaka, through wooded mountains punctuated by wide plains on which rice fields were planted in dead straight lines. That was followed by a further rail trek into the mountains to Mount Koya. The monastic complex sat in a high valley surrounded by eight peaks. Here, in the ninth century, a Japanese monk known as Kobo Daishi had established the *Shingon-shu* or 'True Word' school of tantric Tibetan Buddhism; he reputedly chose the spot because the landscape looked like a lotus flower. The complex had grown over the centuries to become the world headquarters of Shingon Buddhism, and it now contained more than a hundred individual temples: some very large, others tiny. The one I was looking for, named Shino-In, was in the latter category. It was supposed to be the oldest, and dated from 813 AD.

It was much colder up here than it had been in Tokyo and Yokohama, with nearly two metres of snow covering the ground. A sacred pilgrimage path led from the foot of the mountain to Kobo Daishi's mausoleum, with the way shown by engraved stone markers in the trees, each of them built in the symbolic five tiers of a Buddhist pagoda. But the whole place was also a functioning town, with a university, schools and shops, and there was an ordinary road from the railway station too. I discovered that my destination was one of the most remote of all the individual temples. Pulling my woollen hat down low and wishing I had an even warmer coat, I trudge on, eventually arriving at the snow-bound gates of a small wooden building complex – Shino-in, its pointed roof curving into an upturned brim like a hat. I paused before knocking. I had come a long way to reach this point, but now that I was actually here, I had no clear idea what lay in store for me. I could only hope the abbot really would let me in without requiring me to lie for a week in the snow.

The door was opened by a shaven-headed monk in a simple black linen robe, which contrasted starkly with my heavy winter clothing. He looked about ten years older than I was.

I bowed.

I had of course memorised the abbot's name, and I had gleaned the polite way to address a member of the Buddhist clergy from a phrasebook on the train.

"Good afternoon," I said. "I'm looking for Nakamura Jushoku."

The monk returned my bow and gestured for me to come inside.

The interior walls of the temple were of plain whitewashed plaster, and the floor was made of old cedar planks. To my dismay, it was no warmer inside than out, and I could still see my breath in front of me. The monk indicated that I should follow him into a *tatami* room, where a tiny man of about seventy, in a similarly simple – but white – robe, rose to greet me. We bowed at each other.

I began trying to explain myself in some artificial phrases I had pieced together from my phrasebook. But a small woman in similar garb to the men shuffled forward and saved me the effort.

"You are the Englishman who wants to study Buddhism?" she asked. "We are expecting you. Welcome."

"Rhodesian, not English. But yes. My name is Michael. And thank you."

There were just five people living in the monastery: the elderly abbot, who had been there since he was four years old, the monk who let me in plus two other monks, and our interpreter, a Japanese nun, who had been born in Hawaii and was the abbot's housekeeper. She was the only member of the community who spoke any English. I learned later that I was the first Westerner to have been accepted in its almost 1,200 years of existence.

Fortunately Koichi's introduction had been effective, and the good news was that I could stay without having to prostrate myself on the doorstep first. I was allocated a *tatami* room with paper windows, where a daytime temperature of minus four or five degrees was normal in the winter. The next morning the remains of the tea I had left in a cup beside my *futon* (foldable sleeping mattress) had frozen solid. I also discovered that if I spilled water on the floor it would be sheet ice within a couple of minutes, and that I could not write for more than five minutes without warming my hand on a little brazier which was the only heating permitted in the building. Shino-in prided itself on the fact that it had never installed electricity, and that everything was as it was since it was founded nearly one thousand two hundred years ago – fortunately the only exception to this was running water, which provided the one luxury in this temple of extreme austerity – a hot communal bath.

In simplistic terms, the whole monastic tradition is designed to minimise, and ultimately lose, the ego, which, according to Buddhism, is the part of the self that has desires, such as concerns with form, or wanting to be loved or happy. The idea, as I was to learn, was to cut all that off, as if with a scalpel. This applied to all aspects of daily life. The food I was offered on my first evening was minimal. We sat on the floor to a meal of watery rice, rock salt that was meant to be eaten separately, and pickled roots. There was also seaweed and tofu, but that was it – and it all came in tiny rations. This was not poor hospitality, so much as evidencing the whole ethos of the place: food was meant to fuel the body engine but no more, and one was not expected to take pleasure in it.

Originating in India two and a half thousand years ago, Buddhism is a belief system focused on cleansing the mind of agony and suffering, and is therefore fundamentally about human knowledge rather than idol worship. Tantric or esoteric Buddhism (based on a tantra or mystical text, system of learning) is concerned with the situations and meditative practices that lead to enlightenment. The Shingon doctrine expounded by Kobo Daishi holds that enlightenment is a very real possibility, based on the spiritual potential of every living being. If cultivated, it manifests itself as innate wisdom, and with the help of a genuine teacher, via proper training of the body, speech and mind, one can reclaim and liberate this enlightened capacity, for the benefit of oneself and others. But for centuries the doctrines of Shingon had been secret. No book had been published about the sect's teachings and rituals anywhere in the world until some twenty years before I arrived.

As well as choosing a secret sect, I had, entirely by accident, chosen one of the strictest temples in the complex. There may have been others on Mount Koya where monks had wives and children and drank *saké* every night, but not Shino-In. Even today it is the only temple not to have electricity. Nakamura, who, I was to discover farted and belched without any inhibition, was proud of it. "This is the way it was nearly twelve hundred years ago, and this is the way it's going to stay," he told me through his housekeeper.

The strictness of the regime included ablutions. For the first few days I was too embarrassed to ask the housekeeper-nun where the toilet was. Instead I took myself discreetly into the forest and attempted to move my bowels in the snow, risking frostbite to my rear end. Eventually I noticed one of the monks moving at a faster than normal pace; on a hunch that he was answering a call of nature, I followed him, and he did indeed lead me to the proper place. However, I also discovered by observing him that there were particular rules to be obeyed even in the lavatory. Freezing cold as it was, we were supposed to strip off completely in order not to sully our robes. This meant standing naked on below-freezing tiles, and it required a major effort of will just to put oneself through the process.

That was symptomatic of the whole experience of living at the temple, where I came to realise that I had been stripped down to nothing in many other ways. While I was treated with unfailing politeness – which made a pleasant change after the attempts to bully me at the logging camp – there was no likelihood of my developing friendships with the other monks. If I hadn't incurred the obligation of the abbot, as the lowest monk on the totem pole, I would have been very harshly treated as part of the training. In the Buddhist belief system, friendship is about ego, so the focus was on detachment, and my hosts' only interest in me was whether I would learn and make spiritual progress by following their direction – and they were not particularly tolerant of slow or incompetent learners.

I was taught to chant the teachings, which came in the form of *sutras* – Buddhist aphorisms, to meditate and to practise my daily duties. These involved sweeping the *butsudan*, or shrine containing the sculpture of a Buddha figure, cleaning the inside of the temple and presenting offerings in the form of tea, pastries, candles or incense and cleaning the outside areas. A great deal of time was also spent meditating. For me, trying to sit in the lotus position was excruciatingly painful because of my broken femur and ankle. Then there were other bodily tests that were specifically designed to be brutal for everyone. There was one practice called *dai-kan shugyo* or 'great, cold aesthetic experience'. This involved standing naked under a waterfall, still in the depths of winter, and chanting *sutras*. It was so cold that getting any words out was physically difficult.

The real point of that kind of ordeal was to get the body under control, and obviously these practices would have been tough for anyone. For me, as a Westerner, there was an added set of difficulties to overcome. Everything I saw, tasted, smelled, heard and touched was alien. I had no one I could talk to in any common language except the housekeeper, and I could not stop her from performing her daily duties with my idle chatter, for which she had no inclination anyway. There was nothing to read and nothing to do with my mind, except try to adjust to this situation of massive cultural and sensory deprivation, while coping also with the cold and hunger. I prided myself on being independent-minded and resilient, having endured all kinds of indignities and hardships on the odyssey that had brought me here from Rhodesia. But here I discovered loneliness of an order that I had never imagined, even in my apprenticeship in the cabin on Vancouver Island. As one week became two, and two weeks became three, there was no escaping back to the crude conviviality of the logging camp. Not that anyone was stopping me from leaving. I could have walked out of the temple anytime I wanted. But if I did so, I knew I would be passing up an opportunity that I might never have again, and I would also be failing the greatest test I had ever set myself.

I had walked away from plenty of things before: in Ireland I had bailed out of my trek to Belfast, enduring ridicule in the process, as well as giving up the degree studies for which I had crossed a continent. I was therefore more than capable of swallowing my pride and acknowledging that I had chosen the wrong path. But my present circumstances felt very different. Undergoing mental and physical trials in this freezing baptism of fire was precisely the path I wanted to follow. It was too important to allow myself to be defeated. I did not know precisely what the benefits of staying the course would be, because the whole experience was designed to take the initiate on to a spiritual level of which they could not previously conceive. But that alone was goal enough for me. I wanted to see for myself what it felt like to reach that point.

A month passed, and then two. I stopped counting the days, because that defeated the purpose. The goal was to achieve inner change, rather than to hit some external target in the form of a length of time served. I came to see myself as metaphorically clawing my way up a mountain covered with impenetrable trees and brambles. The roots and thorns scratched and grazed me, leaving me sore and tired at the end of every day. But eventually I learned to find my way, hardening myself up as I manoeuvered up the slope, and finally I arrived at the top, to find myself standing on an immense plateau. In the far distance I imagined another set of mountains representing the voyage of spiritual evolution which would perhaps take many lifetimes to achieve. That was when I saw how worthwhile the struggle to get there had been. For I now discovered I was physically capable of standing at the edge of this plateau, without all the baggage of the past. I could sit in the lotus position; I could eat and survive off the minimal food. I had also managed to make loneliness my closest friend, by confronting my solitary state head-on and accepting it as a benefit rather than a problem. That latter achievement alone was a remarkable breakthrough, for which I have had cause to be grateful throughout the rest of my life. I have been in a solitary state many times since then, but I can honestly say I have never been lonely for a minute.

The whole experience had been a deep-end immersion from

which I emerged stronger and with a different outlook on life, and I found that I had genuinely moved to a different plane of being. I had heard that phrase many times before and I understood it in principle. But to experience personally what it meant was a true revelation.

I had also been trying my best to learn Japanese. It was not easy, because people so rarely spoke, but I knew the chants I had repeated so often, and I could function in a basic way. My bigger problem was that I still struggled to make sense of Shingon Buddhism. I did not really understand the teachings, and I could not see myself coming to understand them in my present situation, without enough language skills to follow any sophisticated explanation. So, once I decided that I had mastered the most daunting physical challenges, I began to think that it might be better if I moved on to another monastery or another temple.

Parting was a peculiar experience. I had undergone an intense experience in the company of Nakamura and the others, and I was profoundly grateful to them for what they had taught me and shown me, as well as for their hospitality. But we knew very little about each other, and there was an odd lack of personal attachment – because not forming such emotional bonds had been the point of the whole exercise. I felt cleansed, chastened and wiser as I returned down the mountain, but I did not feel the sadness one usually feels at parting from friends.

Arriving in Japan three months earlier had been a culture shock because everything was so alien and impenetrable. But now, as I made my way back down to Osaka, I experienced a new form of disconnect. My surroundings no longer seemed alien because they were Japanese. Instead, it was the bustle of everyday life – the kind of life that is common to towns and cities in any part of the world – that threw me. I had become used to the devotional silence of monks, and I had to re-accustom myself to how ordinary people went about their business in the real world.

That was true in every sense of the phrase. On arrival at the central railway station I discovered I was bursting for a pee and had no idea where the toilet was. I was still incapable of reading the signs, and passers-by did not seem to be able to help, either.

"*Habakari! Kawaiya!*" I pleaded. These were the two words I had learned in the monastery that related to a toilet. I was also hopping from one foot to another in a manner that I thought left little to the imagination.

But people just shrugged their shoulders.

Finally, an old man, bent over and supporting himself with a stick, seemed to grasp what I wanted.

"*Eh, habakari-ka, ah toirei dai yo!*" Ah, *habakari*, it means toilet.

He burst into a cackle, and now some of the other people I had asked dropped their frowns of incomprehension too and broke into smiles.

It was only later that I properly understood what had happened. I had learned my Japanese from a seventy-year-old monk, who had spent six and a half decades sequestered in a monastery devoting himself to thousand-year-old teachings, so I had picked up an antiquated vocabulary. Imagine a Japanese tourist approaching commuters on Waterloo Station and saying, "Prithee, sirrah, guide me to the privy-stall." That was pretty much what I had done.

In years to come I would learn more about the different registers of the Japanese language. Mercifully, it does not have the system of tones common to many Asian tongues, where a difference in inflection that is virtually inaudible to Western ears can create an entirely different word, but in much of Japanese communication, it is necessary to understand the context in order to grasp the real meaning, and that context can be defined by a tone of voice, an intake of breath or a facial expression. It is a hard concept to explain, but the Japanese understand the point instinctively, and it is best illustrated by an apparently true story about the investment bank SG Warburg, which wanted to open an office in Tokyo in the mid-Sixties. The partners hired a young Englishman who, they were told, spoke fairly fluent Japanese, and then trained him as a banker to a level where he could represent them. Sir Sigmund Warburg then hosted a big party at a smart Tokyo hotel to celebrate the opening of the new office and introduce the young man to the Japanese client base. He watched the young man move from one group of Japanese guests to the next one, and everything seemed to be going well enough as the Englishman engaged the guests in conversation. However, Warburg noticed that every time the young man detached himself from one group to move on to the next, the guests he had just left broke into laughter. Puzzled and unnerved by this, he pulled aside the chairman of a major Japanese industrial conglomerate and asked him what he thought of the new man.

The chairman looked embarrassed.

"Well, dear Sigmund, very difficult," he said. "Can I be very frank?"

Mystified even further, Sir Sigmund said of course he could.

The chairman leaned closer and said confidentially: "Problem is his gestures and spoken Japanese are just like Japanese bar girl from Osaka."

Japanese people found that story hilarious. They understood that foreigners speaking Japanese tended to pick up the idiom, inflection and gestures appropriate to the context in which they had learned the language, and a lot of young Western men acquired it from pillow talk. These Westerners could therefore speak Japanese as fluently as they liked, but what they might never realise was that the original context would be immediately – and sometimes hilariously – obvious to any Japanese listener.

Discovering all that was still some way off for me. All I knew now, as one of the people at Osaka station guided me in the right direction for the toilet, was that I needed to learn some modern Japanese.

I got in touch with a friend I had made on the ship from Hawaii. He lived close to Osaka, and he allowed me to stay for a couple of days with his family. They then arranged for me to teach English at the YMCA in the nearby city of Nara, which had been the original capital of Japan. Packed with gardens, temples and cultural treasures, this was one of the gems of the country, and I jumped at the chance to spend time there. I was advised I could lodge with a member of the YMCA board, a gynaecologist called Dr Tsubomura, who had his own little hospital right in the centre of town. He lived on the premises with his wife and six-year-old son. They put me up in their spare room, and I started teaching English in the afternoons.

After I had been there for a couple of days, a police car pulled up outside. A couple of officers got out and one of them said to Mrs Tsubomura: "Could we please see this young foreigner who is staying with you? We have to take him to the mayor."

My hostess was understandably agitated.

"I hope he hasn't done anything wrong," she said.

I was alarmed by the turn of events as well. I had been just about to go out sightseeing.

"Is there a problem?" I asked.

The policeman said: "No, no. The mayor just wants to see you."

This was some reassurance, but the fact remained that I was expected to get in the squad car and go off to see the city boss, a man named Kagita. He proved to be a huge man with a bull neck, bullet head and arms the size of my thighs.

"You are the only foreigner in Nara," he barked when I was shown into his office. "What are you doing in my city?"

I had heard already that he was a wealthy man and a landowner, and he clearly had the attitude to go with it.

"I've just come out of a monastery on Mount Koya," I said. "I'm here to see if I can learn more about Buddhism, and about Japanese culture."

"Ah," he said, smiling for the first time. "Excellent. You've come to the right person."

I tried to say, as politely as I could, that I had not so much come to him as been summoned.

"True," Kagita said. "But I am still the right person. You have already studied Shingon-shu. Now it is time for you to study

Zen Buddhism, and I will help you. I also want you to study the three samurai disciplines: sword-fencing, flower arranging and the tea ceremony. I have my own private *kendo dojo* at my home, and I practise with my staff every day. I will expect to see you there at six o'clock next Monday morning."

Despite the imperious way in which it was delivered, this was a very good offer. I knew that Zen Buddhism was not an esoteric system, and that it was the principal sect that influenced the samurai class, and placed less emphasis on knowledge of *sutras*, so I had already worked out that this might be a more suitable set of teachings for me to explore. To have a senior figure propose to take me under his wing like this, simply because he had been curious about a rare foreigner turning up in his city, was a great stroke of luck. Without hesitation, I told him I was up for the challenge.

It was to be the beginning of an enormously fruitful relationship. Kagita would beat me black and blue every morning, and then his staff would step in and do the same. I had learned some judo in Rhodesia, but this was *kendo* – the ancient Japanese art of sword-fighting, in which the sword had been replaced by a *shinai* (a bamboo cane the length of a sword split into four slats with a leather cap to keep the slats together). The use of *shinai*, rather than swords, removed the worst of the danger and allowed a much freer exchange of cuts and thrusts. It appeared aggressive and noisy at first, but I soon learned that it required skill and concentration, together with levels of grace and agility that were almost balletic. A kendo-fighter or *kenshi* wears a *keigoki* (a heavy cotton half kimono top) and a *hakama* (a long black skirt). To protect his head and body, he is armoured with a *men* (a heavily padded black helmet with a full visor, plus a *do* (ribcage shield), *kote* (gauntlets) and a *tare* (mini skirt of thick flaps to protect the groin and front hip areas – imagine Darth Vader from *Star Wars* with a stick rather than a light sabre. Despite this protective gear I came away every day with bruises on my wrists and a headache. But it toughened me up as I learned to take it. In the meantime, I also began attending the Soto-shu Zen temple just outside Nara, where the master, a man named Minagawa Eishin, was a good friend of Kagita's. I meditated there regularly, and found this form of Buddhism to be very appealing.

After nine months, I was getting bashed a little less often and had learned to go on the offensive, as well as to defend myself. My regular meditation at the Zen temple also helped considerably. Kagita sat me down for a chat at the end of one of our sessions.

"You have made remarkable progress," he said. "I am now willing to introduce you to my own kendo master. I'll take you to meet him and we will see if he will accept you or not."

This was another immense privilege. Having a good master was the best way to progress, and the only way to meet the best ones was via this kind of introduction. I had done my utmost to justify Kagita's interest in me, and now all those punishing sessions I had undergone were proving their worth.

This new master's name was Murata Kenzo. He taught at a university about ten miles from Nara, and we drove over to meet him the following Saturday. Having grown used to fighting a man of Kagita's bulk, I was expecting to meet someone of similar or even more impressive physique, but the teacher to whom I was now presented was a slight, very calm figure.

Not that he was easily won over. Speaking Japanese to Kagita, he made it clear he was unimpressed.

"Why are you bringing me a Westerner?" he frowned. "Foreigners have no idea of our culture, and I have no time to waste on educating him in basic matters. Besides, he won't understand anything I say."

I could see a twinkle of amusement in Kagita's eyes.

"He does speak some Japanese, and he can probably understand everything you're saying right now," said the mayor. "You should seriously consider taking him, not just as a favour to me. I have been teaching him for months and he has shown me that he has discipline. He has already come out of Mount Koya and is now attending a Zen temple. You have my assurance that he has reached a high enough level to be taught by you. If he had not, I would never have been rude enough to introduce him to you."

Murata considered for a moment.

"If he can answer the following question to my satisfaction I will take him," he said. "If not, he will just have to continue with you."

"That sounds like a good test," said Kagita. "What is your question?"

Murata turned to me. It was the first time he had looked at me properly, and I tried to return his gaze as calmly as I could.

"In the opening position of kendo, if you want to win and you are aggressive, you will lose," he said. "But if you don't want to lose and are defensive, you will also lose. So what must you do?"

I had been nervous about what the question might be. But I relaxed when I heard it. I had been taught that a *kenshi*'s true opponent was his own self. The fighter's goal was the same as for a monk, namely the state of *mushin*, or 'empty mind'.

"The answer is very simple," I said. "I don't care about the result, because the only goal I should have is to be in as balanced a state as possible."

If Murata was surprised that a foreigner with supposedly no idea of Japan's culture could know such a thing, and could express it in somewhat clumsy Japanese, he did not show it.

"All right, I'll take you on," he said simply.

He proved to be a remarkable man. He was modest and kind, yet he was also a hard taskmaster and his mere presence was awe-inspiring. I continued to study Zen at the temple in Nara, Sansho-zenji, and to teach English at the YMCA, but now my kendo practice was at the university with this new guide. The discipline was even more punishing than it had been with Kagita. While Murata might not match the mayor in physical bulk, the level of concentration he brought was extraordinary. I had to work hard to emulate it if I was not to end up as bruised as I had been in my novice days.

The months went by, and I was feeling more and more comfortable in Japan. I stuck out a mile as a tall, thin Caucasian, but as I immersed myself in centuries-old religious philosophy and cultural traditions, I sensed more than ever that this country that baffled the rest of the world might be my spiritual home.

After I had studied with Murata for a year, he sprang a surprise on me. He told me that he had taken the unusual step of entering me directly for the national *shodan* black-belt grading examination, instead of obliging me to progress through the six prior stages. In effect, he had put me on the fast track, which was a rare honour for any pupil, let alone a foreign one.

There were about three hundred of us taking the exam, with myself as the only non-Japanese. It was a noisy and physically exhausting day, but I felt calm at the end. I really was beginning to make some progress in attaining the mental balance for which the *kenshi* strives.

I sat with the other candidates as the head of the examining body made his speech. I could hardly believe my ears when he told the gathering: "There was one foreign student today who demonstrated quite superb fighting spirit. Many Japanese students did not reach the same level, and for this I feel shame. I urge everyone here to study much harder for the sake of Japanese pride."

I came eighth in fighting spirit and sixty-seventh in the competitive bouts, and now I had achieved the rank of *shodan*; first black belt. It usually took three or four years. I had been immensely privileged to learn the discipline under Kagita and then Murata-sensei, and I had undoubtedly worked hard. I had been toughened, both physically and mentally, by this gruelling pursuit of inner balance. I was also sure I could not have done it without both those three months being tested to the limit at Mount Koya and the regular meditation at the Zen temple. It was by no means the last occasion in my life when I would come to that conclusion.

I had been at the temple in Nara for a year and a half when Minagawa, my master there, suggested we make a pilgrimage to the head temple of our Soto-shu sect of Zen Buddhism. The monastery of Eiheji was in the forest about fifteen kilometres from the city of Fukui, north of Kyoto, near the coast of Japan's Inland Sea. The distance by road was not that far, but on a pilgrimage the journey was deliberately difficult: we walked via the summits of mountains rather than valleys, begging for food as we travelled. It would take about three weeks on foot, with overnight stays at temples belonging to our sect along the way, and it would be exhausting. However, it was another step on the road to enlightenment, and there was no way I was going to turn the opportunity down.

We kitted ourselves out in traditional monastic black robes, straw sandals and conical hats, which served as umbrellas as well as keeping the sun off. We stopped to meditate at each peak, and as we sat on one of them, Minagawa told me it was time to choose my *Bukyo no homyo*, the Buddhist name I would take as a lay monk. I was aware that I was receiving an honour that was an immense rarity for a Westerner at that time.

I had known it might be coming, and I had my answer already. I told him I chose Zenku Eison. The character 'Zen' was a mark of my respect for the sect of Buddhism I had learned, and 'Ku' as the second character represented both the sky and emptiness. I chose Eison as my forename because the character for 'Ei' was the first Japanese character for my master's own forename, Eishin, as well as being the first character for the old Japanese rendering of England, and the last character being for respect.

My master agreed that it was a suitable name, and when we returned to Nara he formally ordained me in the temple. After two years in Japan, I was now a Zen Buddhist lay monk called

Zenku Eison.

I was also still only twenty-two years old. I had learned so much from my ordeals and from my masters, but I also knew there was much more out there in the world that I wanted to explore. Although I would carry the Buddhist teachings with me for the rest of my life and I was now a changed man, I still had the heart of an adventurer, and I was itching to try new experiences, as well as to revisit some old ones. I had a strong sense that my fascination with Japan was only just beginning, and I would make it my business to return to the country as soon as I realistically could. Nevertheless, after all the self-denial I had been though, I really did need a bottle of wine, a girl and a steak. I therefore bade Murata, Kagita, Minagawa and all my other friends farewell and set off by sea for Hong Kong, where I was confident I would find abundant supplies of all three.

4:

Other Forms of Enlightenment

THE DARKENED ROOM smelled sweet and musky and there was a fug of smoke in the air. On rice matting all around me lay Laotian men, most of them much older than myself, with their heads on hard, slanting pillows. In front of me a girl prepared my pipe. She took a thin metal spatula and dipped it in a bottle of liquid, then held it over a hot lamp so that the liquid bubbled and became thick enough to roll into a glutinous bead. She coaxed the bead into the pipe, held the bowl over the lamp, and passed me the mouthpiece to draw on. As I inhaled, I felt immediately restful and soothed, as if I was floating off on a soft, warm cloud.

This was my first taste of an opium den, and I rather liked it. It certainly beat the police cell I had been sitting in a couple of days earlier.

Becoming a Buddhist monk had not dampened my curiosity about the world, and I had long been curious to sample opium, which had played a hugely important role in China from the early eighteenth century. In those days, it had been the sole escape permitted to the coolie classes from their otherwise hideous daily grind, and it had continued to be so until the late 1940s, when it had been banned. It was clearly extraordinary stuff, and while I was in the East I was eager to understand for myself by trying it.

I had asked around in Bangkok and discovered that opium was frowned upon in Thailand but not actually illegal. If I wanted to try some, I was told it would be best to go to the north of the country. But I also heard that in neighbouring Laos they still had the kind of opium dens where one could go in and pay to smoke as many pipes as one liked. To me that sounded a much better option.

Getting into the former French colony of Laos had proved harder than I anticipated. I boarded a train in Bangkok bound for the capital, Vientiane, and when we crossed the border, I presented my Rhodesian passport, as usual.

"What is this?" scowled the border official.

"It's my passport," I said.

"We don't recognise this passport," he said, pushing the document away.

"It's from a British colony called Southern Rhodesia and it's a valid passport," I said, trying to sound firm without putting his back up.

But there was no persuading the fellow. He had simply never heard of a country called Rhodesia, North or South, and he was not prepared to let me through. For my part, I was not prepared to turn around and go back to Bangkok just because an ignorant official knew nothing about geography.

As a compromise, he said he would have to consult a higher authority. He would send my passport to Vientiane to have it checked, and meanwhile I would just have to wait.

The waiting facilities consisted of a grotty cell, where I was consigned along with a ragtag bunch of other tired, dirty-looking travellers – most of them Thai – who had also been denied entry. There was no ventilation, and the cell was hot and sticky and reeked of stale sweat. I had proved on Mount Koya that I could cope with physical discomfort and deprivation, but I had no particular inclination to search those conditions out if they could be avoided. All I could do for the moment was find myself a space on the floor and settle down to wait. At least the city was very close to the border, so it should not take too long.

I had reckoned without the painfully slow pace of Laotian bureaucracy. Nobody was in any hurry to process me, and I passed first one night and then two, sustained on miserable portions of rice and tea served in filthy glasses, before the word finally came back that yes, Rhodesia did exist, and I was to be allowed into the country. I arrived in the dilapidated but still airy capital in the same clothes I had been wearing three days earlier, irritable and utterly exhausted. I found a small hotel where I treated myself to a long-overdue shower, and then addressed myself to the reason for my journey. I knew that opium was a way of easing cares away, and after my gruelling treatment on the border, I had never felt more in need of starting this experience.

"Can you tell me where the nearest opium den is?" I said discreetly to the desk clerk in shaky schoolboy French. If I had been misinformed, and Laos actually had zero tolerance of smoking opium, now would be the moment I found that out.

However, he responded as casually as if I had asked the way to the post office. I followed his directions and now here I was, floating away on my cloud, wanting for nothing. I liked it so much that when the effect began to wear off I had another pipe, and then another. It had been worth the trouble of getting here after all.

I was in no hurry to return to Bangkok, so I went back to the opium den the next night, and again the next. For two splendid weeks, I had about twenty pipes a day. Then I just stopped. Everyone I met was astonished that I could take all those pipes every day from scratch, and after two weeks solid not have any addiction at all. But I believe my monastic training and my basic strength of character had set me in good stead. I was as convinced then as I am now that drugs are fundamentally not a good thing, especially for people who have not had any kind of mental training. For anyone with fragilities in their psyche, narcotics may well accentuate those fragilities. Alternatively, for those who have hard lives from which they wish to escape, opium fulfils that wish. The drugs then become a refuge, and they will eventually take the person over. But in my case, I was not trying to escape, and I had not taken enough opium for it to start changing my physio-chemistry. I certainly did not need it to carry on with my life.

A year earlier, I had set out from Japan on a small freighter. I had worked out that this was the cheapest way of getting to Hong Kong, and it had the added benefit that it was scheduled to stop for a week in Shanghai. Foreign tourists were not allowed into China, so this was a rare opportunity for me to visit a city that had once been fabled as the Paris of the East, with the best art, the greatest architecture and the most thriving economy in Asia. Its old colonial buildings still looked very much as they must have done before the Communist revolution, even if Chairman Mao had turned everyone into drab, grey robots wearing jackets like his own. A few short years later, the Cultural Revolution would create an atmosphere of fear that would deter any of the population from engaging with a foreigner. But this had yet to happen, so a few of the locals were curious enough to try to talk to me, and I was able to have a sort of communication by writing Japanese characters on scraps of paper before rejoining the freighter to Hong Kong.

Arriving by sea at one of the greatest natural harbours in the world was a magnificent experience. In those days, Hong Kong still had a real waterfront, and it was not yet as wealthy a financial and commercial centre as it would become. I found my feet quickly. I managed to get a modestly paid but undemanding clerical job through an Italian businessman whom I had helped out while he was on a trip buying antiques in Japan, and I was invited to stay with a couple of English girls, whom I had also met in Japan, in the maid's room of their flat in the residential area of Happy Valley. Thanks to my new boss and flatmates, I made a lot of social contacts very quickly, and was soon having a thoroughly good time. I made tentative steps into a more settled existence by buying my first tailored suit and opening my first bank account, with the Hong Kong and Shanghai Bank; these were the days when, if you were a young white person, you could open an account and they would grant you an overdraft almost immediately. But enjoyable as it all was, Hong Kong was still very much a British territory. There were English street names, English-language newspapers for sale on the street corners and British special constables on the beat, so to me the colony felt like a slightly larger version of what I had known in Rhodesia. In years to come I would make my home very comfortably here, bringing up my children in a fine house on the pinnacle of Hong Kong Island. But for the moment I was still hungry for experiences of the more traditional East, and I was by no means sure that this was the best place to find them. After a few months, I decided it was time to move on. Instead I would explore the unique culture of Thailand, which was the only Asian country to have kept the Western colonial powers at bay.

More than ninety percent of the Thai population is Buddhist, and Bangkok was – and is – a city of immense, awe-inspiring temples, vast monastic complexes with rows of golden Buddha statues and jewel-encrusted towers. The smell of incense hung everywhere in the air, and saffron-robed monks were a common sight in the streets. To walk around the city was to immerse oneself in a centuries-old Buddhist tradition, rather than the British colonial one.

Not that I was any great rarity as a foreigner. There was a thriving expat community, which greatly eased my entry into life in the city. I managed to get a job teaching English and maths at the American International School. I had no teaching qualifications but they were short of teachers, I had some university experience – even if it did not extend to a complete degree – and I imagine I must have been their best available option. I also found a place to live with an expat Englishman who had a spare room at a cheap rent, and whose house was near the school. My job was to teach eleven- and twelve-year-olds, and I approached it in the manner of an Englishman at a colonial school, maintaining strict discipline. The class had to stand up when I entered the room, and after they submitted their first homework assignments on random scraps of paper, I told them they had to buy proper homework books if they wanted any mark at all for their work. Whenever any of them were cheeky, I smacked their backsides with a ruler. I did not see anything old-fashioned or controversial about this: it was entirely normal by the standards of the education I myself had received. It was true I did not regard my schooldays with much affection, but they had equipped me with knowledge and confidence to go out into the world, so it seemed to me a perfectly good approach. And as the level of cheek in my class dramatically plummeted and the presentation and quality of their homework improved considerably, it was clear it was working.

My methods caused something of an uproar among the children, however. They started calling me 'Hitler Higginson' – a nickname that came to my attention when someone daubed it on a lavatory wall. I noticed some boys goose-stepping with one finger held above their upper lip in imitation of a toothbrush moustache, and the fact that they stopped the pantomime as soon as they realised I was watching confirmed that I was the target of their satire. I thwacked them for it, but I did not actually mind.

Unfortunately, I was none too popular with some of their parents, either. I raised eyebrows when I attended a parent-teacher conference wearing an ascot, the kind of silk cravat that people wear nowadays with morning suits at weddings. It was regarded as a sure sign that I was queer. This was seen as a shockingly bad thing in those days, although it was a prejudice I did not share, not least because any form of prejudice was the enemy of curiosity. At the same time, because I was the youngest member of staff, and more presentable than most of my middle-aged colleagues, I had teenage girls hanging around outside my classroom and competing for my attention. I caused further controversy when I sat on my desk in the lotus position during a civics class and talked about the principles of Buddhism. So while part of my class saw me as a Nazi disciplinarian, in some of their parents' eyes I was an eccentric crank who could negatively influence their children. Perhaps it was no surprise that the headmaster did not know quite what to make of me. He would have been even more confused if he had known that I was actually a monk.

I was called into his study one day and told that some of the parents had brought a motion to have me dismissed. This was actually rather interesting: for all my stern approach to classroom behaviour and my flamboyant non-conformism, I took my job seriously and I wanted the children to learn. I was also confident that I was a reasonably good teacher, and I was unwilling to go without a fight.

What saved me was a split among the parents. The children were roughly divided between missionary and military families. The missionaries wanted me fired for having the temerity to beat their children's backsides, but to the military lot I was a hero: they wanted me decorated for gallantry for bringing much-needed discipline to their children. Happily, the military group outnumbered the missionaries. One of their number reminded the headmaster that beating students was perfectly acceptable under Thai law, which reassured him that he was not going to get into any trouble for keeping me on, and I was allowed to continue teaching.

While all this was going on, I was invited one evening to an expat pyjama party. It was the kind of gathering where young men wore lipstick and nighties with balloons for breasts, and to my mind it was a grotesque affair. I ended up sitting on the sofa in my kimono, wondering how long I could leave it before discreetly slipping away. Next to me I noticed a tall, young Englishman in pyjamas and a thick woollen dressing gown that was absurdly out of place in the humid heat of Bangkok. He looked as alienated from the rest of the gathering as I was, so we fell to talking. We got on well, and after about an hour we agreed it would be more civilised to go to his house, where we could talk in peace. We ended up drinking an entire bottle of Jack Daniels and talking until eight the next morning.

The Englishman's name was Kevin O'Sullivan, and he was to become my closest friend, as he remains to this day. By the end of the night, I knew his life story and he knew mine. When we woke up mid-afternoon, he said: "Look I've got all this space and I live here on my own. You'd make a great companion. Why don't you move in?"

Now that I had discovered the delights of opium in Vientiane,

I wanted to take some back so that I could share the experience with Kevin and my other friends in Bangkok. Of course it would be inconceivable to bring opium into Thailand nowadays. It would carry a life sentence in prison, or even the death penalty, if one was caught. Singapore is equally tough, and so is Malaysia. But this was 1964, and while attitudes were not entirely approving, they were nothing like as severe.

I bought an antique opium pipe and I managed to buy a little bottle of raw, unadulterated opium to go with it. Then I set about planning how I could get it over the border. The pipe could be dismantled and packed in my knapsack. If I was questioned about the pipe, I could easily say it was a souvenir. The bottle was more of a problem. I decided the only thing to be done with it was to stuff it down the front of my Y-fronts. It gave me a rather exaggerated codpiece bulge. All I could do was hope that it would play into the common Asian assumption that Westerns are much better endowed than they are.

As I passed through customs I did indeed receive a startled glance in the direction of my crotch, but to my intense relief no one was curious enough to investigate further. My calculation had been spot on, and I was through.

When I arrived back at Kevin's house, I showed him my contraband.

"You really must try this," I said. "It's amazing."

He did not take much persuading.

"Shall we invite some others to join us?" he said. "Who shall we ask?"

We decided to invite a friend who was fairly senior at the British Embassy, his Australian girlfriend and a Chinese-

English fellow whom we were convinced was a spy for MI6. They all came to dinner, and at the end of the meal I asked if they would like to try opium. They reacted just as I had assumed they would: they had all heard so much about this drug, but they had never come into contact with it before, so nobody could resist the opportunity.

At this point I realised I had not given any thought to how I was going to get the opium into my guests. It was generally smoked in a den for good reason: making a pellet from the liquid was a skilled procedure. I had watched it being done in front of me enough times, so I set about doing it myself. But try as I might, I could not get the hang of it. With our guests now waiting expectantly, I racked my brains for another way.

"Tomatoes!" I cried.

We had some little cherry tomatoes in the kitchen, which I now started cutting up so I could drip opium into each one. I passed one to Kevin, who had volunteered to go first. He popped the tomato into his mouth and bit on it to swallow. Almost instantly he started retching dramatically.

"That won't work," he gasped, spitting the tomato onto a plate. "It's the most disgusting thing I've ever tasted. There's no way I can keep it down."

He swigged great gulps of water to try and take the taste away.

It was the MI6 chap who came up with the solution.

"Why don't I go to the pharmacy?" he said. "I'll get those vitamin tablets that come in glycerine pill capsules. We can just empty the powder out and put the opium in with an eye-dropper, and then we can swallow the capsules."

It sounded a much better plan, so off he went, and the rest of the gathering waited in nervous anticipation. Despite the fiasco with the tomatoes, nobody was in the mood to chicken out, and when he came back we set about putting the liquid opium into the capsules.

As a way of swallowing the stuff, it worked well. Kevin went first again, then the embassy fellow, then his girlfriend, then the MI6 chap and finally me. Nobody gagged or retched, and everyone was relaxed and pleasantly excited now.

It took about half an hour for the full effect to kick in this way. When it did, the impact was wonderful. Everyone lay blissed out on the floor saying over and over again how amazingly relaxing it was. I should stress that there was no question of the evening becoming debauched: in contrast to hashish, for example, opium took away any sexual urge and indeed capability to do anything but lie there and drift away, so there was a childlike innocence to it all. It made us feel coddled, nurtured and incredibly safe.

Unfortunately, this state was not to last long. What we had not realised, in our inexperience, was that the dosages we were giving each other were huge. It was not so bad for me because I had already built up a certain immunity after smoking so many pipes every day in Laos. But the others had none whatsoever.

After two or three hours, one guest after another started vomiting in the various toilets around the house. Each of them would recover enough to float off again, so the experience was not completely spoiled, but after a while they would throw up once more. And so it went on all night. It was not an evening that any of us would forget in a hurry, and if there was any apprehension that I was seducing these poor people into becoming opium addicts, it was well and truly dispelled by the end of the night. I am almost certain it put everyone off for life.

I emerged in slightly better shape than my friends, but I now had a particular problem of my own, because I had an unmissable appointment the next morning. I had made up my mind to return to Japan, and I had been accepted on to a one-year course in sixteenth-century history and traditional Japanese architecture at Kyoto University. That morning I had an appointment at the Japanese embassy to secure my student visa. The timing was appalling, but I was due to leave soon and I could not risk putting the appointment off.

So I went off to see the consul and, even though I was feeling groggy, we managed to have a good conversation. In those days, very few Westerners, let alone young ones, spoke Japanese, so he was agreeably surprised that I could talk to him in his own language. He had just stamped the visa into my passport when the exploits of the previous night caught up with me and I had the sudden, unavoidable urge to vomit. I spotted the consul's wastepaper basket and threw up a noxious mixture of opium and breakfast into it.

The consul sat blinking. This was clearly not what he was used to, especially not from a young Westerner seeking a visa.

I looked back at him miserably and wondered what on earth I could do to salvage the situation. There was just one possibility, I decided in my enfeebled state.

"Bangkok belly," I groaned, clasping my stomach.

"Ah!" he said sympathetically. The Japanese are proud of their cleanliness, and he could clearly well understand how a poor foreigner could fall victim to the inferior hygienic standards of, in his eyes, this lesser nation of Thailand.

I went back to Japan by ship to start my course. Through the local Rotary Club in Kyoto, I found a couple who had a beautiful *hanare*, a detached villa at the back of their main home with its own private entrance. It had a little kitchen and bathroom, and a living room/bedroom upstairs. I settled down to study.

Naturally the course was all in Japanese, so it was pretty tough to follow. The historical terms were difficult and there was a lot of dictionary work, but the professor was very kind and patient. Architecture was easier to grasp. Japanese aesthetics are extraordinary, and no other culture I know has the same refined aesthetic sense. The Japanese treasure bare simplicity and equilibrium. The room I am sitting in now in London would be considered fairly tasteful by Western standards — it is full of objects from the East, as well as photographs of family through my long life — but I also know deep down that these things are clutter. This is the way Western and most other cultures operate, but the Japanese would have just one corner of the room with a painting or a hanging scroll, and perhaps a piece of porcelain. Affluent people may have a warehouse at the back of the house where they store things, so they can rotate the works of art according to the season, but they would not have more than one at any given time. It is an incredibly restful and deliberate way of living, and my house in Kyoto was like that — without the warehouse, of course.

I was, as the Japanese say, like white blotting paper — *shiroto* — on which experience was waiting to be written. Having emerged from a country of space and wildlife, I had almost nothing imprinted on my cultural DNA. While passing at speed through Trinity College and parts of Europe and North America, I had absorbed little of those cultures. During my previous stay in Japan, I had acquired a deep understanding of the values of the country by learning its spiritual philosophy. Now, in Kyoto I lived, breathed, worked and studied Japanese art and culture.

Our architectural professor had assembled an eclectic group of people from all over the world, all studying Japanese traditional architecture. He would take some of us to *geisha* houses in the evening. That introduced me to the hidden world of these traditional female entertainers, who act as hostesses and entertainers, and eventually I managed to get a job teaching English to a group of *maiko*, or trainee *geisha*. At the same time, I studied flower arrangements and the tea ceremony — those key elements of the samurai tradition alongside kendo.

At one point I was invited by my tea master to attend an incense-smelling ceremony — *kodo-shikki*, a ritual that had originated in Kyoto in the twelfth century. Incense in a burner was passed around the guests. Then everyone was given seven or eight incenses to smell in separate incense burners, and we each had to try to identify which one was the same as the original. I was the only foreigner there but, to the evident astonishment of everyone in the room, I won. The competition was run by a *tayu*, a courtesan with a higher rank than a *geisha* — today there are none left because the training is too arduous. As a result of my winning, she became interested in me and we became good friends – she subsequently added materially to my knowledge of traditional Japan.

But I was aware that I could not stay in Japan forever. It was now six years since I had left Rhodesia to study in Ireland, and five since I had left Dublin to wander the world. As my course in Kyoto drew to an end, I knew I should eventually get back to Europe and work out what I was going to do with my life.

I had already ruled out being a doctor, and the purpose of my studies in Kyoto was to satisfy my interest in both the Azuchi-Momoyama period (1573-1603) of history, during which the whole of Japan was consolidated under the rule of the first Shoguns, and traditional Japanese architecture began to change, not because I wanted to train and practise as an architect. Now that I was a monk, I could in principle spend my life in a monastery, but I was far too curious about the world at large, and the variety of people and cultures in it, to do that. In truth, my real bent was for trying as wide a variety of experiences as possible. I had proved my entrepreneurial prowess at school, and the idea of starting businesses appealed to my disposition to try new things. I still did not have a university degree, so the most sensible option seemed to be to go to the School of Oriental and African Studies in London to take an honours degree in Japanese. If I focused in particular on business language, this would give me a good grounding to return to Tokyo and start building something for the future. Given the head-start I had in the language, it would hopefully not be too taxing.

Another advantage was that the next available course would not start for a year, so my global odyssey need not end quite yet. I could visit some more countries in the interim, and top of my list was India — the place where Buddhism had first originated, and where my ancestors had been very active.

I made a tantalisingly brief stop in Burma, which is perhaps the most Buddhist country in the whole of Asia. It was also under a military dictatorship, so it was largely closed to foreigners. The longest visa I could get was for forty-eight hours, and they only gave me that because I was a Buddhist monk. It would be another thirty years before I returned and got to know the place properly. Having briefly stepped back in time some fifty years in Rangoon, I then continued to Calcutta, which was a sudden and massive contrast to everything I had been used to in Kyoto. If Japan presents itself in muted colours, India is in full Technicolor.

The old stronghold of the East India Company and the British Raj, Calcutta had once prided itself as a glittering centre of industry, commerce and culture, and as India's largest city. That last boast was still justified when I got there: with a population of more than six million, it was fifty percent bigger than Bombay and more than twice the size of Delhi. But that soaring population had become a problem. After the partition of India in 1947, a massive wave of Hindu refugees had arrived from predominantly Muslim East Pakistan (soon to become Bangladesh). Calcutta's infrastructure had struggled to cope and the city had become a byword for wretched poverty. The misery of so many people's existence was impossible to avoid: there were beggars in all directions, some of them grotesquely mutilated, while women and children sifted through piles of rubbish in search of something to eat. For far too many, being an inhabitant of Calcutta meant sleeping on the pavement. The whole place was choked in fumes, grime and human filth.

This poverty was an eye-opening experience for any traveller, and in principle I well understood the value of knowing how pitiful life could be for the numbers who lived on the streets or in the slums of Calcutta. In truth, however, the impact of facing this appalling poverty and hardship was so intense that I am afraid I had little desire to linger. Instead I made my way north-west to Delhi, which the Raj had made its altogether statelier capital in 1911 – a status that had endured after independence. Here it was more possible to enjoy the chaotic eccentricity of India: the bustling streets where sacred cows, bullock carriages and herds of goats competed for space with rickshaws, bicycles, cars, trucks and pedestrians; the cacophony of car horns, animal noises and human voices; and the distinctive blend of spices, exhaust fumes, incense, sewage and tropical flowers that hung permanently in the air.

India was part of my ancestry, since my ancestors' many involvements in various aspects of Indian life. My great-great-grandfather had spent his life here, as first superintendent of Chittledroog, far to the south, in Mysore, where eventually he became a great friend of the Maharaja of Mysore and helped him improve the lot of his people. But I was also keen to celebrate India's independence from the British Empire. In Old Delhi I sought out the ashram where Mahatma Gandhi had apparently made his devotions. Established there was a wonderful guru called Raihana. She was old and gnarled, with wild hair, and my first reaction – to my shame – was that she was incredibly ugly. But within moments of talking to her, that first impression fell away and I saw instead an amazingly radiant, peaceful person. Such was the power of her aura.

I stayed at the ashram for a couple of months, absorbing the intense spirituality of the place and slipping easily into its rhythms. But my curiosity about artificial forms of enlightenment had not yet been satisfied. I had still not experienced the kind of psychedelic drugs that were the basis of the mind-altering rituals practised for thousands of years in Native American cultures and elsewhere. Before I ended my globetrotting adventure, I wanted at least to try them, so as to be able to make a comparison with my monastic experiences.

I had made a friend in Bangkok who was a dedicated disciple of Timothy Leary, the American counterculture guru. Leary famously believed that artificial psychedelic drugs such as LSD could be of major benefit to humanity. My friend said that since I had been in a monastery exploring spiritual enlightenment, I certainly ought to try LSD; if I wanted, he could arrange for Leary to send me some. That was a perfectly legal thing to do at the time, because no one had got around to criminalising the stuff, so I agreed, and my friend was as good as his word. One day I found a letter with American stamps on it waiting for me at the New Delhi *poste restante*. It was from Leary himself, and inside was a piece of blotting paper with a ring round it and a note saying: "Try this to see how it compares with your monastic experiences." I wish I could have kept and framed that note, but that would have been hard to do: the whole point was that I was meant to swallow the circle of blotting paper.

I fell to thinking about where I should do this. My friend

in Bangkok had given this experience a serious build-up, and it was quite an honour to get the drug from its most celebrated international advocate, so I felt I ought to do it justice by taking it somewhere suitably magical. As I considered the options, I realised the answer was obvious. There are few more entrancing places in the world than the Taj Mahal, the great Mughal mausoleum in Agra, which is just over a hundred and sixty kilometres from Delhi. In those days, it was not besieged by the queues of tourists who flock there today, but it was hardly undiscovered either. Ideally, I wanted a solitary experience, in which I could savour the extraordinary atmosphere while under the influence of the LSD. My best plan, I figured, was to travel to Agra and stay behind after the site closed for the night.

I discovered that the gates closed at midnight and re-opened at four o'clock. On my appointed night, I entered the grounds in the late evening and scouted for a suitable hiding place. I found some thick bushes, and about a quarter of an hour before the place was due to close, I hid inside them and settled down to wait. I watched the final few visitors leave and heard the gates being locked, but even then I was in no hurry to emerge. I stayed for about two hours before I came out. With no guards in sight, I was confident I could now have my psychedelic experience undisturbed. I made my way to the end of the Long Pond, the great ornamental channel in front of the monument which is familiar from every tourist view of the place, and placed myself in the lotus position, which by now was comfortable for me and the best position to take for an experience of this kind. I took my wallet out of my pocket and retrieved the small piece of LSD-impregnated blotting paper.

I hadn't brought any water with me, but it was easy enough to swallow on its own.

I was just about to put it in my mouth when I heard a shout behind me.

"Goodness me, there's a bloody foreigner here!"

"We have to throw him bodily out, isn't it!" said a second voice.

"Hey you, foreigner!" called the first voice.

I was in no mood to be bodily ejected. Instead I sprang up and ran. A long and comical chase ensued as I tore around the grounds of the most majestic monument in Asia, evading a couple of security guards, hiding behind fruit trees and ducking down into sunken parterres to evade capture. I was fitter than the guards, so staying ahead of them was not too hard. I was relieved that I had not yet taken the LSD. Being chased while hallucinating might not have been quite such fun.

Eventually, they got the better of me, and I finally submitted to capture.

"Okay, okay, I'll go peacefully," I panted.

We were all completely exhausted.

"You better had," said the stouter of the two guards, wiping the sweat from his forehead with a handkerchief. "If you don't, we'll have you thrown in jail, isn't it."

As they escorted me back to the main entrance, I looked at my watch. The chase must have lasted the best part of two hours, because it was very nearly four o'clock – the time when the gates were meant to re-open.

I sat outside to get my breath back, and smoked a cigarette. At four o'clock I strolled back through the gates with my head held high.

"You can't bloody well touch me now," I said, mimicking their accents shamelessly.

"Yes, you're right; we can't," they shrugged.

But I was in no longer in any state to have a transcendental experience. After I had made my point to the guards and strolled around the gardens for a short while more, I returned to my hotel for some much-needed sleep.

In the event, it was another few weeks before I took that LSD. Through a mutual friend in Delhi I was introduced to a distinguished Englishwoman in her mid-fifties called Freda Bedi, the first Western woman to become an ordained Tibetan Buddhist nun. She had lived in India for more than thirty years and had been arrested alongside Gandhi in the struggle for independence. When the Dalai Lama and thousands of fellow refugees fled Chinese persecution in their occupied homeland of Tibet, she had been asked by Prime Minister Nehru to help them, and she had built a monastery at a hill station called Dalhousie at the start of the Himalayas. I now went to stay there for three months, and befriended the lamas, or Buddhist teachers there. In this cool, pine-scented spot, surrounded by snow-capped mountains, it was a privilege to deepen my spiritual understanding alongside these wise and enlightened Tibetans. But I had not forgotten my plan, either, and after a few weeks I asked one of my new friends if he would come with me to a guest house which the monastery owned, overlooking the whole plain of India, while I took my LSD.

He was not interested in taking the drug with me, but he said he would be happy to keep me company. He made it clear he found the whole business amusing.

"You Westerners are so funny: you want a short cut to everything," he said. "We take a longer view of how to make spiritual progress."

I knew he was right, but for twelve hours or so I took my short cut, allowing this extraordinary substance to take me on a psychedelic waking dream. The scenic beauty of the location was magnified and spun in fantastic directions as the LSD conspired with my mind to play hallucinatory tricks and took me off on extravagant conversational paths to the amusement of my Tibetan companion. Afterwards, I was not convinced this would offer much lasting benefit to humanity, but I could certainly see why its devotees made such a fuss about it. I was very glad I had taken the trouble to experience it with an understanding and wise companion, and in such majestic surroundings.

Time was moving on, and I was conscious I needed to start travelling back in the direction of Europe. *En route*, I wanted to see Afghanistan, where one of my ancestors; Sir Henry Dobbs, led a mission in 1921 to Kabul, to start the process of establishing diplomatic relations with that country. In the twenty-first century, this benighted place is top of every traveller's danger list. But these were the days before the Soviet invasion and the *jihadist* resistance which led to government by the Taliban. The people were relaxed and hospitable, eager to press glasses of dark, sweet tea on visitors; smiling schoolgirls walked freely in the streets, their skirts above their knees and their heads at best half-heartedly covered; market stalls groaned with apples, cherries, watermelons and fresh dates; strains of music curled constantly in the air. I was entranced.

In the next few years, Kabul was destined to become a major hippie hangout. The big attraction was hashish, and a lot of them started moving on to more dangerous drugs such as heroin, often with tragic consequences. Several years later the American consul told a younger friend of mine: "We should have built a coffin factory. We were shipping so many dead kids back to the States."

For my part, I wanted primarily to see this country because of Sir Henry's involvement, and because another ancestor, also on my mother's side, had fought in the Khyber Pass. But I was not entirely impervious to the other aspect that would subsequently lure the hippies. I was intrigued to learn that the Afghan equivalent of a pub was a hashish den. Being of curious disposition, I was keen to discover what such a place was like.

I was directed to a basement with an earthen floor, a very high ceiling, and cushions around the perimeter, with people slouched all over them in a stuporous daze. In the middle of the room was a granite block on which stood a huge hookah. It was a more picturesque and less squalid version of the opium den in Vientiane. The servers put pure hashish over some hot coals in the hookah and customers would be invited to partake by inhaling the smoke through the hookah's water pipe which cooled it down, before going back to lie on the cushions. The communal mouthpiece did not strike me as very hygienic, and I had done quite enough lying around in Laos, so instead, I decided I would buy some hash to take back to London to share with my Bangkok friends, who were by now back in

London. I asked for one kilo, which came in about ten patties. I wrapped them up and put them in my bag, but it seemed a shame to leave without having a few puffs. So I did my best to wipe the mouthpiece free and took a few deep drags before I proceeded on my way.

I had smoked marijuana leaves before, but not hashish, and I had not realised how powerful it would be. One of the effects of the drug is to induce paranoia, and as I got out in the street I took it into my head that a local branch of the American IDA or Interpol was bound to be on the watch for people like me. I decided to try to outwit these imaginary watchers. For the next three hours, I valiantly dodged in and out of shops, cut down the most obscure alleys I could find, hid behind cars and generally threw myself into this paranoid adventure. Naturally, I got thoroughly lost in the process, which added to my distress, and it was more by luck than anything else that I eventually found my hotel. When I got there, I was still as high as a kite, and I lay on my bed with my heart pounding, imagining that the police would soon be breaking the door down. Finally, I more or less passed out, and by the morning I had recovered my wits.

I was due to leave the country in three days' time, and while I had now developed a wary respect for this substance I had bought, I had no intention of throwing my patties away. Instead I had to work out how to get them back to England undetected. I managed to get a Tupperware container and some Araldite-type glue in the market. I sealed the hash inside, and added a note addressed to myself, saying: "I hope you haven't been stupid enough to open this, but if you have just shut it up and Jim will pick it up from you in London." I signed it 'Chris', who was as fictitious as Jim. The idea was to make it look as if I was merely a dim innocent doing a friend a favour, so I could naively plead ignorance if caught. When I sealed it, one could not smell a thing so I was pleased with my handiwork. But I decided I needed some further distraction to stop any customs people looking through my bag in the first place.

After thinking the problem over, I returned to the market and bought an old Afghan musket, a relic of the Khyber Pass days. I made sure it had been disabled and could not be used. It was also very large – about two metres long – and I hoped it would be a good way to divert attention from my knapsack. I was planning to cross four borders on my journey back to London, so my plan needed to work.

My journey took me first to Persia, as Iran was known in those days, where a fellow student from my architecture course in Kyoto had offered to put me up. I visited the fabled city of Isfahan and the extraordinary ruins of Persepolis, where I saw the tomb of Emperor Darius, who had been a childhood hero of mine. Back in Tehran, I spent hours hanging around antiques shops where scruffy chaps would turn up with sacks over their shoulder. I would stop them before they went in and ask what they had. They would show me jars and other objects they had excavated. I would pull out some money and ask them what they wanted, and they would take some notes. They were not expecting much, and I paid far less than I would have with the dealers' mark-up, but I probably gave them more than they would have got from the dealers. So it was a good arrangement for all concerned – except the dealers, obviously

— and I managed to get four or five superb antique Persian objects that I still treasure.

From Tehran I flew to Lebanon, where I stayed with a professor of English at the American University, who was a close friend of my mother, in his farmhouse halfway up a hill between the snow slopes and the sea. Beirut was a wonderfully cosmopolitan and sophisticated place in those years before civil war broke out, and I spent several enjoyable weeks exploring it. After that I made a brief stop in Belgrade and then continued to London.

At each of the four border posts I passed through, I approached the customs desk and said: "I'd like to declare my Afghan rifle. It's quite safe — it has been disabled. But you can check if you like."

At that point, whatever their nationality, the customs officers would pick the gun up and brandish it around childishly, pretending to shoot one another. As a piece of distraction, it could not have been better. I am also a great believer in the value of poker bluff, so after that I would open my kit-bag and start pulling out the filthiest clothes I had, making the customs men recoil from the stink of my socks. Having given them a flavour of the noxious contents, I would ask them innocently: "Would you like me to empty it out?"

"Oh no, no, please don't worry," they would insist. "That's fine, you can go ahead."

This worked like a charm each time. It helped that there were virtually no kids of my age travelling at that time. I did not have long hair, I still cannot grow a beard, so I did not have one then, and I also made a point of dressing in clean jeans and a clean shirt so I did not look notably scruffy. Nevertheless, those were the days of innocence. Nobody waves a gun around for fun any more at an airport, and today I would be jailed for most of my life, if not actually executed, for smuggling hash in that quantity. Today, it would be fundamentally stupid to risk one's future, if not one's life, and I would strongly advise anyone against taking such a risk.

My parents and brother were living in London by this time, and they came to Heathrow Airport to meet me. As I was going through the final customs post of my long journey, I had an awful vision of being discovered with the hashish and waving to my family through the bars of a Black Maria as I was hauled off to the nearest police station. Fortunately, the mindset of a British customs official in the mid-Sixties was no different from that of a Persian, Lebanese or Yugoslav one. My precautions with the musket and the Araldite held fast to the end. The only problem I had was trying to open that glued-up Tupperware once I got it home.

5:

The Debs' Delight

MY HUNCH THAT the winds of change would have stormy consequences in Rhodesia was proving right. The colonies of Northern Rhodesia and Nyasaland had gained independence from Britain and were now called Zambia and Malawi. Rhodesia wanted to rid itself of colonial shackles too, but not at the price of black majority rule. The new prime minister, a white farmer and former Spitfire pilot called Ian Smith, was now on a collision course with the British government. His 'Unilateral Declaration of Independence' would shortly turn the country into an international pariah.

While I had been wandering the world, my immediate family had come to the same conclusion as I had, and decided that their future lay elsewhere. My brother Brian had come to London to study medicine (and would eventually settle into general practice on the south coast of England), my sister Ann had married a Salisbury boy and moved to Canada, and now my parents had sold up and moved to London too. They had bought the leasehold of a five-storey Victorian house in Glebe Place, a wide, tranquil street just off the King's Road in Chelsea.

It was a smart move because the area was about to become the fashionable heart of 'Swinging London'. But they had a bombshell announcement as we all went out to dinner on my first night back. After twenty-five years of marriage, they told me that they had been separated for some time. They had never been completely compatible, and the move back to Britain had made their differences more apparent than ever. It was my mother's decision to leave, but my father had acquiesced and I think he was probably relieved, because he knew she was at heart an experimenter, and he was a much quieter, more conventional man. Nevertheless, it all came as a complete surprise to me. Aside from one enormously expensive telephone call to my brother from Prince Rupert in northern British Columbia, when I was working on my survey vessel and he was in his last year at school, my only communication with my family had been by letter. They had decided to spare me these details until we saw each other face to face, but I now learned that Mother had moved to a flat in Hampstead and my father had stayed on in Glebe Place (even though the house itself was in my mother's name).

Because they were still on friendly terms, the meal itself was fine, but the evening turned darker when my brother went off back to his medical school digs and my father and I returned to Glebe Place. I had brought him a bottle of very good whisky as a gift, and he now proceeded to drink most of it in one sitting. I realised he was effectively an alcoholic, and I subsequently discovered that this had been one of the main reasons for my parents' separation. While my mother was getting on with life, experimenting and exploring, my father had become a classic displaced colonial, seeking consolation in the bottom of a glass. That night I had to put him to bed, which is an odd thing for a son to have to do for his father, and it was not quite the homecoming I had expected.

He had always been a relatively remote figure in my life, so, while I was shaken by the news, I did not especially grieve for their marriage. But their separation did help me make one decision almost immediately. I wanted to recognise my mother's part in my heritage, so I now began to call myself by the surname Dobbs-Higginson. In due course I would formalise it by deed poll.

In the meantime, I set about preparing for the first year of my Japanese honours degree at SOAS. Term began in September and I applied myself to the course with dedication. But it soon became apparent that I knew more colloquial Japanese than the lecturers. I irritated them enormously by correcting them in front of the other students. It did not help that they were trying to teach us mediaeval Japanese literature and twelfth-century poetry. Much as I valued Japanese culture, my aim in doing this degree was to be able to work in modern Japan in a business context. I was also the oldest student by some years. If there had been a difference in maturity between myself and my fellow freshmen all those years ago in Dublin, now the gulf was vast. I fell to wondering what I was doing there. My doubts were reinforced when I completed my first-year exam papers in about a third of the time we were allocated. I resolved to think hard about my future at SOAS during the summer vacation.

By this time, my social life had pepped up no end. In the months after my return, my father decided he had had enough of London and returned to South Africa. Although we were not close, I appreciated his fundamental decency and I wanted him to be happy, so I welcomed any move that might give him more of a sense of belonging. His departure also gave me the opportunity to split the house – which my mother still owned – into two maisonettes. When my friend Kevin arrived back from Bangkok, I invited him to move in, and I rented the ground floor and basement to four girls who had office jobs in town. One of them was the French goddaughter of Enoch Powell, the Conservative politician, and we became very close for a while.

On a skiing holiday with her over the Christmas holidays, I met some girls who were due to have their debutante season the following year. This was the traditional system designed for the middle-upper and upper classes to introduce their daughters to society once they came of age. It had originally been a highly formal business, centred around a garden party where the debs were presented to the king. Things had become marginally more modern since then and, aside from the very grand Queen Charlotte's Ball as the centrepiece of the season, the rest of it involved going from country house to country house, or to hired venues, for those families who did not own a country house. One of these new skiing friends put my name on the guest list for her deb event, which happened to be right at the start of the season, and for some reason the functionary who controlled the master list for the rest of the season took a shine to me and my name stayed on there. As a consequence, I happily participated in endless weekend parties and cocktail soirées, which provided a welcome contrast to student life. I enjoyed the social anthropology of seeing how these classes lived and behaved, and it also gave me the chance to visit some of the grandest stately homes in England, many of them stuffed full of magnificent art. Because I was older than most of the Hooray Henries who went to these events, I tended to get on well with the parents. From their perspective I was polite, well-mannered and considerate of my surroundings, unlike some of these offspring, who would stub cigarettes out on priceless carpets or start food fights because they could not hold their drink. They had all been to Eton and Harrow, or similar, whereas I was just a bush boy from Rhodesia, but I also knew how to be a good guest and the parents seemed to find me a refreshing change.

At that first event I met an attractive half-Italian girl called Susan, whose father was a wealthy Italian financier. She had a lot more to say for herself than most of the other debs, who tended to be fairly vacuous, and I ended up spending a good deal of time at her parents' smart home in London. I did not see much of her father because he was busy developing the exclusive Costa Esmeralda resort in Sardinia, in partnership with the Aga Khan, but I got on very well with Susan's mother. As I came to the end of my first year at SOAS, they invited me to spend the summer with them at the resort.

At first I jumped at the idea. By all accounts, Costa Smeralda was a stunningly beautiful place so it was an enviable invitation. But as the date for our departure loomed, I began to reconsider. Would I really be able to stand an entire summer surrounded by entitled young brats? They were unlikely to have their parents with them, so I might not even have any grown-ups to talk to.

I was not sure I could stomach it.

Just as I was having these second thoughts, an advert in the personal column of *The Times* caught my eye.

"Wanted," it read: "one navigator and cook to sail the Atlantic."

On a brief visit to Hong Kong while living in Nara, my first sailing experience was on a friend's Chinese junk in Hong Kong. This had intrigued me, so back in Japan, I had actually tried with some Japanese friends to get corporate sponsorship to fund the building of a junk in Hong Kong to sail the Pacific, but we were unsuccessful. Therefore, as I had long been intrigued by the idea of crossing one of the great oceans under sail, the advert rekindled my interest. So, on the spur of the moment I applied for the position and was invited to meet the skipper. He turned out to be a gangly, austere Scot of around my own age called Murrough. He had built a seven-metre sloop himself, and he needed someone to help him sail it across the Atlantic to Florida, where he hoped to sell it. There were only three applicants: one was a drunk, the second had an artificial leg, and I, with my complete lack of experience, was the third. So, *faute de mieux*, I was selected.

We started our preparations to cross the Atlantic. Since I was to be in charge of navigation, I bought a Reed's Almanac. By way of practice I would go out on a rowing boat on the Serpentine, the lake in Hyde Park, and try and get sun shots on a sextant. This prompted hoots of derision from the other boaters. "Hey, Nelson, how's it going?" called the comedians, or "Oi, 'Ornblower, when's your next voyage?" I did my best to rise above their taunts. It was better to be ridiculed now than get hopelessly lost on the high seas in a few weeks' time.

We started off down the English Channel towards Madeira. So that we could get some sleep on the crossing, Murrough had created some rudimentary self-steering gear. I was on duty halfway down the Spanish coast when something woke me up and I saw a large freighter bearing straight down on us, despite our rigging lights and a radar reflector at the top of the mast. I was so new to sailing that I barely knew whether to pull the tiller towards me or away from me. Fortunately, I chose the right direction and we veered sharply to port. We only just missed the ship, and our top spar actually hit her side as she passed. It was a stark reminder that this was a dangerous business.

My first attempt at navigating was little better. We did not know it, but we were actually passing Madeira by a margin of some twenty miles. Fortunately, it was night-time and we realised our error when we saw a distant lighthouse beam. If we had passed that way in the daytime we would probably never have seen the island and might have continued all the way to the South Pole.

Having changed course, we landed in Funchal and prepared for the transatlantic crossing. We had managed to get sponsorship from Heinz, who had donated thirty cases of canned supplies. We also took on a large amount of eggs and granary bread, which was supposed to last longer than white. In these preparations, I followed the terse instructions of my skipper, who did not like to waste words if he could have silence instead. I wondered what kind of company he was going to be on the long crossing, but I was committed to the adventure, and it was too late to back out now.

Having made sure everything was shipshape, we set off for the Caribbean. Now, for the third time in my life, I found myself confronting monotony and isolation. The only things to look at were the sky and the waves, and I fell to thinking about the philosophical idea of solipsism, which says one might only exist because one thinks one does. Ordinarily, our interactions with other people tend to suggest otherwise, but out here there was no one to interact with. Once, a large freighter passed fairly close to us, and I waved excitedly at the sailors looking down on us, because they had finally provided some evidence that we really did exist.

Murrough wanted to know why I was so excited, and I explained my thought process to him.

"You're a curious fellow," he muttered, shaking his head.

Otherwise there was very little conversation, unless it was to bicker. I was clean by nature, and all the more so since my time in Japan. I therefore made it clear I needed to wash every day. I discovered that washing with seawater just made me even stickier, so I was using drinking water. This upset Murrough, who did not share my attachment to cleanliness. Eventually he said: "Fine. You have the port water tank and I'll have the starboard one. If you run out, then too bad."

So I proceeded with my ablutions. I was sparing, but at least I had a sense of being refreshed each day. I had also decided it was pointless wearing swimming trunks, which would need to be washed with valuable water, so I was leaping around the small yacht stark naked. Murrough was not happy about this, but he had little choice in the matter. He continued to wear his bathers the whole way across until they almost rotted off him.

Uninhibited as I was, I recognised the need for a degree of privacy. My shipmate had installed a pump toilet next to the mast, which I did not trust: I could imagine it blowing up, and I had no desire to clean up the filth. Instead I took to clinging to the stern and sitting out over the back stay to open my bowels, while Murrough continued to use the toilet. The one spot looked directly on the other, so we had a convention that whenever one of us wanted to use either method, we would say, "Do you mind old chap?" and the other would say, "Of course, not at all, my dear fellow," and we would keep out of each other's eyeline. One day, however, we happened to be caught short at the same moment. Because we were each bound up in our own needs we did not notice what the other was up to. To our horror we found ourselves staring at each other, he on his throne and myself on the backstay, at a point where it was too late to stop what we were doing. This forced intimacy did not improve the atmosphere between us.

One of the few things that did bring us together was the food. The cases that Heinz had sent us bore the familiar slogan "57 Varieties", and we both naively assumed that each case contained an assortment of different flavours, which would at least be an antidote to the monotony. However, each time we opened a new box, we discovered that it contained only tomato soup. In a sense, it was no different to the dreariness of the repetitive, deliberately unappetising diet on Mount Koya, which I had endured for three months. However, the expectations we had of these supposed dozens of varieties must have played tricks with my mind, because both Murrough and I reacted in exactly the same way. Our disappointment turned into an aversion, and we became revolted by the mere thought of the stuff.

Otherwise there was no meeting of minds. As I got to the point of disliking my companion quite intensely, I started amusing myself by working out a perfect murder plan. I would wait until he was doing something with his back turned, then I would hit him on the head with the spare jib. That would knock him unconscious. Then I would dip his head in a bucket of seawater to finish him off before tossing him overboard. That was important: if he were only unconscious, throwing him in the ocean might revive him, and if he were then picked up by some passing freighter, he could accuse me of attempted murder. As another precaution, I would circle the area for two or three days, again in case some freighter passed. If it did, I would hail it to report his loss overboard in a sudden squall. There were no satellites in those days, so it would be impossible for anyone to prove otherwise. When I finally landed I could simply declare, in a state of distress and exhaustion, that I had lost him at sea and had been lucky to complete the crossing on my own.

Of course it was not really a plan, in the sense that I had no intention of carrying it out. However, I derived a macabre pleasure from devising it in such detail. And it was tantalising, because life does not often put us in situations of such extreme isolation that we really might get away with such a thing.

Unfortunately, that feeling of aversion could work both ways. I had decided that I wanted to swim right in the middle of the Atlantic – not just somewhere out of sight of land, but at the actual mid-point, as far away from land as it was possible to be. Once I had calculated that we were in the right area and it was now or never, I realised how frightened I was of actually doing it. I am a strong swimmer who has always been confident in the water. But the thought of some two miles of ocean under the yacht, with unknown monsters or schools of lethal jellyfish waiting to attack me, virtually paralysed me with fear. At the same time, my idle fantasies about bumping Murrough off had left me all too aware that he might be thinking along exactly the same lines; there was no doubt the antipathy was mutual. I had planned to trail a length of rope over the stern as I swam, so that the boat would not leave me behind. Now I had visions of a fed-up Murrough taking a carving knife and waving goodbye to me as he cut through it.

I hovered at the bows for two whole days without daring to go in. The simplest thing would of course have been not to do so, but that did not feel like an option. It was not unlike staying in the cabin on Vancouver Island or spending those months in the monastery at Mount Koya: having set myself the goal, I would regret it forever if I ducked the challenge. So, on the third day, I finally summoned the courage to dive in. I was full of nervous anticipation of the worst, but I managed to launch myself off the bows of the boat. The water was colder than I expected. However, I was in no mood to linger: I was still far too concerned with what might be in that vast blackness beneath me. I had conquered my fear and done it, which was the main point of the exercise. Now I just had to get back on the boat. I had dived forwards from the bows, and as the boat sped along I managed to grab the stern line. My greatest fear had been that I would miss it, and now I relaxed a little as I slowly pulled myself in along the knots I had tied in it at one-metre intervals. Then I saw Murrough approach the stern and I thought my worst fear was coming true. I looked for the telltale glint of sunlight on whatever knife he might be carrying with him. But I had traduced him. He just lent me a hand and pulled me back on board as any civilised shipmate would. My mind really had been playing tricks.

Just before we reached the Caribbean, we were hit by a hurricane. The waves were taller than the mast. We got the sails down and threw a sea-anchor over the stern to make sure we were pointing into the waves, as otherwise we might have turned turtle. After we had taken all the precautions we could, I decided I was going to enjoy myself. Lightning was flashing everywhere, the rain was pelting down, the waves were monstrous and it was staggeringly beautiful, if one allowed oneself to see it. We were so small against the vast ocean, and since we were so powerless, enjoying the majesty of it all seemed by far the best option. It would also be profoundly liberating to free myself from normal human fear simply by accepting the grandeur of the elements. Still stark naked, I therefore set about strapping myself to the mast with a safety harness.

"Come on, God, let's go!" I screamed into the wind.

This was nature as the ultimate thrill-ride.

After a while I felt bad about enjoying this fabulous experience on my own, and I wanted Murrough to share in it too. So, during a slight lull in the weather, I unclipped myself from the mast, hooked onto the safety line and inched my way back to the cabin.

"You should come up," I shouted to him above the howling weather. "It's absolutely amazing."

He shook his head.

"Can't," he said.

He was hunched over the table writing something.

"What are you doing?" I said.

"I'm writing in the log that we're in a force ten gale, I'm not sure we'll survive, and we're hoping for the best."

I left him to it. That was the fundamental difference between the two of us. I was having the time of my life shouting naked into the storm, while Murrough fretted over something completely beyond his control.

Nearly three weeks after we had set out from Madeira, we caught sight of some dark smudges on the horizon. It was an exciting moment, and I was proud that I had got us so far with the rudimentary navigational skills I had taught myself on the Serpentine.

We hailed a fisherman in a small boat and asked where we were.

"That's Martinique," he pointed. "And that's St Lucia."

My goal had been St Lucia. We were about twenty miles north of the channel between the two islands, so it really was not bad.

We dropped anchor in Castries harbour. Our voyage from Madeira had taken us twenty days, fourteen hours and I forget how many minutes, which we were told was a record for a boat of our class. We spent a few days basking in our achievement – I decided it was acceptable to allow my ego that small indulgence after all we had been through – and the volcanic island of St

Lucia was a lovely place to do so. After we had explored it to our satisfaction we resolved to head north to Martinique, which was more developed. There we could do a thorough clean-up of the yacht before heading on to Florida, where I would disembark and Murrough would try to sell the boat.

Before we left St Lucia, though, there was something important I needed to do. All the way across the Atlantic, I had been dreaming of Susan. The deprivations of the voyage had made me pine for her. In the confines of my bunk with not a great deal else to think about, I had missed her so much that I had decided I was, after all, in love with her. Now I wanted to telephone her, whatever the expense, in order to hear her voice and tell her my feelings.

I scraped together what little cash I had to make the long-distance call to London. Her mother answered the phone, and since we got on well, she naturally wanted to know how I was and how the crossing had been. But the call was costing me a fortune and my money was in danger of running out, so I gave her the briefest account.

She took the hint.

"If you're ringing for Susan," she said hesitantly, "I'm afraid I have bad news for you. She has taken up with a fellow called Robert. He spent the summer with her in Sardinia and — oh dear, I don't know how to tell you this — I'm afraid they might even be planning to get married."

I tried to maintain my dignity and hide my hurt by asking her to wish the happy couple all the best. Then I hung up the phone and returned dejected to my taciturn, unsanitary Scottish shipmate. The irony was horribly clear. I had embarked on this voyage because I did not want to spend the summer with Susan, but because of the wretched nature of the trip I had fallen for her – and now I had lost her. But these feelings did not last long, as there was much to see and do, now that we had finally arrived in the Caribbean.

Sailing from Martinique to Florida was more fraught than crossing the Atlantic. Our sloop had a deep keel for her size, and the Caribbean is full of coral heads which could easily rip the keel off the boat and sink us, so one of us had to be up in the bows the whole time watching out for these underwater hazards. I felt for whoever bought the boat: if they planned to sail it in these waters, they would have a nerve-wracking time. We did a couple of weeks of maintenance in Fort-de-France, then continued carefully through the Caribbean to the Bahamas. There I managed to befriend an attractive, bikini-clad girl in a rowing boat by pretending to run her down – much to Murrough's disapproval – which enlivened our stop in the Bahamas for me and helped ease the loss of Susan. Then we pressed on to Florida.

The final passage involved navigating the powerful coastal current that runs between the island of Bimini and the US coast. But before we reached Bimini, we were becalmed for four or five days. It was infuriating to be trapped with a companion I had no desire to be with, in searing heat, with no other sound but the rigging clacking away in the slight swell, and with the end of the voyage so near and yet so far.

For want of anything better to do, I decided to go for a swim. In these much shallower waters, well within sight of land, I had none of the fears I had suffered in mid-ocean. I dived wearing a face mask and flippers to try to collect conch, which have a delicious nutty flavour, from the sea bottom. It took a few attempts to get to the sea bed but I finally managed it and returned to the surface in triumph, shell in hand. But there must have been a freak gust, because as I looked around, I saw that the boat was now three or four hundred metres away. At the same time, I spotted a long, thin shape in the water. Dipping under the surface to get a better view through my mask, I found myself looking into the ugly, razor-toothed grin of a large barracuda, which was eyeing me back with great interest. It was swimming around me in circles, and I turned in a sort of corkscrew motion to keep facing it, so that I could react if it chose to attack me. All the while I was trying to head back to the boat. I attempted to cover nearly four hundred metres in this corkscrew fashion, which was neither easy nor efficient. Every few strokes I would wave at Murrough and shout to him put the engine on and bring the boat towards me, even though I had little hope that he would, because he was too stingy to waste the petrol. Sure enough, he just waved back. As I finally got close to the boat, I roundly cursed him from the water, giving vent to several weeks of frustration. By this time the barracuda had decided that the boat was more interesting than me, which gave me the chance to clamber back on board.

"Why didn't you turn the motor on and come for me, you bastard?" I demanded.

"I didn't realise that's what you wanted," he shrugged.

"Didn't you see me waving?"

"Yes, but I just thought you were having a good time out there."

In Japan I had learned the proverb "after the thunderstorm the earth is firmer". It means that if you have a fight with someone you have a relationship with — business or personal — you have a better understanding of each other afterwards. My fight with Murrough was either the exception that proves the rule, or, more likely, it illustrated that we had no basis of friendship in the first place. Either way, my open venting of fury did not ease our relationship.

Eventually the wind came up and we finally docked in Fort Lauderdale, where the coastguard told us Murrough's mother had called out a search for us. She knew we had arrived in St Lucia, but because we had been becalmed for so long, she thought we had been lost in the final stretch.

Murrough called her to assure her that we were alive and well, and I checked the time of the first bus for the airport, which left at the crack of dawn. When the time came he walked me to the bus stop, and we simply shook hands and said goodbye. There was no overt rancour, but neither was there any emotion or recognition of the intense experience we had been through together. Instead it was pared down to nothing, like something out of a Hemingway novel. Then the bus arrived and I headed to the airport to catch a plane for New York, where I stayed with some friends I had made in Bangkok and Isfahan.

It took just six hours to fly back from New York to London. I asked the stewardess if I could go into the cockpit, which in those days was fairly easy, and I amused the captain, co-pilot and navigator with my tales of the hot, sticky and disagreeable weeks I had spent going in the opposite direction.

There was a letter waiting for me at Glebe Place with my SOAS exam results. I had breezed through with top marks. But I had reached the conclusion that it was time to stop worrying about my lack of a university qualification, and that I could find something interesting to do in life without that token piece of paper. I went to see the dean, and explained that I meant no disrespect to the school or the lecturers, but I could not see that another three years there would do me any good. She said she quite understood, whereupon my attempts to get a degree officially ended.

The next task was to start earning some decent money.

This was a time when Japanese manufacturing companies and other businesses were starting to arrive in Europe in significant numbers, and I figured they would need representation. So I went to Japan Airlines and the Japanese Chamber of Commerce and told them I could speak pretty good Japanese, which I then proceeded to prove.

"If you need anybody to act as an interpreter, please let me know," I said.

Sure enough, that was exactly what they needed. So I started a company called Japanese Interpreting and Liaison Services, and I secured a succession of engagements for a day or two here, or a week there. Because it was a language that few Westerners at that time were capable of handling, I could charge a hefty fee. It enabled me to live well, and I also had plenty of free time because the engagements were only sporadic. I filled it by going to tea with various women I knew from the debutante season, including some of the married ones. I suspect I irritated a husband or two, but nothing terribly untoward happened and I was careful to maintain more or less the right degree of probity.

With summer over, the Deb Season was once again in full swing. I was dark brown, having spent two months naked on the Atlantic and in the Caribbean, so I must have looked exciting and piratical alongside the pale English society boys. And I was also single again. After a short while I started seeing a girl called Felicity. Dark-haired and petite, she had the most astonishing smile which lit up her whole face. Not everyone knows how to smile, but she certainly did, and every time she did it, I marvelled. She was intelligent and feisty, with a lot of character. She also happened to be one of the world's richest heiresses.

She was the daughter of Viscount X, and she was his only child. Her father had a vast stately home with one of the world's finest collections of Old Masters. The family had its own hunting pack, a squash court inside the building, and a regular array of glittering weekend guests, including Margot Fonteyn and Rudolf Nureyev.

I was invited every weekend unless Felicity and I were going to a ball elsewhere, and I made friends downstairs as well as upstairs. It was a very formal environment, with black tie for dinner and, although I was earning pretty well, I could not afford the three or four dress shirts necessary for a long weekend. So I became friendly with the butler, a chap called Higgs. He was very kind to me, I assume because I was courteous and respectful towards him, unlike some of the other guests, who saw him as a walking piece of furniture. He would arrange for my solitary dress shirt to be taken away every morning, washed, starched and returned in time for dinner. He would also give me guidance so that I, as the colonial outsider, did not make any desperate *faux pas*. I made him a small gesture of thanks in an envelope and he told me I was the first guest of my age who had treated him with respect and consideration.

By this time I had bought the house in Glebe Place from my mother. It was on a very short lease, which was the only reason I could afford it. I set about reconfiguring the building once more, making one large flat on the ground and upper floors, and turning the basement into separate accommodation for my mother. Felicity was a regular presence in the house, and as our relationship progressed we began to think about marriage. We eventually agreed that, in principle, we would like to get married.

At this point I should by rights have formally asked her father for her hand. But I did not do that, and instead it was Felicity who mentioned our plans to him. The next weekend we spent at his home, the Viscount invited me into his study after dinner for a brandy and cigar. His manner was pleasant as he ushered me into a room lined with ancient, leather-bound volumes, but he made a point of sitting behind his massive sixteenth-century desk, with me in front of it. There was no pretence that we were equals in this situation. I respected that, but I was nervous nonetheless. What was I in for?

"I've done some checking with my Japanese contacts in the City," he began.

"Oh yes?" I said.

I reminded myself that I had nothing to fear.

"They report that you do indeed speak very good Japanese," he continued. "So I'm pleased to see your claims are not exaggerated."

I began to relax.

"By the way, what do you think of this statue?" he said. He gestured towards a Chinese terracotta figure on the desk in front of him.

I examined it for a moment.

"It's probably a Tang dynasty funerary figure."

"You're right; it is," he said.

I relaxed a little more.

"Michael, I've watched you these past few months," he continued, as the cigar smoke curled above his head. "My first concern was that you were after Felicity's money. I no longer have that worry. You're too eccentric and candid to be able to disguise it if you were. I believe you genuinely have feelings for her, which I have to tell you is a relief. With the fortune she will inherit, there will be plenty of people who are interested in that alone."

He was right about my attitude to the money. The fortune was by any reckoning colossal, but it would have belonged to someone else, and having to ask every time I spent anything would not have been my style. So I really was not after Felicity for her wealth.

"Having put that behind us, I'm interested to know what kind of career you intend to pursue," the Viscount said. "But that's something for you to work out. In the meantime, could you do one thing for me? Felicity is eighteen and you're twenty-five. I would be very grateful if you would agree not to get married before she turns twenty-one."

I thanked him for his frankness, assured him that his assessment of me was not wrong, and told him that I did care for Felicity very much. Since he had been so fair with me, I would be more than happy to agree to his request and delay until she was of age.

We finished our brandy in an altogether more convivial atmosphere.

As time went on, however, I realised that Felicity and I belonged in different worlds. The most obvious example came after her parents split up and her mother was going to get married again. She bought a place in Tuscany, so Felicity decided she needed one too. It was too far to drive to Italy, but she wanted the use of her car while we were there. Rather than hire one, she put her own car on a plane to Geneva and we then drove to Tuscany from there.

It was all very well being an amateur social anthropologist and observing this kind of money-no-object spending for curiosity value. But I was not sure I could cope with it all the time. I also realised that I was regarded by would-be courtiers as a person of influence, not over her father, but over Felicity. I found people attempting to befriend me as a way of ingratiating themselves with the family, which was an unnerving experience, and felt like a foretaste of a life to come which I did not much want.

The pair of us were also quarrelling a lot, because our perspectives on life were very different. I was too much of a square peg in a round hole, and I insisted on having my own space, which was sometimes not practical. So we decided to part, which we did very amicably, and a few years later Felicity married a man from a distinguished racehorse training family. I wished her every blessing with him, and I am pleased to say that from what I hear, they appear to have a good marriage.

Not long after my arrival in London, I had discovered that a friend I knew from Bangkok was living in the next street to Glebe Place. He had a housemate who was involved in an esoteric self-development discipline called 'The Work', devised by an Armenian mystic called Gurdjieff. This housemate enjoyed testing people to see what they were made of, in spiritual or philosophical terms, and they both knew I had taken LSD in the Himalayas. Additionally, I had given them some of the hashish I had brought from Kabul and, sensing a kindred soul, they invited me round one evening to try some LSD of theirs. So I went for dinner, and afterwards we all took their LSD. The party included a girl who was living there, a French brunette with excellent English, who struck me as uncomplicated and remarkably centred. She seemed barely touched by the drug, even though she had taken the same amount as everyone else.

Her name was Marie-Thérèse and, because she lived so near, I saw her every now and then in the following weeks and months. She came and acted as a sitter for my two Siamese cats when I went away a couple of times, and I ran into her once at someone's house while I was with Felicity. Every time I met her, I remarked to myself how interesting and self-possessed she seemed. Born in the French provinces, she had spent most of her teenage life in Paris. In Buddhist terms, she would be described as an old soul, because she had such moral certainty about what was right and wrong, about good manners, and about being considerate of others and looking after them. In many ways these characteristics were a stark contrast to my own buccaneering approach of attempting to explore and exploit life to the maximum. Even on a limited acquaintance, Marie-Thérèse seemed to personify the kind of moral value system whose importance my mother had dinned into me at such an early age.

One day, after Felicity and I had split up, I met Marie-Thérèse in the street and suggested we get together for a meal. After that, we began spending more time in each other's company, and she made it clear she was getting tired of the environment of endless esoteric experimentation in the house where she lived. I was still sharing with my friend Kevin in Glebe Place, but we had a spare room and I invited her to take it. She moved in, and I think she lasted about two nights in that spare room before she ended up sharing mine.

From then onwards we spent a great deal of time together. She worked part time in a shoe shop while also attending a language school in Kensington to further improve her English. We already felt very close to each other, but one of her former housemates, a chap called John, was still pursuing her, as was a scruffy little Belgian chap who went to the same language school. One day I went to pick her up in my car. John was also there in his car, as was the Belgian, skulking behind a bush.

I made a decision.

"It's time for you to make up your mind," I said as I got out of the car to greet Marie-Thérèse. "You can choose the Belgian over there behind the bush, you can choose John in his car over there, or you can choose me. But you need to make the decision now, because this is a one-off chance. You either get in the car with me and that's it, and it's clear to everybody else that we're together, or you get in the car with him and that's the end of it."

It was a risky strategy, but I was confident as I waited for her answer. And I am pleased to say that, after very little hesitation, she got in the car with me. I have never ceased to be grateful that she did, and I believe she feels the same way.

In the autumn of 1967 I got a job working for a small English travel company based in London and Tokyo, selling holidays in Britain and Europe to Japanese customers. It took me back to Japan for the best part of a year, while Marie-Thérèse returned to Paris and Kevin stayed on at Glebe Place.

It was my first real taste of Japan in a business context, and it reinforced my sense that this was a country where I wanted to spend a good deal of my life. Naturally, I revisited my old haunts, and one night when I was visiting friends in Kyoto they took me to a restaurant called the Ashiya Steak House. It was run by a former American GI called Bob Strickland, who had chosen to be demobilised in Japan because he had fallen in love with and married a Japanese girl. Outwardly, he was a crude hillbilly type, but he spoke excellent colloquial Japanese and was a character of great resourcefulness. As well as starting a very successful restaurant which was famous for its Ohmi beef – the most prestigious meat in the country – he had secured the Japan agency for Continental Trailways, the US intercontinental bus company, which, at that time, was the main competitor for Greyhound. I was introduced to Bob, and we fell to discussing how beneficial it might be if I could secure similar representation with the British tour firm Thomas Cook and its French counterpart Wagons-Lits. If we did that, we mused, we could build up a decent wholesale travel business at a time when Japan was emerging from international isolation and thousands of its people were hankering to travel abroad. I promised to broach the matter with Thomas Cook and Wagons-Lits when I got back to London, and we shook hands.

As we parted, I could have little idea what havoc this man would wreak in my life a few years later.

Early the following summer, I was reunited with Marie-Thérèse in London. We had managed to keep the relationship going by weekly letters during the eleven months I had been away, as we both realised we had something worth holding on to. I had had many relationships, some of them serious, others not, but this one seemed qualitatively different to all of them.

One weekend we were invited by a couple of friends to sail to Brittany with them. My memories of the Atlantic voyage were not fond, but crossing the English Channel was a much shorter trip and I was confident the company would be far more congenial, so we agreed. In St Malo, our friends, a lawyer and a dentist, went off to dine in a famous restaurant, which we could not afford. Instead, Marie-Thérèse cooked us a dinner of mussels on the boat and then the pair of us went for a walk around the port.

Next to the harbour was a tall crane rising about twenty metres into the air.

"Let's climb up and see the view," I suggested.

The climb was strenuous but the view over the lights of the harbour was well worth it. We gazed across the river estuary towards the little town of Dinard on the other bank, and then out into the Channel, back towards England. Marie-Thérèse wrapped her arms around me and sighed.

The house Rufaro, in the Umvukwees (now called Mvurwi), Rhodesia, that my father built with handmade, sun-baked bricks in 1940

My mother with Brian and myself outside the house my father built for us near Salisbury, Rhodesia

Ready for a motor-bike outing on my Indian Warrior in the summer of 1959

Simon Boreham and myself on a practice walk in Dublin, before the Dublin-Belfast marathon walk

Preparing to take sea-water samples on board the *USC&GS Pioneer*, a US Coast Guard geodetic survey ship

With Abbot Nakamura, the other two monks and the housekeeper nun prior to my departure in May, 1963, from Shinno-in, a temple founded in 823AD in the Mount Koya monastic complex, Wakayama Prefecture, Japan

Preparing for my Kendo black belt exam in Nara, Japan, in September, 1964

Murata Kanzo, 8th Black belt, my second Kendo master, whom I met through Kagita, Mayor of Nara

My Zen master, Minagawa Eishin, preparing me for our pilgrimage to Fukui Prefecture in October, 1964

Offering a prayer at the Shinto ground-breaking ceremony for our new building in Tokyo in 1969

Myself with Pygmy hunting party in the Congo jungle, in March, 1984

Euromoney cartoon about my arrival in Hong Kong as new chairman of Merrill Lynch's Asia Pacific Region

As Merrill Lynch non-Executive Director to the board of Sung Hung Kai & Co in Hong Kong, 1985

Peacocks make office crow with delight

By KAVITA DASWANI

JUST outside the spacious suite of offices occupied by Merrill Lynch Asia Pacific Region chairman Michael Dobbs-Higginson is the fruition of months of planning and negotiation – an exotic bird-filled garden.

The financial executive spent months conceiving, planning and building the Japanese-style garden outside his plush offices in St George's Building, Central.

He developed an interest in "the Japanese ability to create gardens in small spaces" after living in Japan and began negotiating with the Kadoorie family, which owns the building.

Four years ago the cement terrace became a green haven.

"I designed the garden, put in a pond and a Japanese bamboo waterfall because it is nice to hear water. Then I felt the garden lacked animation, so I put in rabbits, which ate the plants."

The rabbits were banished and Mr Dobbs-Higginson formed a committee to determine what creatures should live in the garden. It now has mandarin ducks, a golden pheasant and a male and female peacock.

"Their wings are clipped so they can't actually fly, but every so often one of them decides to go for a walk and we have to send a messenger to look for the errant bird."

"We also enjoy playing mild practical jokes on visi-

South China Morning Post article about the eleventh floor roof terrace garden I had created, and populated with peacocks, mandarin ducks and a couple of rabbits, for our Merrill Lynch HQ office in Hong Kong

-Editorial/Opinion-

THE DAILY YOMIURI

India should join Asia-Pacific

Needed as counterweight to China

By M.S. Dobbs-Higginson

Special to The Yomiuri Shimbun

India should be welcomed into the Asian Pacific community— particularly by Japan. But, many will ask, particularly the Japanese, why should Asia-Pacific do so?

There are several reasons.

As the world's largest democracy, India can provide a contrasting role model in bringing democracy to the region—although it is not certain that the other countries of Asia wish to replicate entirely India's populist democratic "demobabel" system!

More importantly, although Japan is economically very powerful, it is Greater China, if not China itself, which could threaten domination of the region.

Another Greater East Asia Coprosperity Sphere led by any country would be a disaster.

In the recent past, India and China have had similar aspirations to be a regional superpower. And India has traditionally seen China as a threat and a rival, owing partly to the intermittent border skirmishes that have disrupted the Indian-Chinese border for decades.

A positive relationship between

Asia-Pacific, India has an important role to play. However, it should not be side-tracked by chasing memberships in organizational chimeras that pro-

growth is being fueled primarily by the overseas Chinese of Hong Kong, Taiwan, and elsewhere.

India has its own pool of overseas

who are investing in China.

At least some of these investors must be worried about the inherent instability of China as it moves

An Op Ed article I wrote in 1990 for the Japanese *Yomiuri* newspaper, concerning the importance of having India included in Asian Pacific regional affairs as a counterweight to China

Let's get together
to face the coming trade war

In an important book just out, banker-turned-writer Michael Dobbs-Higginson argues a compelling case for a new Asia-Pacific grouping to counter the European Union and the US-led Nafta in a Cold War to be fought on the economic and trade front. LESLIE FONG, Straits Times and Sunday Times Editor, discusses the implications of this scenario on countries in the region.

Is THE WORLD IN DANGER OF SLIPPING INTO A global trade war? If so, what can countries in the Asia Pacific like Singapore do about it?

Mr Michael Dobbs-Higginson, 53, a former investment banker who has spent almost his entire adult life living and working in Asia, believes that the risk of a new cold war fought on the economic and trade front is mounting.

He believes it is hugely beneficial, if not imperative, for the Asia Pacific to form a group or forum of its own, modelled after the original European Economic Community, perhaps.

This regional body will be an effective counter-balance against members of the European Union (EU) and the North American Free Trade Agreement (Nafta) should these rich nations turn openly protectionistic and abandon all previous pretences of upholding free trade.

As he sees it, the choice is stark: Countries in the Asia Pacific either hang together or they hang separately as just so many helpless Davids crushed by the two Goliaths.

He thinks the time to start working towards such a forum or community is now, when an ascendant Asia Pacific will be doing so as a pro-active act of faith, and not when a crisis forces a hasty, defensive union out of compromises that cannot stand the test of time.

In his judgment, Asean, which has long experience in regional cooperation, is just the core from which to build this larger regional community.

CONTINUED ON PAGE 6

1993 article in the *Singapore Times* Review about my views on the need to form an Asian Pacific regional grouping, starting from the existing ASEAN grouping, to enable us to deal more effectively with the rising Trade War

A meeting with a Tibetan Yak herder on the Sichuan Provence China border with Tibet to discuss his vet pharmaceutical needs, November, 2005

Aerial view of the fully restored Château de Tourreau showing the château in the background, the farm and the sports complex

The south façade of the château photographed from the South Park

Magic and mystery: the unicorn statue in our park at Le Thor, Provence, by UK sculptor Tom Hiscocks

Our last Xmas at Tourreau. Julien, Justine, Marie-Thérèse, Charlotte and myself, with Simba, our Rhodesian Ridgeback, Christmas, 2013

Three generations of our family in August, 2016, at Thouzon, our new family home in Le Thor, Provence (missing Charlotte's husband and Julien's recent baby daughter)

"I want to spend the rest of my life with you," she said.

I had genuinely not seen this coming. But in that moment I knew that I loved her, and that I could indeed spend the rest of my life with this woman. She was calm and unflashy, with a clear, straightforward moral compass of the kind my mother had urged me to find when I was a child. As we looked down on the harbour, I realised I had found my soulmate, from whom I could learn a great deal and with whom I could build a real life-partnership. I also had a good feeling about a woman who was following my mother's example and effectively proposing to her man.

"I think I could happily do the same," I said. "But I have one condition."

"What's that?"

"You have to learn Japanese."

Whatever she had been expecting, that was not it.

"Why?"

"I'm certain I want to go back to Japan," I said. "That means you'll have to come with me, and I don't want you with me as a passenger. I want someone who can enjoy the place as I much as I do. Come with me and I'll happily fund you through a year of the Japanese examination course. If you pass your exams at the end of that, I'll marry you."

She laughed and gave a classic Gallic shrug. "Of course I will go, and I will learn Japanese, as I certainly do not wish to be a passenger," she said.

And so it was that, by the time we clambered down from that crane, we were conditionally engaged to be married.

The news had to be broken to Marie-Thérèse's parents.

Unlike Felicity, my new fiancée was no heiress. Her father was in the jewellery business, her mother was a housewife, she had two brothers living in Paris and their family home was in the town of Romans-sur-Isère, just north of Provence. I arrived in their lives like a piece of meteorite landing in their back garden.

I went to stay with them, and this time I followed the rules by asking her father for her hand in marriage in what in those days was my fairly basic French. I staggered through my little speech and sat waiting impatiently for their reaction.

Her father turned to his wife and said: *"Que dit-il? Je ne comprends pas."*

He had not understood a word.

His wife understood only too well.

"Je comprends," she said, beginning to cry. *"Il veut épouser notre fille."*

Now her husband understood too.

"Impossible!" he thundered. *"Il n'est pas français, il n'est pas catholique, il est bouddhiste, il vient de Rhodésie... Impossible!"*

At that point, we dropped the further bombshell that we were not planning on getting married immediately: first we were going to Japan, and only after that would we eventually wed.

This was more than Marie-Thérèse's parents could bear. Her father, supported by her brothers, was adamant that it was completely impossible for any daughter of their family to travel, unmarried, all the way to Japan, a far distant place which still had a terrible reputation for wartime atrocities, and was otherwise distinguished only for making cheap goods for the international market. But they had reckoned without Marie-

Thérèse herself. Having accepted my condition to satisfy me, she was now determined to go through with it. As her family already knew, she was a strong-willed character who would not budge from a decision once she had decided it was the right one.

Her father made one last-ditch effort to persuade me this was not going to work. He got wind from Marie-Thérèse that I was in Paris working on the Wagons-Lit contract, and one night he drove all the way from Romans to see me – a journey that took about eight hours. I was out at a business dinner, so he waited patiently outside my hotel until past eleven o'clock. When he finally saw me getting out of my taxi, he jumped out of his car, hurried over to me and crouched down to beat his fists on the pavement.

"You have a heart like this pavement," he said in French. "Hard and impossible! I absolutely do not want you to marry my daughter!"

Without another word, he jumped to his feet again, got back in his car and drove back through the night to Romans.

But Marie-Thérèse gave him her final answer on the matter, to the effect that nothing the family could say would change her mind. Realising he was beaten, he announced that it was clear his daughter had resolved to marry me and the family had no alternative but to accept that it was going to happen, to stop fighting it and to be supportive. He was as good as his word and in time I became closer to my in-laws (including Marie-Thérèse's brothers) than to my own family, not least because I saw much more of them than my own widely-separated father and siblings. In the event, I think everyone recognised that she had chosen the most wisely of the three siblings: both her brothers' marriages ended in painful divorces.

Not long afterwards, I received a letter from Thomas Cook/Wagons-Lits agreeing that I could be their representative in Tokyo. It was perfect timing, and now I was on my way back to Japan with the woman I loved, to begin this major new adventure.

6:

Running for My Life

IT WAS THE WEEK before Christmas 1972, and the life I had painstakingly built for myself and my young family had fallen apart overnight, thanks to a Mr Schwartz. I had never set eyes on this man until twelve hours earlier, and now he was threatening to arrange for me to have an "accident" unless I signed everything I owned in Japan over to my partner. Unfortunately, I had to trust that he meant it, because Schwartz was not some small-time criminal or would-be gangster attempting to muscle in on our business. He was, he led me to believe, the head of the Tokyo CIA station, and he gave every impression that he was perfectly prepared to put his threat into action.

How different everything had seemed the previous evening, when I had been celebrating my good fortune in life with an English friend at a downtown restaurant. We had been living in Japan for five years. Marie-Thérèse spoke the language well and was as fascinated by the country and its culture as I was. We had a large rented home in Tokyo, as well as a beautiful country cabin which we had built for our small but growing family. We were already the proud parents of a strapping young toddler,

Julien, and a few days earlier Marie-Thérèse had given birth
to a baby daughter, Justine. My mother-in-law was over from
France to help with the children, because I was up to my eyes in
the biggest business venture of my career so far, which on paper
would make me worth millions of dollars. I was permitting
myself this celebratory night out because I reckoned I was
allowed a moment of satisfaction.

Relations with my business partner Bob Strickland had had
their ups and downs. Marie-Thérèse decided he was a bad lot
on her first meeting, and she had not altered her opinion. He
and I now had a number of arms to our business, some of them
very profitable, others costing us money. But I had recently had
a brainwave that would raise us into a new league.

Because Bob had a passion for fast cars, one of our businesses
was a garage which carried out repair work on top-of-the-range
vehicles. We did bespoke jobs, and had recently made a replica
delivery tanker, the size of a Mini Cooper, for Mobil Oil to use
for advertising purposes. Mobil was very pleased with the result
and we now had good contacts in the company, including its
number two man in Japan, because he was French and Marie-
Thérèse knew his wife socially.

The company happened to have a petrol station on a major
intersection, Akebanebashi, about ten blocks from our house.
It was an ordinary petrol station, but the location was a highly
strategic one and, to me, the site was ripe for redevelopment
– not just at ground level, but above it. I went to see Mobil's
American executive called Lou Noto, who would later head the
whole company worldwide and would steward its merger with
Exxon.

"Why don't we put a building on this corner?" I said. "If you sell us the air rights to build vertically above your property, we'll construct it. On the ground and first floors we'll give you a showcase petrol station and diagnostic repair centre. Then we can add six floors of offices above it."

I explained that we could put a garage on the floor above the petrol station, with a state-of-the-art testing and tuning centre, which would satisfy Bob. To make a feature of the place, we would have a café behind a window so that people could have a coffee while they watched their car being tuned up. And above it we would have the office floors, with a headquarters for our small group of companies at the very top.

Our pitch to Lou went well. I talked to my bank manager at Standard Chartered into lending us the money we needed to build an eight-storey tower, and our central Tokyo real-estate project was on. I looked after the whole process as the building went up. I had some major fights with Bob, who had an equal fifty percent stake, yet seemed to resent the fact that he was sharing the ownership of this prime site with me. But my legal ownership status was completely watertight, so these tiresome arguments were not worth losing sleep over. I also found all the tenants except one: for some reason Bob was keen to persuade the Libyan Embassy to open their commercial section on the fourth floor. It seemed important to him, and I saw no reason to object as long as they paid the rent.

It was a major coup for two foreigners to pull off something like this in Japan at the time. I was thirty-one years old, and my half share would be worth a small fortune, so I could be forgiven for feeling pleased with myself, as I told my English pal about the project.

But pride comes before a fall, as I was about to find out.

I suggested to my friend at the end of our celebratory evening that he come and see the building, which was nearly ready, so I was keen to show it off. He agreed and we took a taxi to the interchange. It was nearly midnight when we got there, and I expected the building to be deserted. Instead, to my amazement, it was a hive of activity – particularly on the fourth floor, where a group of technicians, including some Westerners, seemed to be wiring up the ceiling.

One of these Westerners was wearing a suit and seemed to be giving out orders.

"Who the hell are you?" I demanded.

He squared up and said: "I could ask you the same question. Who the hell are you?" His accent was American.

"I'm the co-owner of this building and I'm going to call the police," I said.

At this point, his attitude changed dramatically

"Hang on a second," he said. "Let me call my boss."

He picked up one of the few phones that was already connected, and started dialling. I tried to listen in but he was speaking softly with his back to me, so I could not make out a word. I had to wait until he replaced the receiver and turned back to me.

"They'll be here in fifteen minutes."

"They? Who are 'they'?"

"My boss and your partner," he said.

My partner? So this was something to do with Bob!

I waited, trembling with fury, until Bob turned up with

another American – sharper-suited and better spoken than Bob, although that was not difficult – who introduced himself as Schwartz. At this point he simply said he was from the US Embassy. He and my partner were both looking flustered.

"Tell me what's going on, Bob," I demanded.

The pair of them urged me to calm down and asked if we could sort it out tomorrow. By this time I had asked my English friend to go – he was hopefully too drunk to remember much of what he had seen – and I reluctantly agreed.

I did not get a lot of sleep. I had a bad feeling about what I had seen, and I was consumed with anger at my partner. I did not want to trouble Marie-Thérèse yet; she had enough to worry about with the new baby. But I had a feeling of dread when I left home the next morning for my meeting with Bob and Schwartz.

They were both already there, waiting for me. They asked me to join them in Bob's office on the top floor of the tower. As my partner closed the door, Schwartz said: "You shouldn't have seen what you saw last night. But you did, and as you're clearly not stupid, you will have realised we were bugging the office."

He was right. I had worked this much out on my own.

"What the hell do you think gives you the right. . .?" I began.

"Please, let me finish," he said.

I looked at Bob, but he was staring intently at the floor rather than look me in the eye.

"Go on," I said.

"We always want to know what the Libyans are up to. They do a lot of smuggling and false destination shipments. You and your partner didn't arrange it. I did, because I'm the station chief of the CIA in Japan – as Bob here knows, because he has been assisting us with various projects for a number of years."

My partner was still avoiding my eye. This explained any number of strange disappearances or responses on his part over the years we had worked together. But what the hell had he got me into?

I tried to stay calm.

"You don't want me to say anything about it? Fine—I won't say anything about it," I said.

"I'm afraid it's not that simple," said Schwartz. "You know what we'd really like? Come and join us. You're a British citizen, and you could be very useful to us."

"How so?"

"A variety of ways."

"Spying for you"?

He shrugged.

"There's also Philippe," he said.

Philippe was a Frenchman we had working with us in our small consulting company, fresh from a year in Beijing.

"We have a hunch he's with French intelligence, and we know his wife likes you. If you could tape her on video in…shall we say…a compromising situation, it could be of great assistance to us…"

What kind of person did he think I was?

"I wouldn't do that to my wife. She's just had a baby! And I wouldn't do it to his wife," I said.

He put his hands up to calm me down.

"Alright, but we'd still like you to join us," he said.

"I'm not interested."

He looked me in the eye and his tone changed. "In that case we'll need you to come to Yokosuka airbase every month for a lie detector test, to prove you haven't talked."

"I don't think I want to do that," I said. "I don't see why I should."

If I agreed to this, there was no knowing what else they would demand. It was a sure path to enslavement.

"It's your call," said Schwartz. "The only other two options are much less attractive."

"Namely?"

"You sign over everything to us and leave Japan in the next two weeks. And that will be an end to it."

I wanted to pinch myself. This was the kind of thing one expected in the movies, not in real life.

"And the last option?" I said.

"Let's not go into the details. But it's quite likely you'll have an accident of some kind. A bad accident."

So that was the choice. I was faced with handing over everything I had worked for or being found dead in a hit-and-run accident, or pushed in front of a train, or...

We had had such hopes for our life in this country. On our arrival in 1967, we had managed to secure an unusually large house in a central district of Tokyo. It was owned by an elderly woman who ran a small export business with her son. She had promised it to another foreigner but he did not speak Japanese. I fell to my knees on her *tatami* matting and beseeched her to let us have the house instead. My command of the language paid off, and she decided she would prefer us as tenants.

Marie-Thérèse started her language studies. We deliberately lived apart so that she could be immersed in the language, as I had been, and I arranged for her to stay in a series of homes in Kyoto and in the countryside. Her hosts included a leading antiques dealer, an old aristocrat lady with a husband who spent virtually every night at Gion's Geisha houses and an elderly oil painter of some distinction, who had studied in France as a disciple of Matisse, and now lived in slightly scandalous circumstances with the daughter of the head priest of one of the most important Shinto shrines in Japan. All this gave Marie-Thérèse a good exposure to traditional Japan, starting her on her own voyage of discovery into this fascinating country.

Meanwhile I set to work with Bob, selling Western tour services to the Japanese market. He proved to be highly erratic, of limited intellectual capability and strategic vision, and with a huge ego, which was why Marie-Thérèse had disliked him from the day she met him. Unfortunately, she is rarely wrong in her judgement of people. But, for the moment, I countered that he was never meant to be a bosom buddy: he simply provided a decent vehicle for me to set up in business and establish some of my own ideas for what I was going to do with my life.

I was initially vindicated, as the business grew well. We secured the agency for Holiday Inn, striking the deal in person with Kemmons Wilson, the legendary founder of the chain. A famous blunt-speaker, he always flew economy despite his great wealth, saying: "The ass of the plane gets to the other end just as fast as the front, so why pay extra?" That exemplified his no-nonsense business philosophy. We also started representing Avianca Airlines, the Latin American carrier, which was associated with Pan Am. Bob made a big effort to befriend the head of Pan Am in Tokyo, although I thought him a bit of an idiot. But cultivating him served its purpose because we were able to get standby first-class tickets virtually whenever we needed them.

At the end of our year apart, Marie-Thérèse passed her exams, fulfilling her side of the marital bargain. Now it was up to me to honour mine. I had already got hold of the appropriate paperwork from the mayor's office. By some quirk of Japanese law, for a civil wedding, as long as the bridegroom had the signature of the woman he was going to marry on the relevant application form, the bride herself did not need to present herself. In an attempt at a prank, I told Marie-Thérèse the form was for a bank account. Only after she had signed it did I break the news that I could now get us married and she need not attend. I thought this was hilarious, but it was not quite the marriage ceremony that she had envisaged. To say that she did not see the funny side would be an understatement.

She eventually forgave me, and we went together to the mayor's office. We were given a tag with a number 32 on it and told to sit on a bench with several other couples and wait to be called. It was not a romantic environment, even by registry office standards, and my joke about doing the whole thing on my own, which a few days earlier had seemed brutally unromantic, no longer seemed so unreasonable. After a long wait, we were eventually summoned to one of the counters, where we were offered a choice of marriage licences. One was a rubber-stamped printed form, the other a handwritten document in beautiful calligraphy. The second option was five times the price, but having blotted my copybook once, I knew better than to skimp at this stage, and we finally emerged as husband and wife with the deluxe licence. It was just as well: we later found out that most foreign embassies would not recognise the cheaper version. This had become a notorious scam, with unscrupulous Western men using the cheaper licence to lure unworldly Japanese girls into relationships, knowing full well they would not be recognised by any foreign government.

We went back to France that Christmas. Marie-Thérèse wanted to have a proper ceremony which her family and friends could attend – after all, many of them did not expect to see her ever again once we returned to Japan. We went to see the priest in charge of the main Catholic church in Romans, who said he would be delighted to conduct a wedding for Marie-Thérèse, but since I was not a Catholic he would need permission from the Pope. Just as we were losing heart, we met the priest from a small village called Mours about ten miles from Romans, whom we both liked immensely and who was much more sympathetic. His church was a lovely little medieval one, which in its size and modesty suited us perfectly. With a little persuasion, he managed to get over the fact that I was a Buddhist. More troubling for him was my request for the last passage of Fauré's *Requiem*, In Paradisum, to accompany the service.

"Why in heaven's name do you want that?" he asked.

"Don't you know it? It's ethereally beautiful," I said.

"But it's a requiem," he rejoined. "It is highly unusual to have it at a wedding!"

"Well in a sense I'm dying and I'm being reborn as a married man," I said, clutching at straws.

Somehow it worked.

"Just don't tell any of your guests where it comes from," he sighed.

Incredibly kind and modest, he perfectly embodied the best of the Christian faith. He went on to baptise all our children and he became a real fixture in our lives.

We had the ceremony between Christmas and New Year. All Marie-Thérèse's family was there, while my younger brother Brian made the long journey via boat and train from London, as did Kevin, who was my best man. Ann, my younger sister, who lived in Calgary, could not make it. We then embarked on a magnificent honeymoon in Mexico and Tahiti, enjoying our first-class perks with Pan Am to the full. The only dampener was on our last stop in Sydney, where all our luggage was stolen, including every one of our wedding presents. I was not too concerned, but for Marie-Thérèse it was a cruel blow.

In the second year of our business operations, I managed to secure all the bulk travel from the four top agencies in Japan. I was a good salesman, we had a good product and we had a complete lock on the bulk travel business, to the irritation of would-be competitors like Kuoni. To complete the mood of optimism, Marie-Thérèse discovered she was expecting our first child. I was so busy running the travel business that I did not envisage being a hands-on father, but I was excited at the prospect of starting a family, and particularly at doing so in Japan. All being well, our children would be as comfortable in Japanese as they would be in English or French, which could bring them untold benefits, both cultural and professional, in later life.

As we looked forward to the birth, we were also conscious that city living in Japan is dense and crowded. It is particularly unpleasant in the summer when the climate is hot and sticky. We began looking for a plot of land in the countryside, somewhere high enough to escape the heat, for a weekend retreat. We concluded that the best area was just below the mountain resort of Karuizawa, the smart getaway destination for wealthy Tokyo people; if we looked a little further down, we might be able to afford it. We made several research trips, with an increasingly pregnant Marie-Thérèse being bumped up and down on the rough country roads, until we found the perfect spot: an area of rice fields with a huge stone outcrop as a backdrop, a small pine forest on one side, and a slope down to a stream in the middle of a bamboo grove on the other. As well as money, we offered to provide the owner of the land, who was the village headman, a litre of second-class *saké* every month for the rest of our lives, in recognition of his advice and guidance. It was an eccentric gesture, but it seemed to go down well and we reached a deal, whereupon we set about designing a simple cabin. Since the costs were rising we found another couple to go in with us. By doubling the size of the house to make a semi-detached cabin and then splitting the cost of construction and of the land, the project would become much more affordable. Marie-Thérèse had a bad feeling about the husband, but I persuaded her that the benefits outweighed her doubts.

The country retreat proved every bit as idyllic for the three of us as we had hoped. We put in a small swimming pool, fed at one end by the stream, and a sandpit which Julien adored.

The village headman would leave a basket of vegetables on our doorstep every Friday when we arrived after three or four hours on the road. We were looking forward to many years of happiness there – as a family of four, because by the time the house was due to be finished, we were also looking forward to the arrival of our second child, who would be called Justine if a girl, which I very much wanted.

On the business side of things, Bob and I were getting more ambitious, which in hindsight was the root of my downfall. We wanted to be more than just a wholesale travel company, because Japanese travel companies would eventually expand into Europe and the US, at which point they would no longer need our services. In order to diversify, we set up a small export company; it was not particularly active but it added another arrow to our quiver. Then I suggested we start a business consulting company, for which we had brought on board the Frenchman, Philippe. And Bob pushed for his garage. He found another American hillbilly type who could do the engineering work for him, so we went ahead with that venture too.

Bob was obsessed with this side of the business. He insisted we needed more space, so he rented and built another much bigger workshop. But I was worried. While the other companies, led by the travel business, were all making a good profit, the car company haemorrhaged cash and took up a huge amount of time. At one point, Bob had a huge fight with his hillbilly engineer and tried to beat him up with a baseball bat. It was so bad that the police were called. They eventually chose not to get involved, because foreigners in Japan were regarded as a breed apart, and nobody cared if they beat each other up, so long as the dispute did not involve Japanese citizens. But the episode was an example of how tense things were getting.

It was while I was fretting about the amount of money we were spending compared to the revenue coming in that I had my brilliant idea of building a tower above a petrol station. And that was what had got me into my present nightmare situation.

I did not want to tell Marie-Thérèse that I was facing an implicit, unashamed death threat from the station chief of the CIA until I absolutely had to. First I went to the British Embassy, where I knew the ambassador's deputy, Peter Wakefield, very well.

He listened to my story with a grim expression, then said: "I'm afraid these people don't muck around, old man. But let me talk to our people in London to see what they advise, and I'll get back to you."

I waited for an agonising day and night. On Christmas Eve, he called me back.

"This isn't what you want to hear," he said. "I'm afraid there's nothing we can do to help. My colleagues in London say their best advice is leave Japan, no matter what the personal economic damage. At least you'll save yourself. Otherwise you're in great danger. These people play very rough if you don't go along with them. If he has threatened you with an accident, you have to assume he means it."

I have never felt so crushed. I was being robbed blind, by an official government agency, acting entirely unscrupulously, and even though my own government agreed it was entirely unjust, there was not a damn thing I could do about it. My monastic training helped me fend off complete despair, but it could not stop me feeling utter fury at the blatant injustice, and frustration at my powerlessness.

Finally I went back to Marie-Thérèse and told her why I had looked so distracted for the past two days and nights. I felt sick at having to tell her about it, because the news was about to destroy her world as well as mine. But the calm with which she took it was a reminder, if any were needed, of why I had married her. She was upset, of course, and angry with my treacherous partner, about whom her instinct had been entirely justified. But she also buoyed me up, and told me that if leaving Japan was the price to keep our whole family safe, then we must do it, and we would rebuild our lives elsewhere. Bad as things looked, she said, we would find the strength to get through it.

After doing our best to put on a show of Christmas for the sake of my son and mother-in-law, I went back to Bob and Schwartz five days later and duly signed away everything I had in Japan to Bob. As the CIA effectively already owned him, they would now own all of a plum piece of Tokyo real-estate in the shape of our tower block.

Having reinvested almost all my earnings in our group of companies, my only other asset was my small, museum-quality antique art collection, which I took to one of our closest friends, a dealer called Mitsuru Tajima, who went on to become one of the world's top dealers in Japanese, Chinese and Korean antique art. Generous, with impeccable taste, and a true gentleman in the old sense of the word, he and his mother had shared our Tokyo house for a couple of years. He would go all over Japan on antiques-buying trips and I always looked forward to his return to see what treasures he had unearthed. Thanks to his generous tutelage and pricing, we had been able to build up a small collection of museum-quality pieces. When I explained our predicament, he said he was willing to give me a reasonable price, but he had to discuss it with his English business partner. Unfortunately, the latter scented an opportunity, and I was forced to part with everything at a substantial mark-down. It was the only cash we had.

We had no choice but to leave the house in the country, plus a stock of wine we had bought, left over from the Expo '70 World's Fair in Osaka. Marie-Thérèse had been right again, and our co-owner proved to be another greedy opportunist, who saw a chance and grabbed it, knowing there was nothing I could do. I signed my half of the place over to him, along with the obligation to provide the monthly bottle of *saké*; I hope the villager continued to receive it, but I would not stake money on it. I know that my co-owner later sold the house to HSBC to use as a countryside retreat for their staff; for whatever reason, they stopped doing so, and the last I heard, the place was a ruin.

We left Japan in the first week of January. Marie-Thérèse, our two-year-old son Julien and I flew to New York. At least the flights on Pan Am were free. My mother-in-law took Justine back via Moscow to France. As we had no idea what we were going to do, she had very courageously offered to keep our four-week-old daughter with her in Romans-sur-Isère until we had found somewhere to live in London, and preferably a job for me, as well.

7:

Banker in a Kimono

BACK IN THE DAYS when I used to spend weekends with Felicity and her family at their stately home gatherings, I had got to know an American economist called Dr Sidney Rolfe. Twenty years to the day my senior, he was a distinguished academic who was already on his way to becoming a figure of great influence at government level. Because I showed interest in his work, he was kind enough to reciprocate an interest in me, and we had stayed in touch over the years. We had a standing invitation to the Long Island home he shared with his Greek wife Maria, who had previously been married to the shipping tycoon John Carras.

As I sat shell-shocked in our friends the Lenkhs' flat in New York considering my options, Sidney was one of the people I called.

"It sounds utterly appalling," he said when I had told him our story. "Come out and spend the weekend with us. The sea air will do you all good, and we can have a proper talk about what you're going to do next."

So I left Marie-Thérèse and Julien with the Lenkhs and set

off for East Hampton, the hideaway community for affluent New Yorkers.

Sidney and Maria were welcoming hosts, and their ocean-front home was a real tonic for me, even in January, with the Atlantic wind battering the coastline. We had a magnificent dinner in front of a roaring fire and, over brandy, Sidney offered me his advice on what I could do next.

"You need to think what defines you," he said. "As I see it, it's the fact that you speak Japanese. You have self-confidence, so you can manage in just about any situation, and you have great initiative. You have no university degree, so you'll have to find some firm that is smart and flexible enough to see your value. I suggest you look at investment banking. It's very varied, it requires a lot of thinking on your feet, and you need to work hard, bring clients in and get people to trust you. You can do all of those things. The Japanese are just starting to enter the London financial community, and you could be very useful. Would you like me to make some calls?"

I certainly needed something positive to focus on. I was very angry over what had happened. I blamed Bob Strickland for my predicament, because he had not told me of his involvement with the CIA, and he had sided completely with Schwartz once the latter turned on me. He could have tried to negotiate and urged Schwartz to treat me fairly, rather than standing by as the CIA robbed me for having inadvertently got in its way. But he had not done any of those things, nor had he made any effort to contact me before our departure from Tokyo. Because of him, I had lost everything I had worked for in Japan, after my years of investment in our future there. And while our material loss was great, he had robbed us all of something even greater: our entire relationship with a country on which I had focused so much of my adult life. After all that, he had not offered an apology or a word of explanation.

But I also knew it was important not to let my anger spill over into hatred or despair. Hating may feel justified and even cathartic at a time of great injury or upset, but in reality it is a terrible waste of energy. One takes it to bed and wakes up with it in the morning, and it takes up the space of other good, productive thoughts. Although I could think of nothing to excuse my former partner's behaviour, despising him would eat me up inside and make it much harder to move forward.

As for what moving forward might consist of, I promised myself I would never again work for money alone, in the way that I had been doing in Japan. None of the projects I had worked on, with the possible exception of the Mobil tower, had any lasting value to anyone or made any material contribution to humankind. I wanted to take this opportunity to try to make some contribution.

Because banking has now become such a dirty word, it may come as a surprise that what Sidney was suggesting sounded like a breath of fresh air and a step forward morally. But these were the days before rampant greed had corrupted the investment banking industry. His proposal really did represent a complete change from what I had been doing up to that point.

I should provide a word of explanation about what investment banks actually did at that time. Most people's day-to-day experience of banking is with the retail sector – the so-called high-street banks. The lines have become blurred nowadays, but historically, in the United States, a retail bank took deposits (in the form of customers' savings) which it could lend to individuals or businesses to fund their desired activities, from buying a car or a house to financing business ventures. By contrast, investment banks (which the British used to call merchant banks) were formally barred in the US from taking deposits. With no deposits, they could not lend. Instead they were, and remain, in the business of fundraising, which they do by issuing bonds or securities. For example, bonds are sold to investors, who get a specific rate of return after a fixed period, and who may, if they wish, sell them on to someone else. The money invested by the saver in the bond is a way of raising capital for the issuer.

For governments and private companies alike, this is a crucial way of financing large capital projects, such as infrastructure or a new factory, which otherwise might never happen. Investment banks make their money by charging a fee for underwriting (guaranteeing) or just brokering the deal, and while what they do may sound either dry, incomprehensible or rapacious to many people (or a combination of the three), they do, in theory, help make the world a better place, because their work permits economies to grow.

This was the industry into which Sidney was suggesting I would comfortably fit. If I was willing, he would arrange some interviews. It sounded an excellent plan to me.

He was as good as his word, and on my arrival in London, I was invited to go and talk to three banks based there. One was Chase Manhattan, the second was a new consortium between an American bank and a Japanese bank (now defunct), and the third was the small British offshoot of an old white-shoe bank in New York called White, Weld & Company. Chase was big, ponderous and very American, and I could not see myself fitting in there. I was nervous of the consortium, because I had the impression it did not have a clear idea of what it was doing.

As for White Weld, it was a bastion of the East Coast establishment. The uncle of the first President Bush was an executive there at around this time, after selling the family brokerage firm to them, so it was an upper-crust WASP outfit. In London, where it had recently set up in partnership with Credit Suisse, it was run by four partners. One of them, Stani Yassukovitch, was married to a Rhodesian, which immediately made my face more likely to fit. Another was a brilliant, eccentric American anthropologist called Professor Michael von Clemm. He had taught at Harvard before turning to banking, and he had also spent more than a year living with the Wachagga tribe on the slopes of Mount Kilimanjaro. With that background, I hoped he might see the benefit of having someone who spoke good Japanese and understood the Japanese way of thinking at a time when the Japanese banks were just arriving in London.

Fortunately, the two of them did see the possibility and they convinced the other two partners – a South African called John Craven and an archetypal Englishman called John Stancliff – to go along with their decision. In fact, to nobody's greater amazement than mine, I was offered a job by all three banks. But White Weld was the one I chose.

We moved back to London, although at first we had nowhere to live because Glebe Place was let to tenants. While we had been in Japan, my best man Kevin had married Shirley Conran, who was about to become famous as a guru for working mothers with her bestselling book *Superwoman*. They kindly invited us to stay at their Barbican flat for a while. We then moved on to stay with other friends, the Wettons, whom we had known in Tokyo, until we managed to get the tenants out of one of the maisonettes in Glebe Place and move back in there, at which point my wife fetched Justine from France. The joy of this reunion with our two-month-old daughter tempered the frustration we felt at being in England rather than Japan.

I started at the bank in 1973 on the very modest salary of £5,000 a year, which was about one-sixtieth of what I had been making in Japan. Although I was thirty-two, my initial boss, Philip Seers, was only twenty-five. I was on the bottom rung, and there was no point in standing on my dignity or dwelling too much on the fact that until very recently I had run my own mini-business empire and had been worth a great deal of money. I cannot truthfully say that I never gave a thought to my loss of status and material wealth. But this was a good practical example of the benefits of trying to live without ego. Self-pity would take up energy I could otherwise be spending on learning my new profession.

My initial role was to do all the menial tasks, such as staying up all night at the printers to make sure a bond prospectus was correct, running around after the senior bankers and generally acting as a gofer while I learned the ropes. But I soon provided a new revenue stream for the trading department by spotting an opportunity. As the Japanese banks opened their London branches, they needed to raise new funds: their natural base was yen but to lend in the West they would need to raise dollars. I befriended Reichi Shimamoto, the Bank of Japan representative in London. My knowledge of Japan and my ability to speak to him in his own language made a relaxing change for him after his stilted communications with various other players in the City of London. Before our competitors had noticed what was happening, I had secured a lock on virtually all the Japanese bank Eurodollar Certificates of Deposit funding in London.

Having shown I could bring business in, I was asked to create a new department to look after the syndication of our Eurodollar bonds and notes business. A syndicate is where a group of banks work together, for example, to underwrite a bond issue and sell the bonds to investors. We were doing more and more of this kind of work, but the way it was handled internally was fairly shambolic, so I was asked to bring it all under better control. As I was running the syndicate department for the new issue bond and note market, I had every single such issue written down by a group of analysts who had just joined the bank. It was one of the most boring jobs imaginable, and the people we recruited hated me for forcing them to do it. But it enabled us to show prospective issuer clients statistics on our performance and that of our competitors, and it enabled us to track trends, as a forerunner to computerised data analysis.

After I had successfully launched the syndication department and run it for a year or so, I was asked to do something similar for our security sales efforts. In that new role, I talked the directors into letting me have a programmer to do the first computer-generated swaps of securities. A security is any kind of tradeable financial asset. One can analyse any given security in terms of its default risk (from triple A rating to junk status), maturity date and interest rate, and the differences in those values can lead to a market for 'swapping' them. This is all computerised nowadays, but in those days it was not, so starting on that path was a major innovation.

With my training in Japanese aesthetics, which are about functionality as much as appearance, I had become very interested in how people used space in offices and homes. In parallel with my other activities, I was keen to overhaul the bank's headquarters in Leadenhall Street, which were not terribly well organised. A jumble of people sat at various desks with little flow or logic. It led to poor communication and inefficiency. I was confident I knew more about making spaces work better than my colleagues, so I presented my design case to the directors to reconfigure the office at low cost. It went down well and I was allowed to proceed.

I also became so frustrated with secretaries having to retype entire documents because of a few simple mistakes, that I introduced Wang word processors before just about anyone had heard of them in the City. These early devices were ordinary typewriters which stored a line of text before printing it, so one could review the text for errors. That technology may seem laughably primitive nowadays, but it was a significant step forward at the time, and it was characteristic of our firm's embrace of new developments.

While living at Glebe Place, I took out a loan from White Weld, my new employer, to buy a house in Fulham. While not quite as chic a neighbourhood as Chelsea, it was in a good location overlooking a park, Eelbrook Common, which was ideal for a young family. Since this was our first proper home as a unit of four, we set about gutting the house.

Our redesign included a Japanese room on the top floor with *tatami* mats and *shoji* screens for the windows. If we could not live in Japan, we could at least bring something of Japanese life to London. It worked well and we were very pleased with it, even if it was something of a novelty for Parsons Green at that time, and it certainly surprised the estate agent when we eventually came to sell the house. It was also very helpful in entertaining Japanese bankers, who immediately felt at home.

In the meantime, Kevin had broken up with Shirley, so he came to live with us there for six months while Marie-Therese helped him sort out his domestic life by finding an excellent new flat for him in Chelsea. Amusingly, when we were later rebuilding our Chelsea home, the four of us then descended on Kevin's flat near Sloane Square. He was used to sharing with Marie-Thérèse and me, but the invasion of his bachelor space by two very young children was a new experience for him. If he was bothered by it, he did not let on. As a true friend, he put up with us unconditionally in our time of need. Following a longish stint at Kevin's, we were kindly and very generously put up by my former boss, Philip Seers, at his large and rather empty flat – he, too, was very tolerant of Julien and Justine.

So, back at the bank, all in all, I was giving good value, which, I hoped, justified the bank's faith in hiring me without a banking background or a degree. Fortunately, the directors seemed to agree, and in 1981, I was invited on to the board of what had become Credit Suisse White Weld. I was given new business development responsibility for supporting our new issuer client operations in Asia Pacific, from India eastwards, down to New Zealand and up to Japan, as well as Africa.

Subsequently, White Weld Inc, CSWW's sister company in New York, had been bought by the Wall Street bank Merrill Lynch. CSWW rebuffed ML's advances to buy it and remained independent. As a consequence of this, CSWW decided it needed to have a US arm, so it joined forces with another New York bank, First Boston, making the name of my employer now Credit Suisse First Boston. As a member of the CSFB board, I finally had the freedom to generate new clients and businesses, and I found myself dealing with heads of state, central bank governors and captains of industry.

My initial focus was on Japan, Australia and New Zealand, but India also became an important area of activity, followed by a number of other developing countries in the Asian region. I worked closely with Andrew Korner, a younger investment banker who ran our office in Tokyo and reported to me, and together we were responsible for opening up a number of these countries to the international capital markets. This enabled a broader economic development to happen in parts of the world which had previously had no access to international fundraising opportunities from sources other than bank borrowings.

By persuading the Korean, Taiwanese, Philippine, Malaysian, Indonesian and Indian governments that they, or selected government entities, could issue bonds on the Eurodollar markets in London, we enabled them to raise funds from investors who would normally focus only on the developed world. Having arranged those security issues successfully, we then went back to several of these governments to argue the benefits of allowing foreign investment into their domestic stock markets. I showed India's prime minister Indira Gandhi and her finance minister Manmohan Singh the benefits of allowing foreigners to buy shares on the Bombay Stock Exchange for the first time. That boosted the cash flows into the Indian economy, opening the way for major infrastructure projects and capital investments in both the public and private sectors. We did the same thing in Korea and Taiwan, and we did Eurodollar issues for the Philippines, Indonesia, Malaysia and Thailand.

As a nod to my birth and upbringing, Africa had been packaged in with my responsibilities from the outset, and while it was not the easiest place to do business, I enjoyed the challenge. We earned one of our largest fees by trading a block of securities that the Nigerian government needed to sell in a rush because of a sudden fall in oil prices. That meant I became familiar with Lagos, which was a difficult, dangerous city.

One time I was staying at a hotel with a huge pool. The water looked like green pea soup and the bottom of the pool was completely invisible, even at the shallow end. But it was full of Nigerian kids splashing around and one or two hardy adults, so I thought I would go for a swim. I dived in and initially thought that I had touched the bottom – except that it was not. It was a corpse. Goodness knows how long it had been there. It was the first – and I hope will remain the only – time I have ever had to go the front desk of a hotel and tell them:

"I think you'll find there's a dead body at the bottom of your swimming pool."

While I was earning my spurs as an investment banker, Rhodesia's long years of isolation under the white minority rule of Ian Smith had been coming to an end. Abandoned by Britain and regarded as an embarrassment even by apartheid South Africa, Smith was forced by civil war, sanctions and increasing pressure from the UK and other governments to cede power to the nationalist independence leaders, who had fought his rule. At the tail-end of the 1970s, the country of my birth re-emerged as Zimbabwe.

I paid a nostalgic return visit to show my wife and two children the farmhouse in the bush where I had been born. It was now owned by a white Kenyan who had fled that country after independence. Both my grandparents had been dead for years, and my grandfather's farm was now being run by the old lady he had sold it to, and her son.

I also took my family to see our old house in Salisbury, which the new president Robert Mugabe had renamed Harare. This name did not come easily to me. I had nothing against an African city bearing an African name rather than that of a British Victorian prime minister, but when I was growing up, Harare was the name of the poorest slum in the capital. Mugabe had chosen that as the new name of the whole city to make a point about the old order being turned on its head. After I left Rhodesia as a teenager, my mother had subdivided our twenty-five acres and sold the plots to raise enough money to leave the country. When I arrived back at the house with my own family, we found that the entire area was now a housing estate. I understood the need for development, but it was sad to discover that a place whose memory I had treasured no longer existed.

I did not for a moment regret my decision to leave the country twenty years earlier, but I remained proud of my African origins, and not long afterwards I was honoured to be asked by the African Development Bank to manage their first ever Eurodollar note issue. I became a regular visitor to Abidjan, the capital of Ivory Coast, where the bank is based. I used to head automatically for the Hôtel Ivoire, a modern tower on the shore of the lagoon that separates the city from the Atlantic. Mostly this was a trouble-free arrangement, but one doomed evening I arrived at six o'clock off a flight from London only to be told there were no rooms.

"We are completely full, *monsieur*," the desk clerk told me, apologetically.

"But I have a booking," I said. "I'm a very regular guest and I know for a fact that my secretary made the reservation."

"I'm very sorry, *monsieur*. There must have been some confusion. We have a coffee convention here in Abidjan and all the rooms are full."

I took five twenty-dollars bills out of my wallet and slid them across the counter.

"I'm sure you can find something for me."

The clerk slid the money back.

"I want to give you a room, *monsieur*, I really do," he said. "But I don't have any."

I believed him. He looked crushed at having to turn down a hundred-dollar tip.

"I advise you to take a taxi and drive around to see if you can find a hotel," he said. "I am sorry, that's all I can suggest."

Tired after my journey and irritated at the mix-up, I nonetheless recognised that I had little choice but to take his advice. I duly spent the next hour and a half driving around downtown Abidjan looking for a hotel with vacancies. It was a fruitless quest: because of this coffee convention, every bed in town seemed to be taken.

After being turned away from the ninth or tenth hotel we tried, I had an idea. I got back in the taxi and said to the driver: "Can you take me to the best brothel in Abidjan?"

He had been looking fairly doleful until now: even though he was getting a good fare out of it, the hopelessness of our search was affecting his morale as well as mine. But now he brightened.

"I know just the place for you, *monsieur!*" he told me approvingly.

By this time we had been driving around for so long that I had lost all sense of direction, but we finally arrived outside a gaudily lit house. I rang on the door and was invited into the presence of a large and imposing woman, dripping with jewellery and wearing a strong perfume, who was in charge of the brothel.

"*Bonsoir, madame,*" I said. "Tell me please: who is your best girl?"

"Ah, that would be Chantale," she said proudly. "She is excellent."

To emphasise the point she made some elaborate smacking sounds with her lips.

"In that case, please be so kind as to bring me Chantale, if she is not busy."

I was told she was currently engaged, but she was just finishing what she was doing and if I was prepared to wait fifteen minutes I could then be introduced. I took a seat, and a few minutes later a middle-aged Westerner – a delegate at the coffee convention, no doubt – stumbled sheepishly past me, tucking his shirt-tails into his trousers as he prepared to re-emerge into the world of respectability. He was followed a few moments later by Chantale herself, who was a considerable improvement on the madam, even if she was not quite the beauty her employer promised.

"*Bonsoir*, Chantale," I said. "I have a deal for you. Here is one hundred dollars. You go home and have a night off, but first give me your room."

"That is wonderful, *monsieur*," she said. "But are you sure I cannot give you something in return before I go?"

"Thank you, but no. That won't be necessary. I just want a room, as I need to sleep."

She shrugged, tucked my dollar bills into the back of her skirt and showed me to the room, where she gathered together a few personal things and bade me *bonne nuit*. It was not the best room I had ever had for a hundred bucks, but it was not the worst either. It smelled exactly how one would expect a whore's boudoir to smell, with a mixture of cheap scent to mask more noxious odours that I did not want to think too much about. But I was too exhausted to worry about that, and the bed was large and soft. Pleased to have found somewhere to lay my head at last, and congratulating myself on my resourcefulness, I lay down to sleep.

Sadly, even the best-laid plans have their flaws, and I had made one elementary mistake. I had asked for the best girl in the house on the assumption that she would have the best room, and since I had not seen any of the others, it may well have been so, but I had forgotten that the best girl would also be in great demand. All night long there were bangs on the door and needy calls of *"Chantale, est-ce que tu es prête? J'ai besoin de toi!"* ("Are you ready, I need you?")

I ignored them at first, but by the end of a sleepless night I was screaming at them in sailor's French to get lost. It was an effort to concentrate through my meetings with the African Development Bank next day, but I had to put my best face on it. I could hardly tell them I had not had a wink of sleep because I had spent the night in a whorehouse.

Fortunately, my relationship with the bank remained intact, and in December 1979 I was invited under its auspices to a dinner at the palace of Omar Bongo in Libreville to celebrate his tenth anniversary as president of Gabon. No one could accuse the African elite of not knowing how to live it up, and it was a fine dinner, catered by Maxim's of Paris. Under the protective gaze of Foreign Legionnaire bodyguards, I found myself at the same table as an American of my own age called Niles Helmboldt. He had been living for ten years in Liberia, the West African republic originally founded for the resettlement of black Americans. He had started off working for Citibank as the country manager in the capital, Monrovia, and now ran an institution of his own called Equator Bank, which focused on providing investment banking services to

Sub-Saharan Africa.

Niles, who was to become a firm friend, introduced me to the Liberian government. The president, a Baptist minister called William Tolbert, was the grandson of a former slave from South Carolina who had arrived in the late nineteenth century. Most of his government also came from these founding Americo-Liberian families. I became their financial adviser, and I persuaded a small Japanese syndicate led by the Taiyo Kobe Bank to lend them ten million dollars for a mining project. I got to know several ministers quite well, including my closest contact, Ellen Johnson Sirleaf, a US-trained economist whom Tolbert eventually made his finance minister.

I regarded Ellen and a number of other ministers as friends, so I got a horrible shock when I turned on the radio in the spring of 1980 and heard that there had been a coup. A twenty-eight-year-old master sergeant called Samuel Doe had marched on the palace, assassinating President Tolbert in his bedroom and publicly parading thirteen members of the cabinet naked through the streets before having them executed by firing squad on the beach. To add to the barbarity, he had ordered the whole thing to be televised.

Fortunately, Ellen was abroad at the time, or she would probably have suffered the same fate. Niles ended up giving her a job at Equator Bank in Nairobi, and after she returned from exile she became president of Liberia. She was Africa's first elected female head of state, and is still in office, ten years on. She has also been jointly awarded the Nobel Peace Prize.

After the coup I had no desire to continue my advisory relationship with the new regime, but we were owed some fees so I sent a message to the new President Doe.

"I am not sure if you are aware," I wrote to him, "but I am a director of Credit Suisse First Boston and I was a financial adviser to your predecessor. We are owed some retainer fees so I cannot do any more work in helping you raise funds internationally until you pay us the outstanding amounts."

As Doe's new government desperately needed funds, he duly paid up what we were owed, whereupon I severed the connection. I told them that in view of the circumstances, no one abroad was interested in lending money to them. I had implicitly misled him, but we were owed money and the man was a butcher who had callously shot a number of my friends.

Incidentally, he suffered a grisly fate of his own some ten years later when he was overthrown in an even more violent coup by a man called Charles Taylor. Taylor, who was filmed torturing Doe to death, later went on a total rampage, introducing child soldiers and cutting off the hands and feet of anyone who defied government forces. He was eventually convicted at the International Criminal Court and sentenced to fifty years in jail.

I was on another of my trips to Abidjan when I heard that the Ugandan dictator Idi Amin had finally been brought down by a Tanzanian invasion force and had fled his country (April, 1979). Sniffing an opportunity, I flew immediately to Kenya then chartered a small plane to Entebbe, Uganda's "international" airport, and previously the scene of the famous Israeli rescue of a large number of hostages. I arrived to find the place deserted, with some shot-up planes and a few drunken Tanzanian soldiers wandering around. I managed to find a car that would drive me into the capital, Kampala. There was a road-block on the way, staffed by a bunch of Tanzanian peacekeepers – although they looked as if their idea of keeping the peace was to shoot first and ask questions later. Their commander tapped on the passenger window with his AK47. When I wound it down, he proceeded to point the gun at me.

"Give me cigarettes," he said.

I tried gently to push the barrel of the gun so it was not pointing directly at my head, and explained that I did not have any cigarettes because I was trying to give up.

Fortunately, the driver had some, so he gave him those, and I gave him a larger tip when we got into town.

When we arrived in Kampala, which in happier times had been one of Africa's most beautiful capitals, the hotel I checked into was pitted with bullet holes. Even more disconcertingly, my bedroom had not just bullet holes but bloodstains down the wall. I lived on bananas and marmalade for the next three days as I sought out the nominal minister of finance in the interim administration. I told him that we would be willing to buy up the entire coffee crop in order to guarantee some economic stability at this time of upheaval. This poor man had no experience in office and was clearly terrified of being shot for incompetence if he made the wrong decision (not an unreasonable concern, given the fluid state of Ugandan politics at that time). He could not come to a decision, so I gave up and flew back to London.

In the same year that I was appointed to the board of CSFB, the birth of our daughter Charlotte completed our family. By this time we had sold the house in Parsons Green and moved back to Glebe Place, which Marie-Thérèse and I proceeded once more to overhaul. Once again, we set about creating a large, loft-style living room at the top of the house. In half of it I made a mezzanine floor for our bedroom, which then overlooked the living room from a *shoji*-covered gallery window. I also put in a Japanese *ishi-buro* or stone bath. In the Japanese style, one washed and rinsed off before getting into the bath to soak in clean, piping hot water. It needed a special boiler to keep the water at a constant temperature, which I brought through customs at Heathrow.

I declared my *tatami* mats, which the officer proceeded to look up in his vast manual of taxable items. *Tatami* mats were indeed listed, so he noted down the amount I would need to pay. Then I told him about my *shoji* screens, which, I explained, consisted of rice-paper in a wooden frame. But this item was completely unknown to the manual, so he nodded the screens through. He was completely stumped by the bath-boiler. Rather than listen to my lengthy explanation, he let that through too.

As a result, we had a Japanese home in the centre of Chelsea, where I could bring managers from Japanese banks in London, or visiting clients from Japan, to have dinner with their wives. If the man came by himself, I followed the old Japanese tradition that I had enjoyed so often in Japan by inviting him to have a bath first, and then lending him a *yukata* robe; I would be in a *yukata* too, and we would have a Japanese-style home evening. Many of those London branch managers went on to become chief executives or chairmen of their respective banks, and that period of building relationships, creating a Japanese oasis for Japanese bankers to enjoy in a Western home, paid off many times over.

As I felt it was important to have other interests, just after I had been made a board director of CSWW – and my close friend, Niles Helmboldt, was successfully running his own bank, Equator Bank in Hartford, Connecticut – to celebrate our fortieth birthdays, he and I decided to build a small number of extremely high-performance "sports" cars annually. Genesis 40 was inaugurated in 1981, before the rash of small production supercars that came out from the 1990s onwards.

To get the "look" right was essential, but we couldn't afford the cost of designing a new body, so we chose to copy the amazingly timeless Shelby Cobra body, and the rest of the car we had made by specialist engineering shops. The car was designed to attract buyers who greatly preferred servicing and maintaining their own high-performance cars to relying on car workshop mechanics. This was a changing time in the car world; when you opened the bonnet of a powerful car it was so crammed full of different parts that you were barely able to locate the dipstick to check the oil level. However, our car's 'engine room' was designed and laid out to make maintenance and servicing easily accessible.

The Genesis 40 was a powerful, two-seater open roadster, doing 0-60mph in 3.5 seconds – extraordinarily fast at the time – and it was based in Connecticut, USA. The design, the body construction and powertrain were assembled locally, as was the leather and wooden interior. The chassis and suspension were designed and built by another local workshop, which also provided the chassis and suspensions for the Indianapolis 500 race cars. The V-8 engine was based on a 'Chevy 350' block, with all performance components manufactured locally, other than four two-barrel Webers, which were made in Italy. Body construction, interior and painting were also done in Connecticut. Finally, the engine generated 450BHP, and the entire car weighed only 2,100 lbs.

Initial testing of the Genesis 40 took place at Connecticut's Lime Rock racing venue in June 1982. Results were positive and testing continued. Sadly, in the early 1980s, vehicle-destructive crash-testing requirements were stepped up by the US and other countries. These new crash-testing costs far exceeded Genesis 40's resources, so the production plans were shelved and we had to abandon the project with only two cars built. But it was fun, and it certainly made a change to be making something physical rather than trying to create new ways of providing financing for our respective clients.

Subsequently, my primary mentor, Michael von Clemm, had become chairman and chief executive of CSFB, and under his leadership the bank was becoming something of a global powerhouse, in a very different league from its more modest beginnings. At the same time, I had brought in a Swiss-German banker called Hans-Joerg Rudloff, who was brilliant in his field and had a superb sense of where markets were heading. His style was abrasive and the other directors were not keen to have him join us, so Michael and I had to arrange it over a period of some nine months. But after several months of working with him, I regretted having done this. Rudloff demanded slavish obedience from all those working around him, even if he was not formally their superior, and he quickly became disliked. Even though I had championed him, spoiling my relationship with a number of my colleagues in the process, he assumed that I would accept his authority without question.

There were immediate clashes. I was determined to look after the interests of my clients, many of whom were friends and trusted me to give sound objective advice. By contrast, Rudloff was only interested in maximising the fees he could extract from them. His style of dealing with the market, while generally very effective in revenue terms, led to some major internal problems. Thus, in 1983, Michael lost an internal battle and was ousted as CEO by Rainer Gut, Chairman of Credit Suisse, our main shareholder, while retaining the chairman's role. Having effectively been kicked upstairs, he had far less involvement in day-to-day operations.

He was replaced by a macho American from First Boston called Jack Hennessy, whose whole style was very different. When Michael was in charge, he would refer to us as partners or colleagues, but Hennessy talked about his people as "my boys". As the main revenue-generating partners of the bank, we senior members of the firm were used to being treated with a certain amount of respect, so we found his attitude overly crude, and thus unacceptable. The problem was further exacerbated by the fact that Rudloff was clearly in the ascendancy, particularly when Hennessy started treating him as his right-hand man. For me, working at CSFB was becoming much less enjoyable. Eleven years after my first appointment with White Weld, I began to look around for another banking berth.

I spent eighteen months planning my exit. I resolved to treat it like a merger operation – in conditions of utter secrecy. Accordingly, I went out and interviewed secretly with the world's top investment banks. I received an offer from the Industrial Bank of Japan, which was the top Japanese bank at that time, and another from the country's oldest brokerage firm, Nomura Securities, but neither of them would make me a director. Then I talked to Goldman Sachs, but they clearly thought I was beneath them, as did Morgan Stanley.

I did not initially meet with Merrill Lynch, because they were considered more of a stockbroker than an investment bank. A couple of ex-colleagues had joined them several years before and both then left in disgust after only six months, so we at CSFB rather looked down on the firm. But I knew they had an infrastructure already in place in the Asia Pacific region, with offices in Tokyo, Hong Kong, Singapore and Australia, which virtually no other major investment bank had at that time. And I also knew that part of their aim in trying to buy White Weld had been about becoming an investment bank. They were now inching their way towards achieving that.

So I went and talked to them, and to my surprise I found that this was by far my best option, because they wanted me to run Asia Pacific from Hong Kong, and to be a member of their Global Capital Markets Executive Committee in New York. However, I also realised that if I left CSFB on my own, I would be seen by the market and the client base as somehow having failed, or not having been up to the job. It is never a good idea to leave the top of one's profession on one's own, unless one is being headhunted. Furthermore, going as a single new arrival into a new firm would always be risky, because I would have no friends or supporters, and there would be a different culture to adapt to. So I resolved to organise a team from CSFB whose members would walk out simultaneously and join Merrill.

This had to be done in conditions of total secrecy, otherwise we would all have been sacked on the spot. I talked to one of my co-directors, who talked to the head trader, and the head trader talked to his eight key people. I did the initial negotiation with Merrill Lynch, and we agreed that I would be responsible for Asia Pacific, excluding Japan. That made good sense to me because I knew Japan so well and I wanted to get to know the rest of Asia Pacific better, in a banking and cultural sense. Andrew Korner also agreed to join me.

As the whole thing was coming to a head, my father fell very ill. Settled back in England after his time in South Africa, he had managed to overcome lung cancer but now he had heart failure and spent a month in a coma before he died, aged seventy-three. We were told he was brain-dead and I had a long discussion with my brother Brian, a practising GP, about whether we should pull the plug. The final decision would have fallen to Brian, given his medical expertise, and I think he was very relieved when nature intervened. It would have been tough on him to take that irrevocable step, however sure we felt that it was the right thing to do.

I mourned my father's death, but I chiefly felt a sadness at the lack of closeness between us. There had never been antipathy, because I had always considered him a very decent man. But we had had very little in common.

To clear my head after this sad event, to which I didn't really know how I should react, and to get ready for my departure from CSFB, as I was owed lots of leave, I arranged to take my family to East Africa: Kenya (Lamu Island), Rwanda and the Congo.

It was an unusual holiday photograph: there was I, trying to corral members of a pygmy tribe, ranging from four-and-a-half to five-feet tall, into a group shot, a unique memento of our trip, when I felt a jabbing pain in my finger. A younger pygmy had forgotten to put the top on his quiver of poisoned arrows and the tip of one of them had pierced the inside of my forefinger as I tried to reposition him for the photo.

There was instant panic and the pygmies dispersed, at speed, into the forest.

The trip had been arranged by a friend, the progeny of a White Russian *émigré* and a tribal princess, who had his own 'kingdom' in Central Africa, complete with fleet of aging freight planes. We – myself, Marie-Therese and our son, Julien – were spending the day hunting in the equatorial forest with a pygmy tribe. It was remarkable to witness their hunting practices, which had remained unchanged for thousands of years. The poison for their arrows was made from plant extracts beaten into a brown paste. Fresh green leaves were used to fashion the flights of each arrow. Spirals were cut into the arrow tips to allow a greater concentration of poison.

It was one of these tips that had jabbed my finger. Earlier, with the help of an interpreter, we had learned that the poison could kill a man in 30 minutes. It certainly killed the monkeys we had been hunting pretty quickly. Would I meet the same fate? My wife and son were in tears and I became concerned that my sudden death might ruin their holiday.

My arm had gone numb almost to the elbow when, with a loud rustling, the pygmies returned from the forest. They were carrying three 'antidotes' and, in order to distract him from the unfolding drama, I asked Julien to take photos of the ensuing operation. The first pygmy chewed up a leaf and rubbed it on my finger. The second chewed at a root and did the same. The third one blew through a branch until some sap emerged; this too was applied to the broken skin.

After about an hour it became apparent that I wasn't going to die. I had been lucky that only the very tip of the arrow had pierced my skin – little of the poison in the spiral groove had entered my body. Secondly, the arrow had not broken any blood vessels so the poison had spread more slowly than usual.

I counted this expedition, and our earlier gorilla-tracking trip in the forests of Rwanda, as a success. They had, after all, taken my mind off the recent death of my father, off banking for a while and, as importantly, off my forthcoming defection from CSFB to Merrill Lynch.

Less than a month after my father's funeral, in the New Year of 1984, the big day dawned at CFSB. Hennessy had brought over a very senior banker who had just joined First Boston, New York to great fanfare, and he was introducing him around the office to the top management in London. I was a member of the CSFB's Executive Committee, as were the two other key people who were leaving with me. One after another we said:

"Nice to meet you, but goodbye, I'm off."

The management of the bank was knocked for six, because this was the first-ever major walkout of a big team in the Eurobond market. It made the front pages of the *Financial Times* and the *International Herald Tribune*, as well as big headlines in various other papers around the world. It was a dramatic exit, and we had sent out a clear message that all was not well at the firm. Why else would twelve people leave at the same time?

The twelve of us arrived at Merrill Lynch like sharks among a bunch of mackerel. We were ruthless, focused and disciplined, which may sound aggressive but it was exactly what the bank needed if it was to grow in accordance with its ambitions. Sometimes one has to be ruthless in life, and it is by no means inconsistent with a Buddhist outlook to say so. If a relationship or a business endeavour is draining the emotional and physical energy of all concerned, it is better to cut that relationship out and start again, than to have it endure like a cancerous sore, to the benefit of nobody. One casualty of this upheaval was the existing chairman of the European region, who was a genial man, but not a particularly good banker. He was squeezed out and went off to join the World Bank, where I hope he found a more comfortable home.

In my role as chairman of ML, Asia Pacific, I was now a member of the Global Capital Markets Executive Committee in New York. That meant I was just one person away from the chief executive: there was a president of capital markets to whom I reported and he in turn reported to the CEO and chairman. Being so close to the top was another important consideration in joining ML. Andrew Korner and I continued our work persuading Asian governments to allow us to do security issues for them and their banks in the international capital markets. Sometimes it took several years to win them over, because these governments were particularly wary about accepting direct investment into their domestic markets. But the groundwork we had done at CSFB now paid off for Merrill Lynch. Persuading those governments to allow that change made us pioneers. Being from a Rhodesia pioneering family, this was a role I was accustomed to and enjoyed enormously.

I built a reputation for being very independent. Well before becoming an investment banker, I had decided that if there is a lot of competition, and one looks and talks exactly like the last fellow they saw an hour ago, it is hard to make an impact. I therefore continued my natural eccentric ways. Having followed that path, I saw no reason to hide who I was once I rose to a senior position. I believe one should always be willing to risk saying who one is, rather than taking the chameleon approach. Some of my colonial friends made the mistake of trying to become English as soon as possible after arriving in London. I never bothered, because I knew that the English will never let a colonial become a true Englishman, so I was always very open about the fact that I was just a bush boy from Rhodesia. That meant there was nothing to hide, and I was not giving anyone leverage over me. By extension, people also tend to be reluctant to open up for fear of being rejected, but that is another waste of energy.

In my case, I wore a kimono to a signing ceremony in London, and I wore a sarong in Hong Kong when the finance secretary of the colony came for a meal with my chairman from New York. The Asian sarong and the African *kikoy* are essentially the same garment, and one can pack ten of them in a suitcase, to take up the space of one suit. Another time I took two fifteenth-century swords to a dinner we were giving to a Japanese client in London to apologise for withdrawing from a deal because of the general market collapse. I offered to commit *seppuku*, the ritual suicide carried out by disgraced samurai warriors to restore their honour, if one of the Japanese present at the dinner would be willing to accept the traditional role of *Kaishaku-in* – i.e. the person who cuts off the head of the person committing *seppuku*. It was a theatrical gesture, as I was sure that no one would take me up on it. It caused a considerable shock. This was not how most investment bankers behaved in London.

To me, as a roaming citizen of the world, with roots in many places and strong emotional bonds in many more, it was the most natural thing in the world to relate to people from different parts of the world in a way that was appropriate to their own culture. For example, Africans are very physical people, unlike the British, whose men shrink away from being touched by another man. It was therefore perfectly normal for me to walk down Oxford Street holding hands with Babacar Ndiaye, the then chief financial officer of the African Development Bank, even though we received the most astonished looks. He was from Dakar, the capital city of Senegal. It amused him that I was an African, and he liked referring to me as a bush boy, while I would taunt him back by calling him a city-slicker. Africans tend to think that life is to be enjoyed, so they know how to have fun.

Another time, when we were both in Amsterdam for a roadshow event to promote his bank, we hired a tandem bicycle. With me on the front and Babacar on the back, I encouraged him to mime whipping me as we cycled along. He was screaming, "Faster, white slave!" while I panted, "Yes, *massa!*" People stopped and stared, wondering what the hell these two men in business suits were doing. But as far as the two of us were concerned, we were just a kid from Rhodesia and a kid from Senegal messing about on a bike in Europe.

None of that meant that I was a pushover. When the international stock market crashed on Black Monday in October 1987, we were in the middle of arranging a bond issue worth one billion Australian dollars for the celebrated businessman Robert Holmes à Court. Born in South Africa, Holmes à Court had spent most of his childhood on a farm near Bulawayo, not far from my school. He was now a naturalised Australian, and had grown fabulously wealthy as one of Australia's most feared corporate raiders. But however powerful and influential he was, if we went ahead and underwrote a bond issue of this magnitude, we would lose a fortune. In its current turmoil, the market would not want to invest, and we, ML, would have to sell the bonds at sixty or seventy cents on the dollar, incurring a loss of several hundred million dollars. It would therefore be reckless for us to proceed in the way we had agreed.

"I'm very sorry, Robert, but we're going to have to reduce your issue because the market is collapsing around our ears," I told him on the phone from London. "I'm sure you'll understand that we can't possibly take that kind of hit. But since we have an agreement, we won't let you down completely. We can do you an issue for two or three hundred million."

That would still involve significant risk to us, but to us it was an honourable compromise.

Robert, however, was not one of nature's compromisers.

"You promised to do one billion, so I expect you to do one billion," he said.

He did not raise his voice or lose his temper. A man of his stature was used to being obeyed without the need to shout.

I was undaunted.

"Look, Robert," I said. "The market is plummeting. We'll be left with a billion dollars of debt securities that no one will want to buy."

"That's not my problem. You promised one billion and I'm going to hold you to it."

"Is that your final word?"

"It is."

I told him I would look into the matter further and get back to him. In reality I had no intention of conceding. I got straight on to our City lawyers, Linklaters & Paines, who confirmed our view that the stock market crash constituted a situation of *force majeure* – an extraordinary circumstance freeing us from our underwriting commitment.

I conveyed this back to Robert, and there ensued a long exchange of telephone calls in which he insisted we honour our deal and I repeated calmly but firmly that the crash voided it. Finally, on the Thursday after the crash, I sent him a fax saying that if he did not give us his answer to our proposed compromise solution by noon the next day, UK time, we would pull the whole issue.

He immediately tried to get hold of Bill Schreyer, my chairman in New York, but Bill refused to take the call, on my recommendation.

"You can't add anything to what I've told him already, and he will try to shame you into accepting to proceed," I told him.

I knew that one of Robert's most effective ruses was to say nothing during telephone calls. Not just for a few seconds or for a minute or two: he was capable of staying silent for fifteen or twenty minutes. It was remarkable to witness, and for anyone on the receiving end, it took nerve to wait it out. But it was obvious to me that he wanted the other person to step in and fill the vacuum, and in so doing they might well give him an opening. As a rule, I am a great believer in transparency, because it absolves one of game-playing and therefore saves everyone a huge amount of time. But that does not mean I am a pushover if someone is determined to play games. I was happy to sit on the phone with Robert all day, if he wanted, with neither of us saying a word.

Thus, on the Friday morning, a group of us assembled in my office at ML London: the lawyers and the head of syndication, who wanted legal confirmation that he was not going to be sued personally – I told him not to be such a coward – and sundry other colleagues.

We dialled through to Perth.

"Good morning, Robert," I said. "It's now eleven o'clock our time and we must have a decision by noon our time. What do you want to do?"

"I want you to do what you promised," he said.

"Robert, I've explained that we can't do that because there's a *force majeure* condition in the markets. The markets have collapsed."

As I had suspected he would, he fell silent. One minute went by, and then two. My colleagues began gesturing at each other and me in a panic-stricken way. There was not so much as a crackle from the speaker phone for ten, then fifteen minutes. Everyone was passing me notes saying I should say this to him or that to him. But I knew his game and I was not prepared to be intimidated.

"We don't say anything," I mouthed at them. "We just wait."

After about twenty minutes we heard a clearing of the throat. "Are you still there?" Robert said.

"Yes, I'm still here," I said. "I'm waiting for your answer."

Silence descended once more.

A few moments later I was passed a message saying my chairman had called from New York to tell me that Robert was again trying to get hold of him.

I scrawled a message back to Bill: "Just decline. Tell him you've gone fishing."

On we sat, and at a quarter to twelve Robert blinked again.

"What are you going to do?" he said.

"I'm waiting for your answer, Robert," I said calmly.

We heard nothing more, and on the stroke of midday I said: "Robert, in the absence of any response from you, we are officially pulling the issue."

He did not say anything, so I said goodbye and hung up.

It was a testing situation, because it was one of the first cases of a big deal being pulled for *force majeure* reasons. It was even more historic to refuse Robert Holmes à Court like that, given his reputation. I say that not to blow my own trumpet, but to emphasise that life teaches lessons if one is willing to learn them. I had learned from my Zen training that the ego wants to fill in the silence, to come up with some clever solution. What was needed in this situation was sufficient detachment not to be intimidated or embarrassed into talking. I made it a very simple choice for Robert: yes or no. And in so doing, I probably avoided losing several hundred million dollars for my firm.

Although I was frequently in London and New York, we were now based in Hong Kong. We found a very nice house on the Peak, one of the highest points of Hong Kong Island, which has cool air and spectacular views, and as usual we set about re-modelling the place. This involved stress and upheaval, but we ended up with a wonderful home overlooking the South China Sea and the whole of Hong Kong harbour.

Travelling for as much as eight months a year, I was often absent during my children's childhoods. To try to compensate, I made a rule that I would call home every day without fail and try to have a few words with each of them, as well as a lengthy chat with Marie-Thérèse. That way I was not completely out of the loop when I returned home two or three weeks later. However, I was rudely reminded of the limitations of this arrangement when I arrived home one day to find our twelve-year-old Justine arguing furiously with her mother. I asked what was going on, only for my daughter to turn round and say, hands on hips: "Stay out of this, daddy. You're never here, so you won't understand the issue."

It came as a shock to have it spelled out so bluntly, but I

recognised that she was right. From then on I did mostly "stay
out". Instead I would try to catch up with a briefing from
Marie-Thérèse after the various storms had passed.

Our eldest two eventually went off to Middlebury College,
Vermont, USA, famous for its foreign language courses, while
Charlotte was educated in Hong Kong at the Lycée. But for
as long as Marie-Thérèse and I had been married we had also
hankered after a home in France. The children were completely
bilingual in English and French – if anything their French was
then slightly better – they were both going to the French Lycée
in London and spent almost every holiday in France at Marie-
Thérèse's parents' home. We had been actively looking for the
right place for about fifteen years, but we had not found it
because we were unashamedly fussy.

Finally, just after I started at Merrill Lynch, we found the
perfect place. Set in seventeen acres of the Rhone valley, the
Château de Tourreau had been built in the mid-eighteenth
century. With two wings emerging in a semi-circle from the
main house, it was a beautiful Italianate folly. It had an avenue
of plane trees that were over two hundred years old, and a moat
all the way around the south park. It had been commandeered
by the German army in the war, and then bought by the French
ambassador to Czechoslovakia, who had struggled to maintain
it. Under two more recent owners it had fallen into complete
disrepair. When we came across it, both the château and the
adjacent farmhouse were almost complete wrecks: the roof had
fallen in and two staircases had collapsed. We bought it very
cheaply from a *pied noir* from Algeria, who had camped in the
place as it crumbled around his ears, and had been trying to get

rid of it for some time. By coincidence, the billionaire financier Sir Jimmy Goldsmith tried to buy it two weeks later, but I had already signed the contract.

We set about restoring the place as faithfully as we could, using eighteenth-century materials but incorporating twentieth-century mod cons. Since I was earning an investment banker's salary and bonus (albeit modest by the standards of compensation of the 2000 decade), we did not really have a budget. We ordered bronze copies of eighteenth-century door handles and hinges from a bespoke craftsman in Paris, and we bought eighteenth-century oak panelling from distressed châteaux around the country. We converted the barn attached to the farm into a squash court and a gym, and I had a large office with a conference room complete with drop-down screen and projectors. It was a colossal project. I superintended the building work while Marie-Thérèse took charge of the interior decoration. This consisted of a mixture of European and Asian art, just as it would have been in the eighteenth century, when the French aristocracy imported Chinese and Japanese artefacts to decorate their homes.

The renovation process ended up costing many times more than the purchase price, and it took the best part of ten years to complete. But we ended up with a main home for the family to spend its down-time in. For more than thirty years, our family would convene there to spend the summer together.

One of the great privileges of these years came after I helped the secretary to Rajiv Gandhi, who had succeeded his assassinated mother as prime minister, to get her son an internship with

Merrill Lynch. I happened to mention that one of my Dobbs forebears, Major General Richard Stewart Dobbs was the East India Company's district collector for Tumkur in Mysore, or Karnataka as it was now called, and that the village of Dobbspet – "pet" means village in the local language – had been named after him. Further, that, as far as I was aware, it was still there.

As a mark of her gratitude, she promised to arrange a visit. Marie-Thérèse and I were met at Bangalore airport by the state commissioner of Karnataka and driven under police escort to a village of a little over one thousand souls, who all seemed to have turned out for us. They had put up a rather tattered marquee, with an old Marconi loudspeaker system that must have dated back to the 1950s. We were given garlands by the headman of the village and after his welcoming speech, he mentioned that, as my forebear had endowed a scholarship to educate two people from Dobbspet, it would be nice if I could continue that philanthropic tradition by building a factory or a clinic for their village. I told him I would think about it, but in reality something on that scale was way beyond my personal means. I consoled myself that my efforts to open up the Indian economy to foreign investment were a far more effective way of continuing my ancestor's work. I hoped he would be pleased that, in a dramatically changed world, the family was still doing its bit for the subcontinent. He then showed us a large granite block set into the earth near the road, which they swore blind was my ancestor's tomb,

Following this ceremony, we were whisked off to see Dobbs Bungalow, a large, rambling, single-storey house in Tumkur, the state capital of Karnataka, which he had built. Still called

Dobbs Bungalow, it was now the office and residence of our host, who as State Commissioner, was given this house as her official residence. She gave a speech of welcome in which she said my great-great-grandfather was regarded with lasting affection by the people of the state. It was very gratifying to hear that despite the often-expressed resentment of the British Raj period, and the subsequent name changes to expunge the traces of its rule, in my ancestor's case, they had no such resentment, but rather, gratitude for the work he had done.

While occasions like that were a great treat, the culture of banking was beginning to disturb me. We discovered we had a rogue trader at ML in New York, some years before Nick Leeson made that term well-known. He was putting failed deals in his drawer, which lost us somewhere in the region of three hundred million dollars. There was a big scandal and he was fired, but he was immediately offered a job, at a higher salary and bonus, by one of our competitors.

Shortly afterwards we had a meeting of our global capital markets executive committee at Merrill Lynch, and I tried to raise the matter.

"Surely we should be trying to send him to jail," I said.

"We can't," said one of my fellow committee members. "There isn't any legislation that covers what he has done."

There were nods around the table. But to me that was no reason to let the matter lie.

"In that case we ought to insist on legislation. It's a criminal act – it's a form of theft."

But no action was taken and the discussion moved on. I was

astonished by the degree of complacency.

Another time we found two people running a sort of black-box derivatives operation. They were doing complicated things with all manner of exotic financial instruments which none of the top management actually understood. They had been paid bonuses of around five million dollars a year on paper profits, which our accounting firm signed off because they, too, did not understand these instruments. Then someone new arrived at the accounting firm who did understand them, and pointed out that they had not made these profits at all – on the contrary, they had a huge loss. The firm had to write off another few hundred million dollars as a result, but the culprits got away completely unscathed. True to industry form, they were snapped up by another firm.

These were the days before banking careered completely out of control, as it did in the lead-up to the crash of 2008. But there were already signs of the greed that caused that loss of control, and not just by the bankers. The big credit agencies were in on it, because anyone working for one of them would end up knowing a lot of bankers, and there would very often be a job at a bank waiting for them after a period at Moody's, Fitch or Standard & Poor's. National and local governments were complicit too, albeit less consciously, because they raised huge amounts of taxes on the alleged profits made by these paper transactions, whether they were real or not.

As a member of the ML capital market's compensation committee, I learned the truth of the aphorism that the squeaky wheel gets a lot of grease. We used to sit once a year to hand out bonuses, and I would regularly hear colleagues say: "He's a nice guy – he's very good but he won't complain if we don't give him so much. But that other guy is constantly complaining, so we'd better give him something special."

It was very unfair, and I used to try to fight against this tendency, but it was a true fact – and a sad reflection on human nature – that people who are good but difficult are treated better than the good but nice.

The bonus system was also ripe for abuse. If it is agreed that people will receive twenty percent of any profits they make, it is useful to know how those profits are defined. Often someone might say they had made twenty million dollars, so they were due four million. It would then transpire that, after holding that position for a certain amount of time, the trade did not make that profit at all. At least nowadays there is legislation to claw back bonuses, or stop them being given out for three or four years.

The squabbling that went on over individuals claiming credit for particular successes was just as bad. We used to have 'puff sheets' on which we each had to record what we believed we had contributed. Reading people's own inflated accounts of what they claimed to have personally achieved was interesting, to say the least.

One day my chairman's secretary rang me and said that Bill would like me to have dinner with him in New York the following week. I rearranged my schedule and duly turned up at a very smart Manhattan restaurant. After I had given him an account of our progress in Asia Pacific, it was clear there was something else on his mind.

"Michael, I want to have a serious talk with you," he said. "The politics of the firm have changed since the crash (of '87). You have the habit of being extremely frank with everyone, telling them exactly what you think, and not caring very much about whether what you thought would be accepted. It can be quite brutal. We have sixty-odd thousand people working for us, and you're one of the smartest people we have. But you have to realise it's a big firm and there are a lot of average people who need to be treated in a certain way in order to get the best out of them. You've alienated a lot of people by being very candid with your views, by being eccentric, by doing things that no one else would dare to do, and making it very clear that you don't care. This attitude doesn't win you a lot of friends. For your own sake, it would be wise to tone down your behaviour."

As serious talks go, it was pretty heavy. But the truth was, I had it coming. I did indeed have a strong personality and I liked things to be done properly. I did not mind someone having a better idea than me, but I disliked indecision and dithering. I do not believe that bullying should be tolerated in any form, from friends ganging up against someone, as boys will do in the playground, to the modern scourge of being as hurtful as possible on the internet. It is a waste of energy, and this is why I have made a conscious choice, in most cases, not to mention by name in this account most of the people I did not care for. Nevertheless, if someone, at whatever level, did a bad job, I believed in telling them so. I always tried to do it in a dispassionate way, without scolding, but I thought it was important for them to know. By the same token, if someone did a good job, however junior they were, I made a point of seeking them out to tell them so. But this was not most people's way of operating.

I did make some effort to change my ways, but because of the internal politics to which Bill had alluded, it made little difference. I went back to New York the following Christmas and was called in to see the president in charge of global capital markets. He told me there was a need to rationalise expenses and he was not sure whether they could keep me on in my current position. He suggested I could stay for nine months with a pre-agreed bonus, which would give me plenty of time to review my options, or stay on with the risk that a later deal might be less generous.

I told him I would leave in nine months. I had had a wonderful time at Merrill Lynch, but there was no point in outstaying my welcome.

That nine-month scheduled departure gave me the leisure to put my operations in order and think about what to do next. Unfortunately, my long-time investment banking colleague Andrew Korner was doing the same thing, in a way that would test our friendship sorely. Very shortly before my own leaving date, I discovered that he was secretly planning a walkout of his group from the bank. This was exactly what we had both done six years earlier at CSFB, at my instigation. But if my boss at the time had got wind of it, I would have expected him to sack me on the spot: it would have been his responsibility to our employer. Now, to my dismay, I found myself in exactly that position. I was not prepared to turn a blind eye for friendship's sake, even if the action I must take would cost me that friendship.

I called Andrew in.

"I'm sorry, but you just can't do this," I said. "I may be leaving in a couple of months but I'm still chairman of Asia Pacific and I have a responsibility."

I fired him and the other two ringleaders.

He was unhappy with me, as I knew he would be, and I understood why. I honestly felt I had no choice in the matter. All I could do was hope that time would heal the wound.

8:

The Start-up Years

I HAD ENJOYED my years as an investment banker and was proud of the changes I, Andrew and our various national partners, such as Hemedra Kothari in India, had made. We had persuaded a string of governments to open up their countries to new sources of finance which would help to improve the lot of their people. I had also benefited from two very comfortable berths at CSWW and ML, where the element of personal risk was minimal. Now that I was free, the buccaneer in me was itching to enter the entrepreneurial fray again.

On the first day of October 1990 I found myself without a job and needing to post letters. I had no idea where to post them or buy the stamps, because for years I had had an office to do all that. It was a graphic reminder that, seven months short of my fiftieth birthday, I was now completely on my own. However, once I found my feet, my former incredibly efficient and loyal PA from ML, Linda da Cruz joined me, and to this day is still my colleague in my own investment company. This made the transition process much easier.

One of the first things I did, after taking a few weeks to gather my thoughts, was to secure an advisory role at Bangkok Bank, where I knew the founding family well. It was a big regional bank and they took me on to help them set up an investment banking arm. I duly did so, putting together an excellent team. Unfortunately, the idea died when the chairman, whom I liked and respected, but who came from a parsimonious Chinese tradition that did not believe in spending money unnecessarily, was reluctant to pay the salaries that these bankers had come to expect.

I decided to try to use this team elsewhere. I was invited to join Banque Indosuez in Hong Kong as an adviser to help build their investment banking business, and in the first year, this team I had brought in made the largest profit the bank had ever seen in Asia, at a time when most of the big players were losing money. But banks can be political places, and these high profits excited the "barons" in Paris. A turf war ensued, which the friend in Hong Kong who had hired me ended up losing. After three years, we all agreed that enough was enough, and I left.

In parallel, I was asked by the Singapore-based entrepreneur Ong Beng Seng to be a non-executive director of his company Hotel Properties Ltd, his only publicly listed company. Married to Christina Ong, who is also a very successful entrepreneur in her own right, he was held up by Lee Kuan Yew, Singapore's founding father, as a model entrepreneur because he was willing to go international and take risks, which are rare qualities in that rather risk-adverse country. The company has projects in Australia, the US, the UK, Bali, the Seychelles and China, and it is the leading resort owner in the Maldives. I have retained my involvement to this day and am very proud to be on his board.

I was also invited to become one of the hundred members of the Club of Rome. At one time this institution had been a very influential think tank which did good works and pursued interesting initiatives on the international stage. By the time I joined, it had lost some of that cachet and there was a huge amount of talking, which was often not very well directed or focused. After a year when, clearly, I was the odd man out, and had been too frank in my opinion at various conferences, I was asked to leave. I was actually quite relieved, but I had enjoyed attempting to put to good use my expertise on a part of the world I now knew very well.

By this point I had spent a couple of decades observing at first hand the integration of the Asia Pacific region, which was developing a sense of itself in the way the countries of Europe had. I grew tired of explaining the various countries of the region over and over again to people from other Asian countries, and, of course, to Westerners, all of whom were interested but did not have much knowledge, so I sat down to write a book called *Asia Pacific: Its Role in the New World Disorder.* It was translated into both Japanese and Korean, and it ended up on the syllabus of business schools around the world.

The Japanese edition brought me to the attention of the Sasakawa Peace Foundation, set up by a billionaire called Ryoichi Sasakawa, who had built a gambling empire around motorboat racing in Japan. I became the only foreigner invited to be on the foundation's main advisory board in Tokyo.

Amid these new challenges, one very sad event deprived me

of the person who had done so much to give my life direction. My mother had lived in the lower flat of the house in Glebe Place until our children came along and we needed the space, at which point I bought her a house of her own in nearby Gunter Grove. She became the volunteer manager of the first refuge for homeless people established by the charity Shelter, which took up a good deal of her time for some years.

Because I was travelling so much, I used to see her perhaps once every three months, but our relationship remained as important as ever. Since she was the person who had prompted me to travel to the East and enter a monastery, and she had studied Buddhism herself, I naturally told her everything about the spiritual journey I had embarked upon in Japan. She liked the Japanese rooms we had made in our houses in Fulham and Chelsea, and she was more than happy to sit Japanese-style on our *tatami* matting when she came to dinner.

As ever, we treated each other as close friends, as much as mother and son. For example, when she flirted with lesbianism in mid-life, she discussed this development with me without inhibition. I had learned from her and my Asian mentors that one should not pass judgement, so she knew she could tell me anything. On two occasions, at her request, I intervened to fend off the attentions of an unruly and aggressive woman she had met at the Shelter and who was harassing her.

When she was in her late sixties, she had a terrible car accident on the *autostrada* in Italy. It left her with great difficulty in walking, and she became heavily reliant on painkillers, which was not pleasant for her. She remained more or less bed-ridden from that time onwards, with a live-in companion to look after her. It was very tough for her, and not the kind of old age that such an active, adventurous woman had imagined for herself. This long, slow deterioration finally came to an end when she died in London at the age of eighty-one.

We held a big memorial services for her where I wept freely, amid a rush of memories of everything she had done for me, as well as sadness for the difficulties of her last years.

After finishing my advisory stints with Bangkok Bank and Banque Indosuez, there then followed a period in which I initially lost millions as I entered the start-up world. I also received investor money from friends to finance new start-up businesses and then lost some of those friends when the businesses failed. I was cheated out of one deal by a giant corporation, and I lost another when world economic events thwarted the most ambitious venture I had ever contemplated, before or since. Such, I suppose, is the life of an adventurer.

At this time we were still living in Hong Kong, but the expiry of Britain's ninety-nine year lease on the territory from China was now only a couple of years away. There were already signs that the place was going to become less inclusive. For most of the years we had lived there, if Marie-Thérèse and I turned up at a cocktail or dinner party and there were Chinese people speaking their own language to each other, they would as a courtesy switch to English. But now I noticed that happening less often. The Cantonese are not known even within China for being especially polite or courteous to strangers. For example, if one stepped aside to let someone take a taxi, they were more like to just take it without demurring, let alone saying thank you first. Since I had been brought up to believe that courtesy to strangers is an important quality, I did not look forward to the prospect of a further deterioration of general manners. I also anticipated that the pollution in the adjacent Chinese city of Shenzhen and its industrial zones would affect the air quality in Hong Kong, and that there was likely to be conflict between the Hong Kongers, with their perfectly reasonable democratic aspirations, and the central Chinese government. Finally, I predicted that Hong Kong would change from being a regional base to being a very China-centric one, which was of no interest to me.

I already knew, having been there many times, that Singapore was an extremely courteous society where complete strangers would go out of their way to be helpful. The best example came when I parked too close to the car behind me in a parallel parking zone. A pedestrian knocked on my window and said: "I think you should move forward, because otherwise the car behind won't be able to get out." In the West this would be regarded as busy-body behaviour and might result in an earful of abuse, but to me it was the hallmark of a socially considerate society.

Singapore is also very efficient, clean and green, and it is just as favourable a financial and tax jurisdiction as Hong Kong. It therefore seemed an extremely comfortable place to live. The only downsides were likely to be the constant humid climate and the lack of discernible seasons. We would be able to avoid the worst of that by going to back to Europe every summer. So, in the year before the handover in July 1997, we moved to a flat just three minutes' walk from the Singapore Botanic

Gardens, which is Asia's version of Kew Gardens. We have never regretted the move.

Meanwhile we still had our property in France, which was an undeniable extravagance, now that I no longer had the security of my regular investment banking income. The banks holding the mortgage on the château were pestering me to sell it, which we were loath to do. After spending so many years over the renovation, we had made it into a beautiful home and were not ready to part with it. Even if we were, the property would not have been easy to sell: there are not many buyers in the market for a place that large, and disposing of it would probably have meant selling at a loss. Nevertheless, the annual maintenance of around a quarter of a million euros would not pay itself, so I needed to find another source of income.

As a possible solution to the problem, my thoughts turned to Myanmar. Previously known to the rest of the world as Burma, the name its British colonial rulers had given it, this isolated, heavily repressed country had exerted a fascination on me ever since my fleeting, forty-eight hour visit in 1965. I now began to take a fresh interest, which would lead me to pursue the most ambitious project I had ever attempted. If it worked out, I might end up spending the rest of my life there. If it did not…well, so be it – there were always other opportunities.

The country has rich natural resources, such as gold, copper, oil, gas, jade and teak, and, in general, its people are remarkably gentle and courteous to foreigners. As I had briefly discovered in the Sixties, it is the most Buddhist of all the countries in Asia, and even its military rulers had always considered themselves deeply devout, for all their corrupt practices and their regular tendency to turn guns on whichever of their fifty-odd ethnic groups had fallen out of favour. For decades, however, it had been kept in a time warp by the military dictator, General Ne Win. He eventually had to step down in 1988, and by the mid-Nineties it was run by a junta which called itself the State Law and Order Restoration Council. This was usually abbreviated to Slorc, an acronym reminiscent of the evil agency Smersh in the James Bond film *From Russia With Love*. It did nothing for the regime's international image.

In Hong Kong, I had met a striking Australian woman called Miriam Segal. Of indeterminate age, she was the daughter of Polish Jews and had actually been born on a fishing boat off the coast of Palestine, before being raised in Australia. She had clearly been a great beauty in her youth and she had made her fortune in the Sixties with a chain of fashion accessory boutiques in Manhattan. She had now settled in crumbling, down-at-heel Yangon (which the British had called Rangoon), where she was an unusual sight in her designer outfits and her long, crimson-painted fingernails. She had first arrived in Myanmar in the mid-Seventies in search of handicrafts to sell in New York, but along the way she had befriended the generals and she now proposed introducing me to them. She wanted to see if we could marry her unlikely connection to the military government with my expertise in the financial markets in order to help the country develop.

It was without doubt a very interesting opportunity. Unlike Miriam, I had no liking for generals and no illusions about the tyrannical record of the regime. I could see, however, that this desperately poor nation with virtually no modern infrastructure was ripe for the kind of development that had launched Japan and Korea on the road to post-war success. Those countries had moved forward via vast conglomerates involved in all aspects of economic life in their respective countries; what the Japanese call *zaibatsu* or the Koreans *chaebol*.

As I saw it, economic growth in Myanmar would lead to the development of a middle class. A larger middle class would mean more educated people who could then put the legitimate argument that they needed democracy to progress further. This had been a key stage in the process towards liberalisation in all the other countries of Asia, and while it had not worked perfectly everywhere, it still struck me as Myanmar's best hope, by far.

I therefore developed the idea of forming an industrial/agricultural conglomerate for Myanmar, with the likes of Mitsubishi, Sumitomo, Samsung and Hyundai as my models. Its role would be to facilitate any project – from a cement plant to a dairy or meat ranch, from growing timber to building a port – as long as it looked financially viable and was something the country needed. That last part was important. If the venture worked, it could give its investors a handsome reward, but it should not just be about making money. It would help an impoverished nation enjoy the basic modern developments that most of the rest of the world took for granted. Industrial or infrastructural development might not sound as romantic as a popular uprising to free the oppressed Burmese people from the yolk of military dictatorship, but I knew from my years in the investment banking world that arid-sounding financial deals could, in the right circumstances, make a huge difference to ordinary people's lives.

My initial task was to get the military government to see the advantages of opening up to foreign investment, and in order to do that I needed to set up a base in Yangon. When learning of my plans, the regime kindly offered me, for a nominal rent by international standards, the former mayor's house as my headquarters and home. It had a wonderful view of the Shwedagon Pagoda – the beautiful gold-leaf-covered Buddhist structure which is the city's most famous landmark – through the branches of a *durian* tree. The fruit of this tree is famous for its off-putting smell but is nevertheless regarded by many people as a great delicacy. I also planted a nice little vegetable garden along the side of the house, and tending it was a good way of relaxing from the stresses of trying to put my series of ambitious deals together.

Despite this comfortable home environment, I quickly learned that Myanmar was not the easiest country to live in. The foreign exchange situation was a nightmare because there was a black market rate that was ten times the official one, and lots of ordinary consumer goods were simply not available, which meant stocking up in Singapore or Hong Kong. But the whole enterprise was the kind of challenge I enjoyed, and I had never been daunted by the prospect of living in tough territory. I felt like a pioneer, which naturally appealed to my sense of adventure.

A more formidable obstacle was the political campaign led by Aung San Suu Kyi, the opposition leader who had been under house arrest since her return to the country some six years earlier. Her strong links to the West, with her British husband and two sons back in Oxford, had done a great deal to put Burmese human rights on the global agenda, which was, naturally, a good thing. She was now calling for a level of democracy which the generals had made clear they were not prepared to grant, and the world was listening. To counter their refusal, she had demanded international sanctions on Myanmar. Her campaign was getting a lot of traction abroad, with the influential support of the prominent US Senator Pat Moynihan. He had a Burmese left-winger on his staff who persuaded him to adopt the cause, and apparently he then struck a horse-trading deal to get the support of President Clinton, so it became official US policy.

To me, however well-intentioned all this was, it was a retrograde step: sanctions would restrict the kind of normal economic growth which, to my mind, was key. The transition to democracy was not guaranteed, but I was convinced this would be a better option for the Burmese people than isolating the country still further.

I therefore wrote a public letter to the government newspaper saying that Aung San Suu Kyi was wrong to insist on sanctions. This position was regarded as sacrilege by most of the outside world. My letter was published in full, and I was subsequently interviewed about it on CNN in New York, which earned me a degree of instant notoriety. I got used to being attacked as a Slorc stooge every time I went on the internet. My monastic training was once more invaluable in helping me deal with the brickbats. Personal attacks are hurtful because they damage the ego. If one can successfully minimise the ego, it is possible to stand back from the personal criticism and assess dispassionately whether or not it is justified.

In this case, I was convinced that it was not. I reckoned I understood the situation in Myanmar and the prospects for its development better than the vocal *émigrés* and their supporters around the world. So I pressed on with my plans and, little by little, I made progress. After some months, I had managed to get a number of Asian firms interested in investing in a series of projects that we had identified.

The most important component of the investment was due to come from a syndicate of Japanese banks and companies. It took a lot of long, patient work to put it together, culminating in a make-or-break meeting at the Tokyo headquarters of one of the banks. I had sunk all the money I had left into this project and, if I did not get the funding, I would be flat on my back. As I went up in the lift to the boardroom, I remember saying quietly: "Please, please; this needs to work." It was the only time in my life I had ever sought divine intercession.

To my intense relief, the syndicate's answer was that they would provide the seed funding of US$4 million to get the venture started. I now had around US$250 million dollars in "soft circles", whereby investors agreed that, subject to the government granting the relevant licences, they were interested in putting in amounts of, say, ten or twenty million dollars. I had a list of specific projects earmarked with partners, and we had provisional interest in each one from the relevant section of the regime. I was euphoric. All that time, effort and patience really had paid off, and I was now on the brink of something very big, which could dramatically change both Myanmar's fortunes and mine.

I had, however, reckoned without the Asian financial crash.

Our fund was predicated on the Association of South East Asian Nations, ASEAN for short, formally admitting Myanmar as an accredited member. ASEAN announced in early 1996 that it was prepared to do so, with formal ratification due to take place in July 1997, so that element of my plan seemed to be in place. But at the beginning of the very month when ratification was supposed to happen, the Thai economy collapsed. That led to the domino collapse of some of the other Asian economies, in particular Indonesia and Korea, and it had a serious negative effect on Asian economies in general. The only one largely unaffected was Japan. The crash did not destroy Myanmar's chances of admission to ASEAN; that happened on schedule. By that time, however, my US$250 million of interest had disappeared like an ice-cream in the Sahara. The entire region had suddenly become risk-averse, so for my investors it was now inconceivable to put money into a blighted, backward country living under a rigid military dictatorship.

Having been so excited by the vision of the development I could facilitate, I now found myself on the verge of bankruptcy. I moved out of my house overlooking the Shwedagon Pagoda and went to live in a dank room in a warehouse belonging to a business contact. I lived there for two months, surviving on chicken, rice and fruit, and conserving what few funds I had left to pay for my two older children at university in the United States, as well as to provide for Marie-Thérèse and Charlotte in Singapore. The situation was bleak and depressing, and it would have been very easy to lapse into self-pity. Once again, however, my training on the Japanese mountaintop was my bedrock. It enabled me to detach myself from my sudden change in physical circumstances and from the enormous disappointment. This setback had been another of life's adventures, I was able to assure myself, from which I would learn and move on.

Fortunately, I had not spent all the seed capital and so the company had no debts. That meant I was able to give a modest amount back to my founding investors. As my share, I collected what equipment was left in the office in Yangon and took it back to Singapore, to start the next adventure.

As it turned out, Myanmar did open up to outside investment eventually: I was merely ten years ahead of my time. Looking back, I suppose I am grateful that this massively ambitious scheme did not come off: if it had done, I would have had to live in Yangon almost full time. That would have appealed to my pioneering instinct, but it would have been intellectually relatively barren, as well as very difficult for Marie-Thérèse and our children. I would be totally immersed in Myanmar today, rather than pursuing the diverse and hugely exciting range of projects that have occupied me since then.

But I cannot deny that the whole experience was very tough.

The most uplifting element was the generosity of my friends. To my eternal gratitude, they helped tide me over financially at a time when I was close to ruin. One was a close Thai friend called Varin Pulsirivong, who lent me a substantial sum with no questions asked nor any conditions imposed. Another was Andrew Korner, whom I had sacked for attempting to lead his own walk-out from Merrill Lynch. We had repaired our friendship a couple of years earlier, after my book *Asia Pacific* was published, when I used it as an excuse to knock on the door of his office and offer him a copy with a signed dedication. He graciously accepted it and we resumed our close friendship. Andrew was another of the people who now simply asked how much I needed and wrote out a cheque on the spot; he did not say a word about when he wanted it back or whether he wanted interest. In the event, I was able to repay it in full a year later, but I could never have reached that position without the enormous help of these friends. Andrew's willingness to put our past animosity behind him and come to my assistance when I needed it most was a mark of very considerable friendship, which I will never forget. The episode was a perfect example of that Japanese proverb about the earth being firmer after a thunderstorm. Then another close Asian friend of mine simply made me a large gift. I haven't mentioned his name, as his country's tax office can be very difficult sometimes.

As I looked around me and began to pick up the pieces, I still had the problem of owning an absurdly extravagant château that cost a fortune to run but was virtually impossible to dispose of in a hurry.

A close Japanese friend of mine, Hideo Ishihara, the chairman of Goldman Sachs in Tokyo, spoke highly of a thirty-something American protégé of his, by the name of David Heller. By coincidence, my daughter Justine had just started working for Goldman Sachs in London (with no help from me: it took her no fewer than twenty-eight interviews before they accepted her). She happened to meet David in the office, they embarked on a relationship, and she invited him to Tourreau for the weekend. When he arrived, it was clear he was impressed by the house. After I had showed him around, including my extensive wine cellar, I told him that I was looking to see the house and would offer half of my cellar if he could introduce a buyer. He said that he would think about it. Then, while we were having a cognac and a cigar after our last dinner, while sitting listening to Gregorian Chant booming out into the park, with the brilliant night sky as the ceiling to this extraordinary music, he proposed entering into a partnership, in which he would buy fifty per cent of the estate. He explained that acquiring fifty per cent made more sense, as he would have our local knowledge to help him run the place, and we would not need to part with somewhere we had put so much effort into. Having established that this proposal had nothing to do with Justine – I was naturally concerned about what might happen to the partnership if their relationship foundered – we concluded an agreement. In the event, the relationship did not last, and David and Justine both moved amicably on. But he did become a superb partner.

With his participation, we embarked on the second round of restoration. We put in central cooling, and we adapted the swimming pool so that it had a waterfall around all four edges. It was a wonderful pool, dug to a depth of five metres so I could dive from a one-metre Olympic springboard. It was big enough for vigorous games of water polo – and for small children we had a second one alongside it. We also populated the place with animals. We had some sheep for a while, and a couple of donkeys, until a donkey kicked a sheep into the moat, where it drowned. We also discovered that donkey dung smells awful in the hot Provençal sun: whenever there was a cross-wind we would leave the swimming pool retching because of the stench. So we got rid of the donkeys and the sheep, and concentrated instead on wildfowl. At one point we had pairs of around thirty different species from all over the world. These included peacocks, Canada geese, and white and black swans. The whole park was animated with the movement of these birds, either marching across the lawns or dropping onto the octagonal basin or the moat. We loved having them, but sadly, so did our Rhodesian ridgebacks. Male peacocks fan their tail feathers into an astonishing display, but when they do so, they expose a bare rear end. This presented our dogs with a perfect target. The local fox population did not help, and our wildfowl flock steadily diminished, to the point where we were left with a couple of geese, one of which had gone mad, and two white swans. The crazed goose attacked everyone in sight, and one guest was so startled that he leapt back, fell down and broke his elbow. He spent three days in hospital, and we decided it was time to get rid of this particular goose – and had him for supper.

The château was not just about indulgent summers. I started a Tourreau Foundation with the aim of bringing together Japanese – and, later, other Asian – leaders with their top British or European counterparts. We had some very senior people: central bank governors, ministers of finance and major global company heads, such as the chairman of Unilever.

I invited between ten and fourteen people at a time. They would arrive on the Friday evening, leave on the Monday, and nobody was allowed to go out of the front gates once they came in. We provided extremely good food and wine, and my children would serve the cocktails and canapés. The point was to show Europeans, and particularly the British, a side of the Japanese that they would not normally see.

When the Japanese visit Europe, they normally do a whistle-stop tour, rushing around during the day and then relaxing with Mitsubishi Corporation or Nomura Securities at a Japanese restaurant in the evening. There is no real interaction on a personal basis. So the idea was to arrange gatherings with five, six or seven participants from each side, all at an equivalent level. There was a clear understanding that everything was off the record so people could have very frank discussions, and I would make sure everyone sat next to a different person for each meal. The former British Cabinet minister Lord Jenkin, the first chairman of the UK-Japan 2000 Group, said he had been to many meetings with his Japanese counterparts but had never had this level of intimacy and personal contact.

I held these gatherings for about five years. There was no commercial purpose. I simply felt I owed the Japanese a great deal from their kindness when I was a student in Japan, as well as from my banking years. They have a saying, *"Koko made marimashita no wa mina-san no o-kage-san de, dakara nanika-wo, o-kaishi shitai"*, which roughly translates as: "I have arrived at this point in my career thanks to everyone's help and now I would like to give something back."

Although my misfortune in Myanmar had nearly cost me everything I owned, I remained committed to the idea of applying the skills I had learned over my long career to business start-ups.

In the dot-com boom of 1999 and 2000, I advised a Silicon Valley company called Intertrust, which pioneered the field of data privacy. Instead of a retainer, I received a number of share options at fifty cents. At around this time we found a flat in Cadogan Square, London, which we very much liked. To buy it, I exercised a number of my options at ninety-five dollars. It was a good thing I did, because, in a less smart move, I kept the rest. Not being very interested in shares, I did not watch the price every day after the company had gone public, and I stupidly rode this investment down and down because I was too busy doing other things. After the dot-com crash, my remaining options plunged to around four dollars, when the company was bought jointly by Sony and Phillips.

I continued to pick up advisory assignments. I was retained by a couple of wealth management bankers from the now defunct New York investment bank Bear Stearns, who were running a private fund. My role was to help them meet wealthy investors in Japan, and I managed to get them in contact with the billionaire founder of a Japanese credit service company. In the course of negotiations, I had a long telephone conversation with Warren Buffett, the legendary US investor, who was interested in the possibility of investing in this company. I told him he would have to come to Japan and see the place for himself.

"I'll do it on one condition," he said. "You eat all that *sushi* crap and I'll just have my hamburgers and coke."

I assured him I would, and I looked forward to meeting him in person and introducing him to Japan. It was not to be, however, as the deal collapsed before we could get that far.

Instead, another big start-up now presented itself. I got to know an Australian who had acquired the licensing rights from the Australian government agency for scientific research, CISRO. This agency provided a lot of new technology to the agricultural sector, and the fellow I met had borrowed money against very little security in order to develop one technology in particular, which he had identified as having great promise. Following the crash, he had run out of funds and the National Australian Bank foreclosed on the company. The bank was then trying to find a buyer for the asset, as it had no idea what to do with the technology. This fellow's idea was to make a very low-ball offer to take the technology off the bank's hands, and I agreed to fund it.

The invention itself was undeniably brilliant. It was an osmotic process that removed the liquids from organic products – anything from oranges to the bark of a tree – to get the highest possible rate of extraction and, just as importantly, to leave a non-putrescible residue. Pressing an orange to extract the juice leaves the pulp and peel, which still contain residual liquids and will rot over time. With our process, what was left over could not rot, and it could be used as a filler for other foods because it was completely dry and neutral fibrous material. So we were improving efficiency in three different ways: by increasing the volume and quality of the juice extracted, cutting down on waste, and leaving what remained as a usable product rather than landfill.

The problem was the capital expenditure: this revolutionary equipment was expensive to install. We were approaching companies who had millions of dollars already invested in existing equipment. Asking them to toss it all out and spend millions of dollars on our new equipment was a tough sell, however good the technology. We quickly worked out that the only way it would work was if we sold the invention to a large international company which was building a new factory.

In our case we went to Ocean Spray, the giant US producer of cranberry juice. They liked our technology a great deal and could see the advantage in it for them – so much so, in fact, that they simply appropriated some of it.

The first time I tried to get a deal with them, we arranged to meet at the Mayfair Regent Hotel in New York. We talked in my room and then they repaired to their's to discuss it. They kept telling me: "We're going to have a win-win situation." But I had the strong sense that they meant: "We're going to win and you're going to lose."

We had known all along that we had to prioritise intellectual property. But getting patents is hugely expensive, especially if they are to apply all over the world. We spent a vast amount of money that we could ill-afford in the attempt to secure them. Now we discovered that having the law on our side and a patent in our back pocket was not enough, because going up against big companies is virtually impossible.

Thus, when we complained that they were stealing our technology and that any court would agree, Ocean Spray effectively said: "So – sue us."

That, as they well knew, was easier said than done. They had a department of in-house lawyers waiting to bury a case like this in paperwork, whereas we had to pay an external lawyer who would no doubt cost us hundreds of thousands of dollars over the several years the case was likely to run. At that stage we could hardly afford a can of baked beans, let alone the cost of taking on a giant American company. The case became impossible to pursue and they ended up acquiring our company.

It was a dispiriting experience. I had learned fairly early in adult life that to enjoy any enduring relationship – personal or business – there had to be a measure of mutual respect, and in my view, mutual respect was based on fairness. The Japanese use a system called *omakase shimasu* which essentially means "I leave it to you". In a business negotiation, provided there is trust between the two parties, the idea is to say: "Okay, tell me what you think is fair." As long as the other party is serious about building a long-term relationship, that puts a moral obligation on them to try to be fair. It often works very well, because the other party may suggest the sort of deal that they would have accepted at the end of the negotiation, and both parties get straight to the baseline without wasting time and energy on bartering or negotiating every last penny. To me it is closely connected with the English concept of fairness, where it is generally accepted that one should not try to take advantage of the other person, and that so doing could open up a can of worms in which all the rules are altered.

Unfortunately this approach seems incomprehensible to most Americans, who live in such a litigious environment, and have what is effectively such a young national culture, that they are still really a bunch of teenagers, in historical terms. They will try anything, and they rely on the legal equivalent of the school authorities to keep them on the straight and narrow.

Their lawyers make sure the contracts are written to favour their client, or have loopholes that can be exploited later, and moral responsibility becomes an alien concept. The only exception in my experience is the Midwest. In that part of the United States they have a work and moral ethic that came from Germany and Scandinavia, and handshake deals still exist.

There was no such attitude at Ocean Spray. Their lawyers were obdurate and absurd, with no respect for any kind of fairness. At the same time, I was learning other key lessons, most notably that, in the pre-internet days, it was not sensible to have our management sitting in Hong Kong, with an operating guy in Sydney, and another operating guy in Melbourne.

To make matters worse, along with this technology came the fellow who had invented it. While he was an undoubted scientific genius, he turned out to be a very difficult person, as did his wife. She tried to interfere in everything, and had hysterics whenever her husband disappeared from the house for more than half an hour. The record was when she called my hotel room in Sydney fifty-five times in two hours. The hotel operator got so fed up she reported it to the management of the hotel, who pleaded with me to get a restraining order because this woman was wasting so much of their staff's time.

The Australian who introduced me to this mad inventor dropped out, because I held him responsible for a lot of problems and we fell out. In the end, I had to give up as well, because it was all too much of a drain on my limited resources. The venture had eaten up a lot of my own capital – I am talking millions – and I had raised finance from good friends who were not very happy with the result. I lost two of them permanently. They felt I handled the situation badly, and they may have been right.

Not everything I touched turned to mud, even if it sometimes felt like that. I have never played golf, but I became the proud co-owner of a golf course in Chiang Mai in northern Thailand. I founded it with Varin, the Thai friend who was one of my rescuers during my quasi-bankruptcy. We spent four years looking for a site, and we then had it built by a Japanese construction company. We opened our fifteen-hundred-acre Royal Chiangmai Golf Resort in 1998. We hosted all kinds of people there, including General Prem, the former Thai prime minister, who remains today a figure of immense influence. I could see that the grounds would be a wonderful location to set up an Asian institute for the Sasakawa Peace Foundation back in Japan, of whose advisory board I was still a member. We got as far as producing architect's drawings, but the foundation had a change of management after Sasakawa himself died, and they decided they did not want to embark on this "foreign adventure". It was a shame, because one of Japan's biggest problems is that its people do not really have the ability to mix easily culturally in an open forum, even with other Asians.

Mixing with very influential people came with the territory where Varin was concerned. A few years earlier I had been at a dinner party at his home in Bangkok at which one of the guests was General Suchinda, the then supreme commander of the Thai armed forces. During the meal Suchinda revealed what was going to happen the next morning: Prime Minister Chatichai was due to fly to visit King Bhumibol at his palace in Chiang Mai, but the plane would be diverted back to Bangkok and

Chatichai would be placed under house arrest. He was planning a coup, in other words, and explaining it in uninhibited detail to the assembled guests. I would have taken this as quite an honour if he had not, at one point in this explanation, noticed me at the end of the table and said: "Michael! I had forgotten you were here."

At that moment I began to wish I had not been.

"I'm sure you know that Thai jails are not very pleasant," the General continued, "so I advise you to keep your mouth shut about what you are hearing."

I did indeed know that.

"Don't worry, General, don't worry," I assured him.

I have rarely been more sincere.

The next morning, Prime Minister Chatichai was indeed ousted in precisely the way Suchinda had described. He had presided over a famously corrupt administration and had been ridiculed in the country for it, so he was no loss. But I was relieved that no physical harm came to him, and after a short period of exile he was able to return to Thai politics.

Elsewhere in South-East Asia I did some work for a large Indonesian conglomerate called Texmaco, which bought used equipment from other parts of the world and applied it using very cheap Indonesian labour. This was a difficult restructuring job and there were some big consultancy firms helping too. Despite their efforts and mine, the owner would not let go, and, unfortunately, he ended up losing his empire for a pittance. In a more successful engagement, I became an advisor to a company called Sithe International, run by a French entrepreneur in New York, which built and acquired power stations in Asia.

My contribution was to help acquire two power stations from Hyundai Engineering, after South Korea had been badly hit by the Asian crash and a lot of its big conglomerates had to sell off assets. I had good Korean contacts and was able to play a pivotal role, for which I earned a substantial advisory fee. I knew I could put it to good use if I could only find the right start-up.

A new candidate now emerged in the telecommunications sector. I was approached by a fellow based in the Isle of Man who asked if he could come to see me in France. He had found a way of generating very cheap international calls from SIM cards, in a system he called Call Key. This was long before Skype and WhatsApp developed technologies which made international communication free to anyone with the right hardware, and calling abroad was still very expensive. Affordable mobile services would be very attractive to the huge numbers of people who were beginning to migrate around the world in search of work.

Unfortunately, I had not learned my lesson from the food-processing venture, because once again we had the problem of being scattered all over the world as we developed the project. The Isle of Man fellow had as his partner an ageing hippie friend based in Tucson, Arizona. I brought on board a close friend of mine who was based in Scotland, and I myself divided my time between Singapore, London and France. Furthermore, the whole enterprise turned out to be a complete mismatch in terms of discipline and focus. My Isle of Man partner was a bright IT man but the hippie turned out to be a flake and we were constantly frustrated with him. Despite their difference in ability and attitude, the pair of them were somehow bonded together, and the IT man always came to the hippie's defence, right or wrong. As a result, my relations with both of them grew steadily worse. Then my Scottish friend had a stroke and was out of action for a while, and when he returned he could only function at around fifty percent intellectual capacity.

I tried my best to bring order to our affairs. Having come from the investment banking world, it was natural for me to be structured and organised, and to have a proper understanding of corporate governance. To my other two partners this was all new. I tried in vain to convince them that they needed proper documentation for everything, that there had to be a paper trail, and that every expense needed to be accounted for.

"Remember that you have shareholders," I said. "You are responsible to them, and you can't just do what you like."

But they would not accept the importance of it, and we ended up fighting all the time.

I would say: "Why the hell didn't you do this?"

And the IT fellow would say: "Who are you to tell me what to do?"

"I'm your chairman," I would say. "I and my friends have put up the money."

"I don't care," came the response.

It was not very mature.

In the end they combined to ask me to remove myself from the group, which I happily did, and they ended up cheating me out of a fairly large payment. Again, the law turned out to be a strange animal when I tried to recover what I was owed. It was a clear case of being cheated, but I got a bad feeling when the lawyer who wanted to take the task on said: "I hope I'll get a successful result for you."

"What do you mean?" I said. "It's quite clear that they are in the wrong."

"That doesn't necessarily mean that the law will agree," he said.

I let the matter lie, not wishing to throw good money after bad if there was no guarantee of a just resolution. I had also persuaded some friends to put money in, but this time I had been a little smarter. I said to them: "Don't put in a sum more than you would spend on a weekend jaunt somewhere with your friends. So if it goes, it goes, and you're not going to blame me afterwards."

That worked, and I did not lose any more friendships.

Despite this latest failure, I was still determined to make one of these ventures work. After my success with Intertrust, I remained fascinated by technology, and was keen to be part of a breakthrough. My goal was to make a big killing with massive leverage, which I knew was possible because I had witnessed it with the dot-com venture, Intertrust. My problem remained that I was an ex-investment banker who had never really done any investing in that part of my career, so I was not particularly good at it.

My third start-up was another telecoms business called Global Mobile Technologies. The idea was to provide various responses on a mobile phone: for example, tsunami alerts could be put out, so that every mobile phone in the area of the alert could pick up an emergency message. There was quite a lot of interest in this, and again I got friends in, on the same principle of not committing more than they could afford to lose.

The original idea came from a business partner called Jeff, who was an American lawyer based in the Philippines. He had found a true geek, who completely looked the part, with white hair and skeletal face. Our venture looked promising: we even persuaded people like Sony and DoCoMo, the biggest mobile phone operator in Japan, to take a good look. Once again, however, we were plagued by our poor management: we had two people in Manila (one of whom was in California half the time) and myself in Singapore, and I could not follow what they were doing on a day-to-day basis. We eventually brought in a Hong Kong investor – a successful, hard-nosed Chinese businessman – who put up the US$ 6 million dollars we needed, but there was immediate conflict between him and my two partners in Manila. Then the American lawyer was arrested returning to the US, when police at Los Angeles airport found obscene pictures of underage children on his computer – I immediately fired him but my Chinese investor's response was "Shit happens and we need him". So he re-hired him.

So it all seemed to be unravelling, but suddenly, out of the blue, I found myself with a major personal problem of my own to worry about.

We were in London in the New Year of 2007, and Marie-Thérèse and I were due to spend a weekend in the country with my old friend Kevin and his second wife, Victoria Glendinning. Based on a strong, intuitive desire, I had persuaded Marie-

Thérèse that we should have a colonoscopy and gastroscopy. We had arranged to go together and the plan was that, once we had got the all-clear, we would head off immediately afterwards to Kevin and Victoria's house in Somerset.

The afternoon did not begin well, as the specialist was two hours late. When he eventually turned up, we were each lightly sedated and he did what he had to do. Once we came round, he gave Marie-Thérèse the good news.

"Mrs Dobbs-Higginson, you're fine," he said. "There's no problem at all."

Then he turned to me, and his expression was less reassuring.

"Unfortunately, Mr. Dobbs-Higginson, you have a tumour the size of a golf ball in your colon."

By this stage I was something of a veteran of minor cancers: over the past few years I had had basal skin cancers removed from my face and an early-stage melanoma taken from my upper back, along with a long strip of muscle. That last procedure had been a day-patient job, and three days later I was travelling, so it had not any great impact on me. But it was clear from the specialist's face that we were now dealing with something of a different order.

"It would be inappropriate for me to pretend that it's not a big problem," he said. "There is an eighty percent chance it is cancer, but we have to wait for the biopsy results to be certain. I strongly advise you to get it seen to by a surgeon."

Emerging a little dazed into the chilly January afternoon, I called Kevin and Victoria. We were already late, I apologised, and we would now have to cancel completely.

After an unsettled, unhappy weekend at our flat in London,

I went on the Monday morning to see a surgeon in Harley Street. He wanted to remove the tumour right away, but I had an important business trip to Japan a few days later, and then we already had our flights booked back to Singapore. We lived five minutes' walk from one of its two top hospitals, so it made sense to have the operation there.

In the event, we decided to head straight for Singapore before my trip to Tokyo. When we got there, I asked around for colonic cancer specialists and was given two names. I made appointments to see them both.

The first of the two had green slime on his teeth, which did not seem a good start. If he could not look after his own dental hygiene, how was he going to look after my intestines? I was not impressed by his bitten fingernails either. He suggested two options, one minimally invasive, the other full surgery. He made it clear that he recommended the former.

"Just as a matter of interest," I said, "is the fee for the minimally invasive option more than the fee for an open surgery?"

"Well, yes, it is actually," he said. "It's more complicated."

"I see," I said. "I'll think about it properly and get back to you."

As I was leaving, the receptionist called me over and said: "Here's your bill for the consultation."

"I wasn't actually consulting him," I said. "I was interviewing him, and he failed the interview."

I walked out, leaving the receptionist and her two colleagues with their mouths agape. Clearly nobody had said that to them before.

The second surgeon, Dr. Ngoi Sing-Sang (known as Ngoi to his friends), recommended the opposite approach.

"I would prefer open surgery, because I can have an unobstructed view of your abdominal sac, and I will be able to do a much better job," he said. "There's always a risk that cancers have spread, and you're at stage four already, so that's what I strongly advise."

I was to discover that he was one of the best surgeons in Asia. He was willing to undertake risky operations, where people's lives were under serious threat, unlike most surgeons who gave those cases a wide berth because they did not want a death on their record. To me, that showed he had guts and integrity.

I checked into the hospital as soon as I got back from Japan. At this point I was very relaxed. As with every other hurdle in my life, it promised to be an interesting experience. If the worst came to the worst and I did not survive, my only real regret would be to have to leave my family and close friends behind – especially Marie-Thérèse, whom I worried about much more than myself. She had been an extraordinary life companion and deserved better than to be left alone at sixty.

I was very touched that our younger daughter Charlotte had taken some precious holiday allowance from her new job in Paris to keep Marie-Thérèse company while I was in hospital. They were both there while I was sedated.

I came round about six hours later, at around one in the morning. The pair of them were still there, looking rather anxious. I tried a few drugged quips to lighten their spirits.

But soon enough I was in no mood to quip any further. I had never known such confusion. In my intensive care bed I was surrounded by beeping machines, and I had tubes in my veins, nostrils and lungs, as well as a drain in my side and a catheter. Added to all that, I had a sense of evisceration. Most Asians believe that a person's life energy, or *chi*, is centred in the abdomen. According to that view of the body, the surgery had played havoc with my normal energy flows. No wonder I was in such physical distress. I was given a click-plunger for voluntary self-doses of morphine. To reassure myself that I still had some say in what was happening to me, I resolutely refused to use it. I may have been placing too much faith in my own very high pain threshold, but I needed that sense of control more than I needed the pain relief.

Dr Ngoi told me the operation had gone very well and he had removed forty-four centimetres of my colon, plus twenty-three centimetres of my small intestine, because it looked in poor shape, and he thought it made make sense to get rid of it while he was there. I also learned that he had removed eight kilos of what he described as "fatty apron". He told me he did it with a very elegant, swift swipe of his scalpel and then plunked it in a bucket. As a quick weight-loss method, it beat going on a diet.

I was moved out of intensive care, but despite the reassurance that everything had gone well, I was beginning to feel thoroughly beaten by this experience. I had had other hideous and extremely adverse experiences before – falling out of a tree when I was fourteen and spending two months being tied up to weights in hospital; losing five years of work and a fortune in Japan due to the CIA, and a few years previously I had undergone a seven-hour operation to rebuild my shoulder after a riding accident in the United States – but as I retched noxious green liquid, this felt much worse. I hated being so feeble and pathetic. The presence of Marie-Thérèse and Charlotte made a huge difference, as did Julien and Justine's daily phone calls, but there was no getting away from how miserable I felt. The highlight of my day was having to learn how to use my bowels again. In front of the whole medical team I was encouraged to try and break wind and then pass solids, right there in my hospital bed. I rose to the occasion and managed both, to rapturous applause. I half-sat, half-lay there, with my own filth lapping at my bare buttocks, totally bemused by the Kafkaesque situation in which I found myself.

Finally, after six days, I began to feel better, and after a week I was allowed to go home. I now embarked on six months of chemotherapy. I was constantly exhausted, I could no longer feel my feet because of peripheral neuropathy, and on top of that I was having to work eighteen hours a day on the telecoms start-up. I was reduced to tears a couple of times by the awful weight of it, not just being reduced to sub-par, but sub-sub-sub-par. But thanks to the skill of the surgeon, the advances of medical science, the care of the hospital, and the tireless support of my family and friends, I had come through.

Unfortunately, the prospects for my business venture had not improved while I was out of action. My main partner committed suicide before he could face trial. Replacing him proved extremely difficult, and relations deteriorated with our Chinese investor business partner. Eventually I signed a drop-hands agreement, allowing me to walk away, and the Chinese businessman took over. The final straw for me was the discovery that my skeletal geek partner had only been working about three days a week in the office; we found out that he spent the rest of his time in his second apartment in Manila, separate from the one he was living in, with three prostitutes. It was his very own harem.

Again, my friends and I lost our money. They had not put much up, and this time I had not either, but it was a fairly awful experience. I did not seem to be very good at the start-up business. I had done three, they were all disasters, and I had lost millions of dollars for myself and my friends.

9:

A Raindrop
in the Ocean

WE FINALLY FOUND a Chinese buyer for the château and its
entire contents. He bought it sight unseen and now runs the
place as a rental business. I hope our loving restoration is still
valued by those who go to stay there. We, meanwhile, have
happily downsized to a large farmhouse near the village of Le
Thor, about twenty-five kilometres to the south of our former
home, and surrounded by wheat fields and apple orchards. We
have two and a half acres, instead of the seventeen we had at
Tourreau.

The house, which looks decrepit from the outside, is very
different inside, and large enough to accommodate all of our
three children's families (including six grandchildren aged
between five months and six years, and their respective nannies
– all of them, fortunately, in a separate wing). They are all
growing up in different countries, so we and their parents are
very keen for them to enjoy holidays together in this house. In
this way they can develop strong, supportive bonds with each

other. The fact that their parents – our children – are so close, will facilitate this process.

In the garden there is a copse of old and very tall poplar trees in an oval. To give my young grandchildren a sense of magic and the mysterious, into this copse I have placed a life-sized unicorn with a narwhal horn, a taxidermist's horse glass eye and a smooth lead forehead and nose, commissioned by a well-known UK sculptor, Tom Hiscocks. I also had him make it with its head turned towards the house, as though it was looking at the humans there with some surprise. Each time the grandchildren come to stay, I take them to stroke the unicorn's nose and make a wish.

Our son Julien lives in New York, where he works in contemporary art and his wife Alexandra is a film producer. They have two daughters.

Justine lives in London. She has two daughters with Tom Aikens, a Michelin-starred chef, who has restaurants across London, and in Birmingham, as well as in Istanbul, Hong Kong and Dubai. She runs all Tom's business affairs as well as her own boutique finance firm, which raises capital for private equity deals and funds.

Charlotte lives in Paris. She went into advertising, and works as an executive producer for a production company. She has two sons with her partner Philippe Simonet, who co-heads an American advertising firm's operations in France.

My children are good company and providers of great delight and joy. They have repeatedly told me that, although I was physically absent a great deal while they were growing up, I was always there for them when they needed me. I suppose that is the best that one can reasonably expect one's children to acknowledge, as one approaches the end of one's life.

I use that last phrase very deliberately. I am now in my mid-seventies, and in today's world, getting to eighty, eight-five or ninety is by no means unthinkable. Marie-Thérèse and I have several friends who are well into their nineties and still going strong. But, as things stand, it is unlikely that I will reach even the first of those landmarks.

As a child, I had mild case of a condition called atrial fibrillation, where the heart beats irregularly and can go from forty pulses a minute up to two hundred. It is not good for the heart or for the body overall. As I grew into adulthood, the condition became steadily worse, but I had been living with it for so long, I stopped thinking about it. Eventually, however, I reached the point where I was getting quite tired, and I had a thorough cardiology examination. The doctors told me they would need to insert a pacemaker. This is done using a local anaesthetic and, being an insatiably curious creature, I was able to watch the entire proceedings as they inserted it sub-cutaneously between my skin and my rib cage and then fed the electrode through an artery into my heart.

Despite this operation, the condition continued to worsen, so my doctor in Singapore prescribed a drug called amiodarone. For a while, this was used extensively for treating chronic atrial fibrillation, but what my doctor did not tell me was that a percentage of patients on it develop an incurable secondary condition called pulmonary fibrosis. This is like a creeping lichen in the lungs that steadily reduces oxygen intake until one cannot get any at all. The patient basically suffocates, in nature's extreme, slow-motion version of waterboarding.

I learned all this only after I myself was diagnosed with pulmonary fibrosis. I was furious with the doctor who prescribed the drug and probably would have sued him, had he not been a grand old member of the Singapore medical establishment; doubtless they would all have rallied around to defend him. Instead, I changed to a London-based cardiologist, Laura Corr, who was a magnificent doctor and has now become a friend. She put me on a different drug, which works very well combined with the pacemaker.

The principal side-effect of atrial fibrillation is, in my case, constant exhaustion. It can also cause the blood to clot, which can in turn lead to a stroke, as happened to me in January 2013. So I now have two separate conditions that each reduce the lungs' capacity to take in oxygen and produce exhaustion. The net result is that I live in a miasma of fatigue which gets worse as the day wears on. By the evening, unless I have had some solid rest in the afternoon, I am a basket case.

Nevertheless, I had not quite realised how bad the outlook was until I was referred to a new respiratory specialist, a very nice Irishman, who thought I had already been told of the consequences by my previous consultant.

"As you know, once diagnosed with pulmonary fibrosis, the average lifespan is between two and three years," he said.

"Can you explain that?" I said slowly.

"Well, with this disease, as your previous consultant has already told you..."

"She hasn't, actually," I said. "But carry on."

The consultant was now making a visible effort to choose his words with great care.

"You have survived extremely well because you seem to have an unusual variant of this disease," he said. "It was first seen in you four years ago, and normally you would be dead by now. To be perfectly honest, we're not quite sure why you aren't. But I'm afraid you probably only have another two or three years to live."

My Buddhist training, which has given me the ability to detach myself where possible from the demands of the ego, has helped me deal with all manner of difficult situations in my life, both physical and emotional. But it does not work magically. With my three cancers, there was at least some possibility of repair, and one gets used to the notion that one can go and get medical problems fixed. This, by contrast, was an entirely new state of affairs.

Perhaps it was a defence mechanism that made me lapse into a stage brogue with this Irish consultant.

"Ah, to be sure, if you haven't knocked me for a bit of a six there," I said.

He was profusely apologetic.

"You have no need to apologise," I said, still attempting to process this new information. "At least you've told me what to expect, so I know what I have to deal with and I can now try and make plans."

Two or three years, he had said. This conversation took place about a year ago, as I write this account, and it will be another six months at the earliest before this book is published. So the clock is ticking pretty quickly.

Since that day, I have sought out the best possible advice

to find ways to slow down the process, but only time will tell with what result. I should also mention my GP in Chelsea, London, Dr. Kristina Brovig, who is without question the best GP I have ever had anywhere in the world. With my multiple ailments she guides me skillfully through the labyrinth of the different specialists I need, and double checks the various drugs they prescribe.

After the initial shock, I have become much calmer about what lies ahead. I console myself that I am relatively lucky that I have no pain, which so many others with medical problems have to deal with on a daily basis. However, I am somewhat concerned about the physical ordeal still to come. No specialist has yet been prepared to tell me what the final stage is like. It is obviously pretty horrific, and I have already been in touch with a clinic in Switzerland, because I have no desire to slowly suffocate to death, with my wife, in particular, forced to watch. I have also looked at ending my life myself. I have worked out how to do it, because I was a medical student and I have spoken to enough doctors. The trouble is getting hold of the necessary drug.

I am dispassionate when I think about these matters, and it does not make me feel emotional, although I probably will get emotionally involved when I say goodbye. My only serious regret is leaving Marie-Thérèse. Of course I shall be sad not to be there for my own children, but they all have very busy and seemingly stressful lives, to the point that we sadly don't see much of them – thank goodness for Skype and Whatsapp, which partly address this lacuna! People often mourn not being able to see their grandchildren grow up, but with the world changing so fast in what drives the children of today, I am not sure how well I would be able to communicate with my grandchildren. I also think the world in is in for a pretty rough ride, with terrorism and global warming and its increasingly enslaving communications technology. It is difficult to fight enemies we cannot see, and unless the venality of self-interest and corporate interest take a back step to the realisation that we truly have a global problem with climate change, it will overwhelm the next, or next generation but one. Therefore, I am not so unhappy to be leaving that possible world scenario behind.

Nearing the end of one's life, it is normal to look back and review it. Not in the sense of regret or wishing one had done this or that, both of which are futile mental exercises at this stage, but to observe any lessons to be drawn, in the hope that others may find them useful.

My mother taught her children that anything is possible if we put our minds to it, but she also insisted that we should never accept any belief or maxim until we had metaphorically tasted, touched and kicked it. I hope I have followed both precepts.

Having left behind the racial segregation and injustice of Rhodesia at the age of eighteen, I went to a series of universities in Europe, North America and Asia, without completing a degree at any of them. At every stage I was driven by intense curiosity which gave me a craving for new adventures, new knowledge. My urge to live for a while in a Buddhist monastery in Japan led me to the most important, formative experience of my life. Those months taught me discipline: how to prioritise, to establish a sense of purpose and, above all, to minimise the role of ego. This was a difficult lesson for a Westerner, because we are not accustomed to this way of thinking. But it has guided my every move since then, and helped me to live life, rather than merely to survive it.

I emerged from that mountain-top monastery determined to approach life with what I like to call a 'dispassionate passion'. The dispassion is the standing back, looking at oneself and others objectively, without any prejudicial judgement, and trying to see the substance of the person. It is a key part of Buddhist philosophy. But one also needs the passion in order to communicate the value of doing so, which is one of my principal aims in writing this book. In the monastery itself there was no passion at all: nobody cheered or slapped me on the back as I made spiritual progress. In the outside world, by contrast, passion is required to talk about these ideas — because they really are worth talking about.

Having been ordained a lay Buddhist monk, I could have spent my life in a monastery. But I chose not to, and when I eventually stopped wandering, I turned to commerce. For me, there was — and is — no contradiction between being a Buddhist and pursuing a commercial career. An entrepreneur, like a monk, can cultivate his own identity while participating in the greater whole, and there is no reason one cannot aspire towards spiritual experience and truth while also leading an outwardly successful life. Far from being inconsistent, the two are often mutually supportive.

My Buddhist training helped me get through the adversity of what was effectively my expulsion from Japan, the country I loved and where I had hoped to build a life for my family and myself. With the help of loyal friends, I reinvented myself as an investment banker. Banking has a terrible reputation nowadays, but for me at that time it was a worthwhile occupation which fulfilled my desire to help create something of tangible and lasting value to humankind, rather than just to make money for its own sake. In the course of my banking career I did a great deal to facilitate the economic and infrastructural development of various Asian and African countries. I emphasise that, not to burnish my own ego, but to stress that banking was once, and could again be, a socially useful occupation.

I gravitated towards Buddhism because it does not have dogma in the way of other religions (and really it is a philosophy not a religion). The Christian church inserts itself between man and his God as the interpreter, the forgiveness-giver. But, like the medieval Cathars in Languedoc, France, who were wiped out by the Roman Church with the aid of Louis VIII, because they said that, as they talked directly to God, they did not need the Church, I have seen no reason to have a formalised intermediary.

I do not mean to imply that all priests are doing nothing but an elaborate dance of form. There are many remarkable ones, such as the man who married Marie-Thérèse and me, who was an absolute embodiment of the idea that God is love. He gave love unconditionally and it was an honour to be with a person like that. The same was true of the abbot of my monastery on Mount Koya. There are also some remarkable people, period – such as my guru in the ashram in Old Delhi. It is very hard to make progress in anything without teachers, and I was the fortunate recipient of the kindness of several such spiritually advanced people who taught me a great deal. This was not entirely a matter of luck: since it was in my nature to go out and seek knowledge, I met many different kinds of people.

As I have grown older, I have tried to give back some of this kindness, and to grow it. When I was in Myanmar, I employed a medical student who was unable to continue his studies because the junta had closed down his university. Instead, he worked in my start-up for a while, and he later contacted me asking for my help to get into university in Singapore. I gave him a reference, and I subsequently helped him get into the Insead business school in Paris by lending him his first-year tuition money. He eventually graduated and got a very good job, at which point he got in touch with me again.

"I am now ready to pay you back," he said.

"I don't want to be paid back," I told him. "I want you to pass it on to somebody else who needs it."

I have no idea whether he did so, or how. He was under no obligation to tell me about it, and the measure of my success would be his doing it of his own volition, guided by whatever he thought was right.

So what of leading a good moral life? As in business, what matters is the profit-and-loss account. In my Buddhist philosophy, life is about a daily P&L, a weekly P&L, an annual P&L, a lifetime P&L. One should try and have more credit in the bank than debits, and if one does a wrong action, try to compensate by recognising that and avoiding repeating it, but also by doing a good action, so that there is credit in the bank at the end of one's life, and hopefully at the end of each day. I have not always managed to stay in the black. Occasionally there were long periods where I was a considerable debtor. But it was not a comfortable experience because I was aware of it, as opposed to being oblivious. I had no such easy mechanism, as the Catholics do, of going off to confession and getting absolved.

Many religions impose guilt for bad actions, which in my view is corrosive. Having followed my particular path, I have really not felt guilty about anything. That does not mean I have done nothing wrong — far from it. I have regretted certain actions, because they incurred an unnecessary P&L debt. But feeling guilt or regretful is unhelpful because it is a waste of energy. As far as bad actions are concerned, what is done is done. What really matters is what is done next. If the goal is to end up as a creditor and not a debtor, that in itself should make one's next action better.

At the moment, I am busier than ever with business ventures, all of which are examples of this approach. Indeed, the main impact of my current medical condition is to have made me extremely impatient, because I have lots of things to do and it is frustrating to have so little time in which to do them.

As my body falls apart around me — as I explain to my friends, my "car" is always in the garage getting fixed, but the "driver" is fine — so to keep the "driver" active, I am engaged with three new start-ups, which I hope will build and become considerable successes, even if I am not there to see it happen. The first involves making affordable, non-polluting, electric vehicles for the Asian markets, including cars, vans, *tuk-tuks* (the auto-rickshaws which are a major form of urban transport all over South-East Asia) and bicycles. This company, Shado International, Singapore, was founded by a close friend, Ben Lim, who asked me to invest and chair his company. We have orders already and it will be a worthwhile achievement for me to have played my part in getting them onto the polluted city streets of these and other emerging markets.

The second involves commercial drones. Drones have a negative image because of legitimate anxieties about privacy and unchecked use of airspace, but they have a huge range of benevolent applications, such as monitoring for traffic, crops, disturbances or fires, or maintaining remote pipelines over rugged terrain. They will dramatically cut down carbon emissions by reducing the need for manned flights in planes or helicopters for remote locations, provided we can develop sophisticated air traffic control systems, which is already happening. This company, H3 Dynamics Holdings, Singapore, specialises in fuel cells, certain hardware and software applications for all types of drones. I co-founded this company with Taras Wankewycz, a very focused and disciplined forty-three-year-old engineer, who was born in the Ukraine and is now a French national, and who will hopefully lead it to great success and be of benefit to our global society.

The last company takes me back to my roots because it focuses on Africa. It is a business-to-business (B2B) e-commerce platform called goafrica.com, also founded in Singapore. I am working with my American partner and close friend, Niles Helmboldt, who has spent his entire adult life dealing with investment banking in Africa. He came up with this idea and asked me to be his co-founder. We believe our timing is good because Africa now has about six hundred million mobile phone users and more than a hundred and twenty million Facebook users. Various non-governmental organisations are working to create solar-powered charging stations in the bush for mobile phones and village laptops, and satellite systems now exist which offer full coverage of the continent relatively affordably.

There are lots of pitfalls, because nothing is ever easy – especially in Africa – but if we pull it off, it will be amusing to have a company of this potential magnitude started by two seventy-five-year-olds. We are also being very materially assisted by Andrew Korner and his firm, Asia Capital Partners, Hong Kong, in producing a well-structured business plan to ensure that we attract key strategic investors going forward. Our dream is that it will make a huge difference in terms of giving Africans more efficient access to their counterparts throughout Africa, as well as to the rest of the world, and similarly allowing the rest of the world to understand and have better access to the constituent countries of Africa and their respective cultures. This project will also be providing ten per cent of its pre-tax earnings to charitable projects in Africa for the empowerment of women in Africa.

All these ventures have been incorporated in Singapore simply because Singapore offers a degree of excellence as a jurisdiction for companies, including, *inter alia*, start-ups, such that in my forty plus years of being involved in businesses globally, I have not found a better one. The fact that I have happily lived there for more than twenty years also helps.

I have attempted to learn the lessons of some of my previous disasters. What unites all of them is that they aim to put twenty-first century technology to the global good. It is also about giving back, and passing on, both of which I can do even if I am no longer alive.

This is what I believe it means to contribute to a wider community from which one cannot be separated, which is what being a raindrop in the ocean is all about. To me, that is the essence of a good life.

It may be controversial to say so, but I do not believe that happiness is the most useful goal in life. In my experience, it is balance that gives calm and dispassion, which in turn bring peace. In fact, I see the world primarily in terms of whether or not it is in balance – a perspective which applies equally to countries or regions, as well as to individuals. Where balance does not exist, energy which could be used for something else is required to help compensate. This is central to Buddhist teachings, and it was implicit in my kendo master's question about the twin dangers of wanting very much to win or being frightened of losing For him, the right answer was that the goal is to be in equilibrium, without the demands of the ego clouding one's vision. If that happens, it is easier to make the right decisions in an intuitive rather than a calculated way.

In my endeavour to live a full life and follow my own star, the ego has been my principal enemy. One of the key points of Buddhist philosophy, as I learned during my monastic experience, is to minimise the ego – eradicating it completely would need many lives to complete. The ego is the aspect of oneself that constantly demands satisfaction, in the way that a *gourmand* stuffs himself with endless eating.

In resisting ego demands, the goal should be to attempt to separate one's fundamental self from the banal desires that we are constantly told we should have: to buy a Gucci bag to become a better person, or to eat a particular brand of ice cream to achieve true satisfaction. Learning to monitor one's activities and to observe oneself is crucial. My rather primitive way of doing this is to have a little imaginary fellow sitting on my shoulder who points out that I have exaggerated something, been a little loose with the truth, or allowed a certain subjective animosity to intrude into whatever I am doing. It can be irritating at times to have my thoughts and conduct restrained by this little man. But he stood me in very good stead when I got to the monastery, because in all that loneliness there was nobody else to observe me and, overall, I would much rather have him there than not.

Ego intrudes into so many areas of life. It is hugely relevant in the world of digital communications, where people send a message into the ether and expect a reply as soon as possible; it is hard to think of a better example of the *gourmand* requirement for instant gratification. I remember when the fax machine was heralded as a dramatic new breakthrough. It was indeed, but one did not have to carry a fax machine around in one's pocket, so there were limits to how far it imposed itself on one's life.

I fear this new 24/7 communication enslavement is really going to have a negative effect on society. Before that permanent worry about missing the latest tweet or email, of being left out of a conversation, we had time to smell the flowers or to engage in a relaxing pursuit, and we had space to think about more substantive things. I mourn the passing of those days, and I am pleased that I will not be around much longer to face even more ghastly developments along these lines, such as some chip in one's head that tells one that a message is waiting.

I obviously have some fundamental concerns about the way technology is transforming our lives, especially the lives of children and young people today – and often with negative results. I need not dwell on the positive aspects as they are well known, but I do feel it is necessary to sound a warning about these negative influences.

Firstly, the world of emails, tweets, SMSs, and Facebook, Instagram and Snapchat postings and other such internet-related forms of communication, leads to a short-form transfer of ideas and feelings. By their very nature, they tend to be short and thus superficial, often banal in the extreme and therefore do not involve the sender in thinking carefully, in depth about their message and what the recipient is likely to feel. Further, there is the sense of entitlement that the recipients must give an immediate answer – and if they don't, there must be something wrong. This puts unnecessary pressure on both sides and, indeed, in some cases, guilt for not responding at once. All such a waste of energy – and for such trivial reasons.

What has happened to those long, face-to-face conversations with both friends, colleagues, and indeed, sometimes with strangers, where one not only heard the words but also captured the look in the eye, the facial movements and the hand gestures, all of which gave one a number of contextual reference points to better understand the words one was hearing – and more about the person uttering them. These person-to-person exchanges very importantly give one the time and opportunity to hear new ideas and to think new thoughts – to craft one's ideas, so as both to capture subtle nuances of one's thoughts to better articulate them, and for them to be more easily understood by others. This process is not just about hearing and talking. It is also about using one's body to provide a variety of signals as to one's emotional position on the subject, and the generation of a profound sense of companionship in tackling together this fascinating adventure of living. The current evolving alternative from of communication via the internet mainly in sound bites or fleeting images, results in a largely two-dimensional life, with perforce its aridity AND the diminishment of the multi-dimensional excitement and true creativity that face-to-face occasions allow.

Evidence of this is abundantly clear in the millennia-old tradition of enjoying a meal together with family or friends, whether at home or in restaurants. In the past this was an event looked forward to, as it brought everyone together, and conversation was lively and enjoyable. Today, however, how often do the smartphones come out during the meal and the meal's participants metaphorically leave the table to be with someone else? How often does one go into restaurants and see all the members of a family having Sunday lunch on their individual mobile phones or tablets, with hardly a word being exchanged with those around the table? And the resultant ill-effects on the use of the imagination and the development of real curiosity…

All this is further exacerbated by the fact that there is just too much information available, which overwhelms people so they resort to truncating what they have to say, such that life ends up as a series of soundbites, often misleading and lacking in real colour. All this is rather sad, and it hardly bodes well for the future.

It is clear that our global community is evolving technologically to the point where most of our transactions on virtually any subject will take place on specialised internet-based platforms, further reducing the physical, intra-human contact process. This in turn removes part of the colour and passion involved in dealing face-to-face with all different kinds of people.

All of this does not suggest a future that will cause me to regret having to leave somewhat prematurely.

Finally, I need to say that what is usually lacking in such internet exchanges, and indeed, very often in human-to-human direct contact exchanges, is "empathy". This ability to share someone else's feeling or experiences by trying to understand the other person's feelings, or indeed imagining what it would be like to experience those feelings and/or to be in that other person's situation, is directly related to ego minimisation. Thus, as an important part of making spiritual growth, it is very important to develop the ability to be empathetic to the condition of others. However, it has a curious side effect, especially for a man, as it often leads, in sharing the joy or pain, or whatever the other person is feeling, to crying – which I often do, to the embarrassment of my daughters – funnily enough, not my son. Women are much better at empathy, no doubt because it is part of their genetic make-up, but also because bringing up children as mothers gives them a crash course in the importance of empathy.

I am not trying to tell anyone how to live his or her life. But these are the issues that I have grappled with and learned largely to overcome.

I recognise that I started out with advantages that not everyone enjoys. If one is brought up, as I was, with lots of space — particularly space that one owns as far as the eye could see, as my family did in Rhodesia — it is bound to change one's outlook on life. It bestows a confidence that those brought up in a concrete jungle are unlikely to have, unless they have a very strong inherent sense of self. Nor is it easy or possible for many people to spend a few months of their life in the mountaintop isolation of a Buddhist monastery — although I am convinced the world would be a better place if everyone did.

But even without those advantages, it is possible for everyone to try to minimise the ego and to learn to be dispassionate. That will bring a confidence and an ability to accept the various blows and obstacles that life delivers in a more neutral way, without taking everything personally, as so many people do. If someone makes a cutting comment about me at a meeting, I could waste time and energy fretting about whether they dislike me, or whether I had said something stupid. But that is the ego's response. The ego is so fragile, demanding and energy-consuming. If I look at myself dispassionately, I realise that I have faults, that I am not always efficient, and that I make mistakes — sometimes serious ones. If I do this, and that is a normal part of evolving, there is no need to be defensive.

The next step is to learn how to forgive oneself; to say: "All right, I did such-and-such, I really messed up, and I'll learn from it by trying not to do it again." The alternative is to think:

"Oh God, I really messed up and now everyone is going to hate me." The first approach is far more constructive.

If one can learn how to forgive oneself, it is then possible to move to the next stage, namely to learn how to love oneself. That may sound indulgent, but it is a necessary condition for loving others. Loving is fundamentally about having the ability to forgive, oneself included, because nobody is perfect. And once one has that, one has a huge fund of energy to draw on. Imagine no longer wasting energy on guilt, regrets and dislike or criticism of others. It will provide a huge bank of additional energy that can be used for a constructive approach to life: helping to make things happen, make oneself better, helping one's neighbour to get better, and so on – all for the cumulative betterment of our global society.

Over the years, many people have told me that they found my philosophy of living – focusing on substance not form, driven by curiosity, and attempting to minimise ego – to be interesting, and that I should write about it. I have used what limited time I have left to write this book in the hope that my views and approach to life may strike a chord with some readers, and give them a different perspective on how to deal with themselves and the world around them.

A few days ago, I received an email from a young Frenchwoman doing her master's degree in Canada. Her parents are younger friends of ours, and she used to do some babysitting for us. In her email, she wrote: "I recall our conversation about it not being essential to have an ego in order to succeed in life. I can assure you that, ever since our conversation at Christmas, I have tried to bury mine deep in the earth and it feels great! Just as if I had lost twenty pounds in weight. It is not always easy but will hopefully become a built-in asset after a few months of training." A few months is optimistic, but just having a different perspective has already helped her a lot.

I have not always minimised my ego as much as I would have liked, but I am glad that my passing on my ideas to this young woman has had such an impact. Hopefully, these ideas will prove to be of interest to others.

In this overall context, I have often been asked what my profession was, and my response is invariably that my hobbies were my various jobs and projects, but my actual profession was the art of living in as fully engaged and substantive a manner as possible – and to be ruthless about ensuring that I did so.

In conclusion, I am enormously grateful to all those people who, through their support, interest and, often, affection, have collectively made such an important contribution to my being able to make this wonderful voyage through life, albeit with many painful or very challenging moments, which were equally interesting – and very instructive!

All that being said, I was particularly blessed to have Marie-Thérèse as my wife. Picking up the baton from my mother, she became my closest friend and life partner – as well as, very importantly, my ultimate judge of what she considered acceptable behaviour. She was, after all, "substance" personified, with a simple moral value system which never wavered. I can't begin to imagine what life would have been like without her.

Acknowledgements

I would like to acknowledge, with deep gratitude, the following individuals, who taught me so much and/or opened new doors of experience and thought:

My mother

Abbot Nakamura, Shino-in Temple, Mt. Koya, Japan

Master Eishin Minagawa, Sansho-zenji Temple, Nara, Japan

Guru Raihana, Gandhi Ashram, Old Delhi, India

My wife, Marie-Thérèse

I would also like to express my gratitude to the following individuals for their friendship, and for their giving me the opportunity to share many things together and to learn much from them (listed alphabetically):

Asia Pacific

In Asia Pacific, I would particularly like to single out in Japan: Mayor Kagita, Master Murata Kanzo, Hideo and Keiko Ishihara, Tomomitsu Oba and Mitsuru Tajima; in Hong Kong: David Halperin and Andrew and Ruth Korner, in India: Hemendra Kothari, and in Thailand: Varin Pulsirivong, all of whom became members of my extended family and who added immeasurably to my appreciation of their respective cultures, and/or taught and/or gave me so much. In addition, my thanks also go to other friends in Asia Pacific:

Australia

Dorothy and Geoffrey Heeley, Barbara and John Ralph and Patricia and Philip Spry-Bailey, with all of whom I had a great affinity, no doubt partly because of my Rhodesian background, and all of whom allowed me to prod them unmercifully on the subject of why Australia should look north.

Hong Kong

Ronald Chao, David Halperin, Andrew and Ruth Korner, K C Kwan, David K P Li, Alasdair Morrison, Barbara Rust, Manfred Schoeni, Anna and Helmut Sohmen, Tang Kwok-Yew, France and Bertrand Viriot and Eric Winkler, who in their different ways, and from widely different backgrounds, helped give a fascinating kaleidoscope of perceptions into what makes up Hong Kong and how it relates both to the Peoples' Republic of China and the rest of the world.

India

D Basu, S K Birla, R P Goenka, Vikram and Gutenjali Kiloskar, Biki and Mirjana Oberoi, S S Nadkarni, MJ Pherwani and S Venkitaramanan. As various members of my mother's family had spent some 150 years in India, I was particularly interested in how it was evolving after its independence. So I was grateful to these friends for allowing me the privilege of giving affectionate and concerned criticism and suggestions as to how, and in which direction, India should evolve.

Indonesia

Arafin Siregar, Ali Wadana and Jusuf Wanandi, who so many years ago started me off in my attempts to learn more about Indonesia.

Japan (family name first)

I am grateful to have had the friendship of: Akimoto Minoru, Endo Shigeru, Hashimoto Toru, Hazama Kimiko and Koichi, Horie Tetsuo, Koizumi Takashi, Miyauchi Yoshihiko, Kogo Nobutsune, Kurosawa Yoh, the Miwa family, Owada Hisashi, Orita Masaki and Masako Shimamoto Reiichi, the Tsubomura family, Tsushima Yuji, Tsutsumi Yuji, Yamada Shohei and so many, many others in Japan. Individually, in so many different ways, they allowed me to explore their country and the hearts and minds of its people, as well as allowing me to encourage them to be more integrated with the rest of the world.

Korea (family name first)

Chang In-Yong, Choi Dong-Ik, Choi Won-Suk, Chung Yong-Eui, Ha Yong-Ki, Kim Hong-Suk, Kim Sang-Ha, Lee Phil-Sun, Song In-Sang, Suh Hyung-Suk, Min-Jong and John Wiesniewski,

Yang Jae-Bong, Yoo Byung-Chul and Yoo Chang-Soon, who with many others, put up with my enthusiastic probing, and have guided me in my many decades long drive to understand what is Korea, who the Koreans are and where they fit into the world, in particular their relations with North Korea, China and Japan.

Malaysia

Tun Ismail bin Mohamed, my mentor and close friend. Tunku Tan Sri Dato, Seri Ahmad Yaha and Tan Sri Basir bin Ismail, Tan Sri Zain Azraai, who allowed me to dream wild dreams of an Asian Pacific community grouping; starting with ASEAN and the possibility of such grouping to include Australia, China, India, Japan, Korea and New Zealand to counterbalance NAFTA and the EU.

Myanmar

Brigadier General David Abel, who was a decent man, and in his various ministerial roles did his best for the people of Myanmar. He also did his best to help me with my Myanmar project, which was sadly torpedoed by the Asian financial crash.

New Zealand

Gillian and Roderick Deane, Vicky and Tony Ellis, Hugh Fletcher, Margaret and Ron Trotter and Judy and John Wrightson, who all made not only myself, but my family as well, so welcome, and who gave me over the years, interesting perspectives on both New Zealand and its relationships with the rest of the world.

Philippines

Caesar Virata, who was a paragon of virtue and who helped me understand the conflicting threads that have made this country's history, and have led to to-day's somewhat chaotic society.

Singapore

Ong Beng-Seng, who has had me on his listed company board for some 24 years, and for whom I have great admiration for his global perspective and reach. Ben and Susan Lim, Chris and Chantal Tan and the Ngoi family, who are an important part of our extended family.

Koh Beng-Seng, Tommy Koh, Sim Kee-Boon, George Yeoh and Patrick Yeoh, who have allowed me to have the same wild dreams about ASEAN leading the way to a regional grouping, all the while allowing me to tease them about the sometimes excessive rigidity of Singapore's approach to managing its population.

Taiwan

Chen S Yu and W T Tsai and his sons Richard and Daniel, who enabled me to better understand Taiwan, its people and its difference from the People's Republic of China, despite the infrequency of visits, and who gave me so much of their time.

Thailand

Varin Pulsirivong and his family who welcomed me into their midst. Nukun and Jane Prachuabmoh, Chatri and his son Tony Sophonpanich and Daeng and Vichit Surapongchai, who are still constantly educating me with great patience and affection into the subtleties of the Thai culture and its peoples.

The West

I have obviously some mentors and many friends in the West, who have taught me so much about Western value systems and the cultural differences between the countries that make up the West.

In particular, I wish to acknowledge the considerable influence and/or the help that Kevin O'Sullivan, Dr. Sydney Rolfe and Peter Luthy provided me with during this journey.

I would also like to emphasise the importance of the following individuals' and family's friendships, which have enriched me and oft-times helped me considerably, both to better understand myself and to have a better understanding of the world I was travelling through:

The three generations of the André and Dominique Barret family, Sir John and Julia Boyd, Elizabeth and Dick Bristow, Jeremy Brown, Father Raoul des Cielleuils, Michael von Clemm, Chiara de Bonnecourse, Anne-Marie and John Edwards, Michael von Clemm, Claudie and Jehan Duhamel and their two sons Augustin and Gauillaume, Duncan Davidson, Barry Friedberg, Maryese and Jean Gabriel, David Gemmill, Don Gershuny, Julian Hartland-Swann, Niles Helmboldt, Jayne and Rupert Hughes, Bruno and Francois Israel, Loula, Eric and Vasilis and Irina Kertsikoff, Dominique and Alain Langlois and their children, Annie and Georg Lennkh, Candace Luthy, Arlene and Reuben Mark, Boulie and Jim Marlas, Rogan McLellan, Samir Nahas, Babacar N'Diaye, Paul and Kathy Neff, Onno and Renee Ruding, Felicity Samuel, Bill Schreyer, Philip Seers, Charles Shanock, the three generations of the Manee and Michel Verdet family, Sir Peter and Felicity Wakefield,

Jim Watkins, Andrea and Jason Wilson, and last, but certainly not least, Dinny and Stani Yassukovitch.

It goes without saying that there are also a great number of other people throughout Asia Pacific and the West who have, in so many different ways, also been so generous with their time and support.

There is an excellent Japanese saying which very eloquently summarises my feelings: *"Koko made marimashita no wa mina-san no o-kage-san de"* which translates as "thanks to everyone's help, I have been fortunate to arrive at this point".

Finally, my grateful thanks go to Billy Sandlund and Simon Edge for their help in transcribing my stories and my description of my own philosophy, and to Simon Edge for his excellent research to ensure that my recollections as to certain facts were correct.